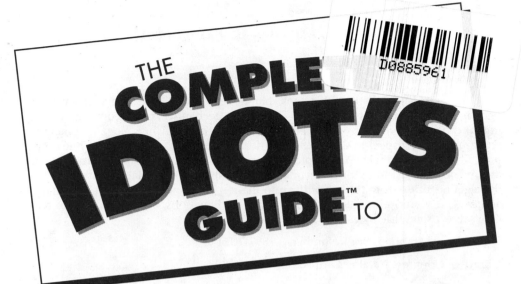

THE COMPLETE IDIOT'S GUIDE™ TO

Microsoft®
Access 97

by Joe Habraken

A Division of Macmillan Computer Publishing
201 W.103rd Street, Indianapolis, IN 46290

*To my brilliant and patient spouse—thanks for being
a great pal, Kim.*

© 1997 Que ® Corporation

International Standard Book Number: 0-7897-1051-X

Library of Congress Catalog Card Number: 96-72208

99 98 97   8 7 6 5 4 3 2 1

Interpretation of the printing code: the rightmost double-digit number is the year of
the book's first printing; the rightmost single-digit number is the number of the
book's printing. For example, a printing code of 97-1 shows that this copy of the book
was printed during the first printing of the book in 1997.

Screen reproductions in this book were created by means of the program Collage Plus
from Inner Media, Inc., Hollis, NH.

Printed in the United States of America

Publisher
Roland Elgey

Publishing Director
Lynn E. Zingraf

Director of Marketing
Lynn E. Zingraf

Editorial Services Director
Elizabeth Keaffaber

Managing Editor
Michael Cunningham

Acquisitions Editor
Martha O'Sullivan

Product Development Specialists
Lorna Gentry and Henly Wolin

Production Editor
Katie Purdum

Copy Editor
San Dee Phillips

Technical Editor
Jim O'Connor

Technical Support Specialist
Nadeem Muhammed

Illustrator
Judd Winick

Cover Designer
Dan Armstrong and Barbara Kordesh

Book Designer
Kim Scott

Production Team
*Janelle Herber, Mary Hunt, Malinda Kuhn
Daniela Raderstorf, Pamela Woolf*

Indexers
Becky Hornyak, Nadia Ibrahim, Tim Taylor

Contents at a Glance

Contents

Part 2: Catching the Brass Ring: Creating Databases 33

4 Database Creation: More Fun, Less Filling 35

5 Turning the Tables: Table Design 51

6 Going On Record: Adding and Editing Data 67

7 Being Manipulative: Different Ways to View Your Records 81

8 Between You and Me and Access: Table Relationships 97

Lights, Camera, Access: Introducing Microsoft Access 97

In today's fast-paced business world, we are constantly bombarded with facts and figures. With electronic media the rule, the Internet and World Wide Web bring massive amounts of data right into your office and home via the personal computer. There is not doubt that we are living in the information age.

How well you manage all this information will certainly have a bearing on your own success. Whether you judge success in professional terms, such as building an important corporate database, or in personal terms, such as managing your ever expanding compact disc collection, Microsoft Access is the database management tool to get you there.

Now the above paragraphs may lead you to think that this book is very serious. And in one respect you would be right. This book takes its job very seriously— the job of teaching you the ins and outs of Microsoft Access. However, this book's approach to covering material that normally would give you a near fatal migraine is one of clever (at least my mother thinks so) yet controlled humorous abandon. This means we are going to have loads of fun and lots of laughs (at least some giggles) as we tackle a very powerful database management software application and win!

But I'd Rather Walk on Hot Coals Than Work with Databases

Databases have really gotten a bad rap since the advent of the personal computer. Early database software was quite arcane and very user-unfriendly. It was not that uncommon to see a coworker run screaming from the office—a complete nervous wreck—after tussling with a poorly designed database with an indecipherable interface.

Tackling Databases with Access

Microsoft Access 97 is extremely powerful, and very friendly. It's easy-to-use features can help you build very complex and very usable databases for both business and home. You certainly don't have to be a computer guru to dive right into this software application and start building your own databases either. This book is here to help you and you will quickly learn great things, like:

➤ How to plan a proper database that will really work for you.

➤ How Access makes it easy for you to build a database.

➤ Ways to make data entry easy in your database tables and forms.

➤ Clever features like queries that allow you to quickly and easily manipulate the data in your database.

➤ How to report and print the information that you have in your databases so that it looks nice.

➤ Strategies that help protect and maintain the valuable information that you place in your databases.

This book will get you up and running in Access almost immediately. In the first three chapters you will learn how to work with Access, how to get help when you need it, and the niceties of designing a database. After that you will dive right in and work with a multitude of the database objects and features that Microsoft Access has to offer. You will certainly get your chance to build and troubleshoot databases as you become familiar with this great database software package.

This Book's For You (and Why)

As I sat down to write this book, I was thinking about you. I figured you were probably a lot like me; you've worked on a computer before and when you have to learn a new software package (like Access) you like to cut to the chase and get up and running quickly.

I'll admit that this book is actually a little bit of an enigma. While it will serve the novice Access user very well, I also think that the intermediate Access user will find a lot of new information and useful tricks and tips in these pages.

Using (Not Abusing) this Book

Certain conventions have been followed in this book to make things easy for you. When you are asked to select an item, or type some text it will appear in bold. For example, Click the **File** menu, or type **Kim** in the First Name field. The various Toolbar buttons that you are asked to select will be represented by a graphic in the text, which should help you locate the correct button.

Since I really do want you to feel good about Access and its features when you finish this book, you will find that the text remains pretty focused when it discusses a particular subject. However, for those of you who crave more information or just enjoy pleasant asides, additional information on certain subjects has been provided in special sidebars.

Office 97

These boxes will highlight hot new features that you will only find in Access 97, the most recent version of this fantastic database software program. It's no crime for you to stay up-to-date or be informed on the latest and greatest and these boxes will help you.

Check This Out These boxes will include notes, tips, and warnings about the Access features and database concepts covered in this book. A few may even contain sarcastic remarks, but hey, nobody is perfect.

Techno Talk These boxes contain higher level information or additional background information on various subjects. It's stuff that you might find comforting to know. On the other hand, if you don't feel that you have to know everything in the world, you can skip these tasty morsels of information.

Trademark Courtesy

While you may think that I am being quite courteous by listing the software manufacturers who have created the programs referenced in this book, I am in fact putting an enemy list together for the National Luddite Foundation (just kidding). Below the trademarks and service marks that were totally obvious to us all are listed.

Microsoft Windows 95, Microsoft NT Workstation, Microsoft Access, Microsoft Word, Microsoft Excel, and Microsoft PowerPoint are all registered trademarks of Microsoft Corporation.

Microsoft ActiveX and Microsoft Internet Explorer are also trademarks of Microsoft Corporation.

If any trademark or service mark appearing in this book does not appear on the list, it was probably either a small error or petty jealously, so no big deal.

Trademarks

All terms mentioned in this book that are known to be trademarks have been appropriately capitalized. Que Corporation cannot attest to the accuracy of this information. Use of a term in this book should not be regarded as affecting the validity of any trademark or service mark.

Part 1
The Secrets of Life and Databases

Details, details—we live on a planet of over-managed minutia; a world where experts focus on specifics, a place where most of us can't seem to see the forest for the trees. When you're learning something new, it's extremely difficult (and often frustrating) to attempt a jump right into the specifics.

Never fear, you're in good hands. This part of the book will help you get a handle on the big picture concepts of database management, provide you with a test drive of Microsoft Access—a powerful and easy-to-use database software package (or minutia manager if you prefer), and show you how to get help when you get stuck. It's a world of database fun and excitement that awaits you; so go ahead, turn the page, and jump right in.

BAD COMPUTER PRODUCTS: LIGHTHOUSE SCREENSAVERS.

Databases, Access, and You

The Almost Unspeakable Question— What Is a Database?

What is a *database*? Well, that's a question that strikes fear into the hearts of many people. Tomes have been written on the subject. Governments have fallen because of this question. In fact, in some countries, it is illegal to utter this question (when I want to get rid of house guests who have stayed too long, I ask them this question).

All right, so maybe I'm exaggerating a little bit. You will find, however, that most people view databases as horribly complex entities. Fortunately for you, Access makes database management a breeze. And as for the unutterable question? Well, I'm not afraid to answer it, and by the time you finish reading this book, you'll be able to stop people on the street and describe the makings of a database—whether or not anyone wants to listen.

A database is simply a collection of organized information relating to a topic: a list of very important clients, a collection of classic vinyl records, or a group of friends who all owe you money. Databases don't have to be the Darth Vaders of the personal computer software world; you can set up a database to be just as user-friendly as anything you create in a word processing or a spreadsheet software package.

Selling You on Databases

Databases are all around you: the phone book, the dictionary, even your home filing cabinet. And while some of these databases are more organized than others (let's not even start on my filing cabinet), each is a repository of information. You will also find that just about everyone around you uses databases.

The check-out clerks at the grocery store rely on a product database to give them a price every time they scan an item. The mechanic at the service station uses a parts database to see if he can find a supplier that carries that thing that just fell off your car as you drove past the Lexus dealership (or was that the Saturn dealer?). You probably even use a computerized database when you look up books at your local library (see, databases aren't scary, although the Dewy Decimal system can be).

The main reason to use a database is to keep track of information. But, there is much more to database management than just putting information in the database; you also want to be able to retrieve, sort, collate, edit, and report the information. Access can do all this and more. So setting up a database of important clients, for instance, requires that you input all the information relating to the clients. This sounds like a lot of work, especially if you have hundreds of clients, but eventually you can manipulate and track the information easily and thoroughly—this is what makes Access (and a database, in general) an incredibly useful business or personal tool.

Hopefully, the panic-ridden urge to drop this book and run screaming from the room has subsided and you are feeling more comfortable with the whole concept of the database. You may even be thinking about all the things you can organize using a database.

Relating to Access

Microsoft Access is a special kind of database software package and it will help you build a special kind of database: a *relational database*. Yeah, I know, this book isn't supposed to get super-technical. And besides most people don't need a database to keep track of their relations. Bright red T-shirts at the family picnic usually do the trick. Well, don't worry, relational databases are really not that hard to understand, and they are extremely useful when you want to manipulate data (and they won't manipulate you like your in-laws in Idaho).

A relational database divides information into discreet groups that can then be related to each other. For instance, one grouping may contain customers, another grouping will show products, a third grouping may consist of suppliers, and a fourth grouping of information in this database may contain orders. A relational database allows you to set up relationships between these different groups and then create reports and forms that tie together and display the information in the different groups.

A relational database is like a fisherman's net; each discreet group will potentially relate to another discreet group, so that all the information can be pulled together when you go fishing for it (this metaphor is making me sea-sick).

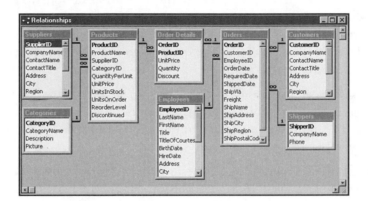

The relationships between the tables in an Access relational database give you incredible powers of manipulation over your data.

It's All in the Table

The core component of a relational database is a *table*. Each table holds the data relating to a particular area of information, such as your customers or suppliers.

Database tables look very much like a spreadsheet; you arrange the information in rows and columns. Each row holds all the information for a particular person, place, or thing. Each column contains a different piece of information pertaining to that person, place, or thing.

In database terms, each row in the table is a *record*. So each person in a customer table has his own discreet record. Each discreet piece of information in the record is a *field*. For instance, a person's first name is a field. You will learn a lot more about tables and records in Chapters 5 and 6 and how to design a relational database in Chapter 8. So at this point, just try embracing the concept of the relational database, which groups your information in discreet tables.

A typical database table.

III Customers : Table						_ □ ×
CustNo	First Name	Last Name	Address	City	State	Postal Code
1	Pierre	Manger	111 Eiffel Blvd.	Paris	MN	55330-4433
2	Janet	Dugong	12 Coastal Way	Waterford	NC	44240-5567
3	Bob	Jones	1340 America Dr.	Crystal	NV	35012-6894
4	Alice	Barney	4443 Maine Ave.	Spokane	WA	65437-1234
5	Kim	Reech	55 Platinum St.	Los Angeles	CA	85434-9354
(AutoNumber)						

Gathering Your Relations(hips) Around the Table

As I said before, it is the tables in your database that you relate together. This is done by a field or piece of information that is common to the tables. An example would be your Customer table, which will assign a customer number to each of your clients. Then, when you place a new order in your Orders table, you can type in the customer number of the person placing the order. See how the data in the two tables tie together, by a common piece of information, the customer number.

An example of how you can use this type of relationship between tables is to create a report for a hardware store that shows how a particular hand tool is selling and who is buying it. This type of report requires related information from your Customer table, an Order table, and probably a Product table.

Relational databases are far superior to their less-evolved cousins, the *flat-file database*. A good example of a flat-file database is a spreadsheet program such as Microsoft Excel. If you use a spreadsheet to track your customer orders, you have to repeat all the information related to the customer (his address, phone number) each time he places a new order. In Access, you only have to repeat the customer's number in the Order table; all the related information for the customer resides in the Customer table. Voilà! It all makes sense; now you see how a relational database works!

A Database with a View: Access Objects

Access does not limit your database work to tables; it provides you with a number of different ways to view and manipulate your data. Access categorizes each of these viewing and manipulating containers as *objects*.

You will probably find that you will use most of the common objects in your databases, especially tables, queries, forms, and reports.

Macros and Modules

Two of the more complex objects that you can create for your databases are *macros* and *modules*. You can create macros simply by using some Visual Basic code to automate certain repetitive tasks such as the steps for printing a certain form. A module is a little more complicated; it can contain a great deal of code that invokes a particular complex procedure. Both of these objects are complex productivity tools that may not be for the average user. (For more about macros, see Chapter 20.)

Access Queries, Forms, and Reports

A *query* is the way that you ask your database questions, such as how many left-handed can openers do you have in stock, and whether you have any regular customers that are left-handed that you can sell them to. The answer to a query can sort and select data in a particular table or tables. You will learn all about queries in Chapters 10 and 11.

A *form* is an excellent way to view, enter, and edit the data that you have in your table. It allows you to look at each record individually—a record by record view. Forms will be the topic of discussion in Chapters 9 and 10.

You can use a *report* to pull and summarize information from one or more table in the database. Reports are a great way to present information in a very readable and attractive format. You will get your feet wet with reports in Chapter 13. Then you will expand your reporting techniques with Chapters 14 and 15.

In essence, each of these objects gives you a different view of your data. You will find that after you finish this book, you will want to have a number of objects set up for each database. Once the various objects are in place, most of your database work will either consist of data input or reporting.

Planning Your Database

Rome wasn't built in a day, and neither were the sets for most of Cecil B. DeMille's film epics. (You remember Charlton Heston flying around the Roman amphitheater in his chariot in *Ben Hur,* don't you?) Taking a little time to plan your database will pay off the very first time you print a successful report for your boss. You must keep in mind that you must set up the database data so that it is easy to manipulate. Below are a few tried and true rules that may help you design your database (I'm not saying "don't ever break the rules," but they will at least help you get started).

➤ Grab a piece of paper and think through the database design; decide what tables, forms, and reports your database will most likely need. You can then build on this foundation.

➤ Set up the first table for the database. Make sure it provides all the information you will need for that particular category of data. If you design the table for customer data, make sure you include a column for ZIP code and phone number.

➤ Use forms for data entry. Forms allow you to concentrate on one record at a time and see each piece of information that needs to be input into the record. Incomplete records can be a real drag.

➤ Remember Access is a relational database. Each table should contain information that relates directly back to the table's purpose. For instance, a customer table should hold information on customers, not on products. If you want product data listed, design another table for your products.

➤ Reports are the icing on the cake. They present your data in a positive and clear format. Design them carefully. They are probably the only thing related to your database that other people will see.

➤ Save your work and save it often. Don't even turn on the computer if you are going to spend hours inputting data and then not save the information. A power failure can happen at any moment; protect your data!

The Least You Need to Know

➤ Access stores the data that you put in your database in tables. Each row in the table contains all the information for one particular person, place, or thing.

➤ Access is a relational database. You will have multiple tables in your database that relate the various groups of information together.

➤ Database objects—queries, forms, and reports—let you manipulate and view your data. Queries allow you to sort and order your data by asking the table questions. Forms are very useful for data input. Reports allow you to show off your data in a desktop-published format.

➤ Take the time to design your database up front. It will save you many headaches and database snafus in the long run.

Chapter 2

Putting Access Through Its Paces

In This Chapter

➤ Start Microsoft Access

➤ Open a sample database

➤ Make your way around the Access work space

➤ View the database objects (now from both sides)

➤ Close your database

➤ Exit Microsoft Access

Now that we've discussed the tough stuff such as relational databases and database objects, you can start having fun! You will find that once you learn the basics, Access is a pleasure to work with.

Start your exploration of Access and its database capabilities by viewing one of the sample databases that Microsoft ships with Access: the Northwind Trading Company database. Before you can start perusing this database, however, you need to start Access.

One Giant Step for Humankind (Launching Microsoft Access)

There is almost as much built-in redundancy for starting a program as you would find on a NASA spacecraft. However, because you actually want to start the Access software and build a database before they put an astronaut on Pluto (and you reach retirement age), you can skip some of the more esoteric possibilities and go with the **Start** button on the Windows taskbar.

Take a Shortcut

You can easily create a shortcut icon for Access that will reside on your Windows desktop. Double-click the **My Computer** icon on the Windows desktop. Double-click your local drive (usually C:); a list of all the folders on your hard drive appears. Open the folder that contains the Access software (that folder is most likely labeled **ACCESS** and you can find it in the **MSOFFICE** folder). Use the mouse to drag the Access executable file, **access.exe** (its icon looks like a key), out onto the desktop. Windows automatically creates a shortcut icon.

Click the **Start** button on the Windows taskbar. Place the mouse pointer on the **Programs** group icon. A Start menu for all your applications appears.

Locate your Access program icon and place the mouse pointer on it. Click the mouse button to start the application.

Location Is Everything

The Start menu displays folders that contain program icons (such as Access). Program icons can also appear directly on the menu. Unless you did some weird custom installation, the Access icon should appear directly on the Applications Start menu. Just be aware that every computer can have a slightly different Start menu configuration.

Starting Microsoft Access is a one-click proposition.

Click here to launch Access

Opening a Database File

When you launch Access, the first thing you see when the application opens is the Microsoft Acces dialog box. This dialog box allows you to create a new blank database, use the Database Wizard to create a new database, or open an existing database.

The Microsoft Access dialog box lets you choose what to do next.

Your Databases Up in Lights

Once you have used Access for a while, you will also find that the Database dialog box displays a list of the last four databases that you opened. You can also get to database files that are not on your most used list by clicking **More Files**.

Take a look at one of the sample databases that comes—ready for your enjoyment and edification—with Access 97. First, you need to open an existing database. By default, the **Open an Existing Database** option button appears selected, but if it's not, click it now. Then click the **OK** button.

A Northwind Database Sampling

An Open dialog box appears. Locate the directory that holds the sample database files; this probably will be the SAMPLES directory in your MSOFFICE directory.

Once you locate the SAMPLES directory and click it, a list of the sample databases appears. Double-click the **Northwind.mdb** database file to open it.

Open Season on Databases If the database you want to open appears in the "recently used" list in the Microsoft Access opening dialog box, select the database name and then click **OK**.

You will find the sample databases in the SAMPLE directory.

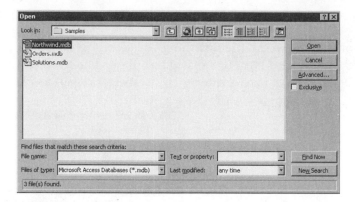

Understanding Extensions
The file extension *.mdb* stands for Microsoft database. Access uses the file extension to identify Access databases files you see when you look in directories and want to open a file.

When you open the Northwind database, a rather annoying and somewhat flamboyant screen appears with information regarding this sample database. This screen is little more than an announcement and serves no real purpose. Click the screen's **OK** button and it will go away (if it really annoys you, click *the* **Don't Show this Screen Again** check box and it disappears forever). You will find yourself face to face with the Northwind Database window and a lot of great tools that will help you as you work with your databases. Welcome to the Access application window!

Taking a Look Through the Access Window

Take a moment to look around the Access workspace. Access resides in a typical application window; in this window, you will do your database thing. At the top of the Window is the *title bar*. On the far right of the title bar are the *Minimize, Maximize/Restore*, and *Close* buttons; these buttons allow you to manipulate the size of your application window. Just below the title bar is the *menu bar*. The menu bar gives you access to all your software commands and features.

Beneath the menu bar is the *toolbar*. Toolbars hold command buttons that give you one-click entry to powerful software features. Access has a number of toolbars, each with a different general purpose. When you open a database, the Database toolbar appears. This particular toolbar allows you to quickly initiate commands and features related to the creation and maintenance of databases.

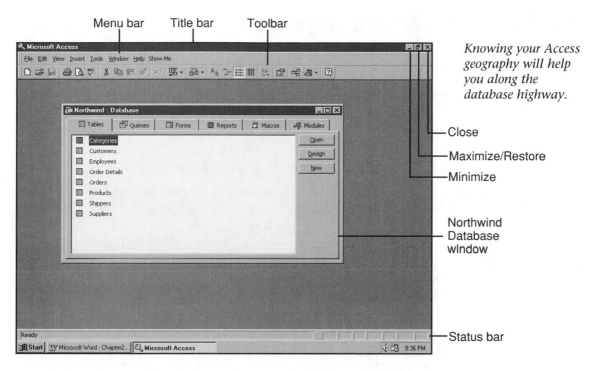

Menu bar   Title bar   Toolbar

Knowing your Access geography will help you along the database highway.

Close

Maximize/Restore

Minimize

Northwind Database window

Status bar

When you work with the various objects that make up databases, such as tables, forms, or reports, you will find that each has a toolbar that gives you quick access to features related to that particular object.

At the bottom of the Access window (just above the taskbar, remember it's always there) is the *status bar*. The status bar tells you what you have going on in the application window. For instance, when you work with a particular feature or command, this activity appears on the status bar. The status bar will also let you know if you have your Caps Lock on or if you have activated the Number Lock.

The Database Window

One of the most important (if not *the* most important) items in the Access workspace is the Database window. The tabs on this window let you view, manipulate, create, delete, and format all the objects that make up databases. And you can remember their names: tables, queries, forms, reports, macros, and modules. The following sections take a look at all these objects except macros and modules; they require just a little too much programming knowledge and I don't want you to become a total PC gear-head (however, you will learn about macros in a later chapter in this book).

13

Getting to Know Your Objects

The Northwind database provides you with an excellent way to get your feet wet with the objects that you will eventually create for your own databases. Start with tables.

Get Your Feet Off the Table

As I've stated more than once already and will no doubt state several more times before you complete this handsomely bound book (my middle name is Superfluity), database tables are where you put your data. Each particular piece of data is a *field*.

Click the **Tables** tab in the Northwind Database window. (It's the tab you saw back in the last figure, and it should appear by default, but perhaps you've been messing around and clicking the other object tabs in the window. Okay, now, pay attention.) You can see all the tables in the Northwind database, each represented by a table icon. Double-click the **Orders** table icon.

The Orders table in Datasheet view shows all the Access bells and whistles you use to create great tables.

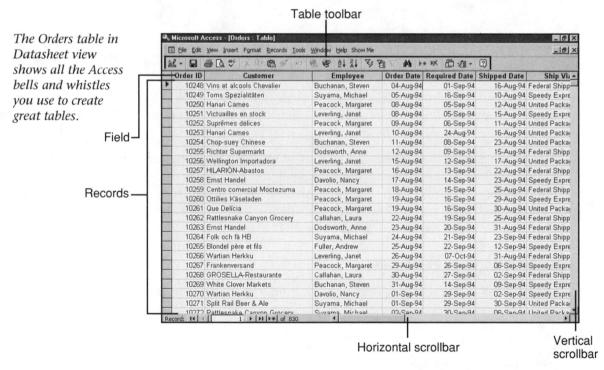

Wow! This thing is big. It kind of looks like a spreadsheet, doesn't it? This particular view of a table is *Datasheet* view. Use the vertical and horizontal scrollbars to peruse the data in the table. Notice that the datasheet divides into columns of information; these are your fields. Each row is a *record*. It's all pretty simple stuff, actually.

A Toolbar for Every Object

When you opened the Customers table, Access pulled a switch on you. It changed the Database toolbar to the Table Datasheet toolbar, which gives you buttons for features and commands unique to table maintenance. Take a look at how the toolbar changes each time you open a new object type.

Click the **Close** button to close the table. Now, take a look at another one of the database objects.

The Million-Dollar Question—The Query

Queries allow you to pull data from one or more table; they are basically questions that you ask the database. Queries look like tables and are often subsets of data in your tables. Click the **Queries** tab in the Database window. Double-click the **Sales by Category** query.

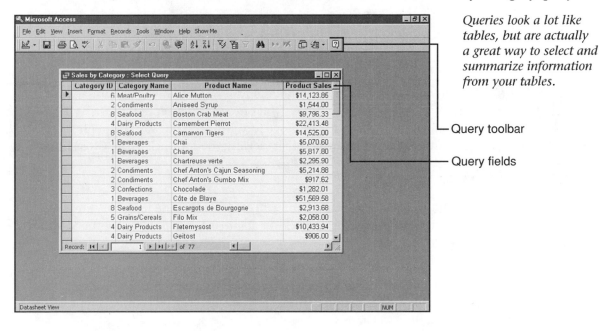

Queries look a lot like tables, but are actually a great way to select and summarize information from your tables.

— Query toolbar

— Query fields

This query pulls information from the Orders table (the actual sales) and the Products table (take a look at the Products table; that's where the categories are). This query also does some math and totals the dollar amounts of the orders for each category. Pretty cool, huh? And while you may be a little intimidated now, you will be designing queries like this one in no time.

15

Close the query by clicking its **Close** button. Click the **Forms** tab in the Database window. Let's take a look at the next object on your list.

Forming Your Own Opinion About Forms

Forms are great for entering and editing data. You can design forms for use with one table, or you can build them to service more than one table at a time. Double-click the **Customers** form.

Forms are a great way to look at one record at a time.

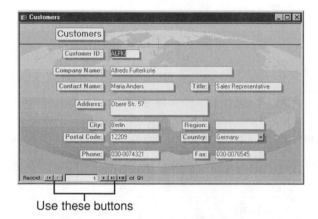

Use these buttons

This form takes advantage of one of several different layouts that you can use to build attractive forms. Notice that the form shows you one record. A set of buttons at the bottom of the form window allow you to move forward and backward through the records. Try the buttons out. When you finish viewing the form, click the **Close** button.

Let's Have Your Report

Another one of the database objects that you will encounter is the report—a great way to summarize, list, and publish your data. Click the **Reports** tab. Double-click the **Sales by Category** report.

Reports are interesting in that they have some of the capabilities typically associated with queries. Reports are great at summarizing your data and making it look great. Not only can a report show your data as text, it can also provide you with a graphical representation of your information—a chart.

Reports are the culmination of all your data gathering and input. You build your tables, queries, and forms, and once you have your data in the database just like you want it, then you print out a great report and *shazaam*! You're promoted to middle management. Click the **Close** button to close the report.

Relationships Are Where It Is At

Really the bottom line in working with Access is understanding how different tables in the database relate; Access builds (with your help) relational databases, remember? To get a preview of how the various tables in a complex database can be related, click the **Relationships** button on the Database toolbar.

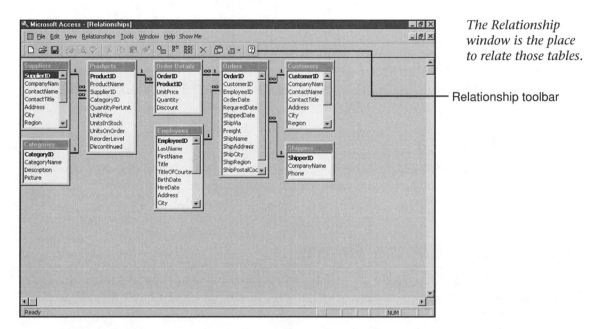

The Relationship window is the place to relate those tables.

———— Relationship toolbar

Access shows you how each of the tables link and by what field. (You will read about the possible types of relationships in Chapter 8). For now, just concentrate on the type of fields used to relate the tables. When you finish checking out the relationships (sounds like a guy with no date at the prom), click the **Close** button to shut down the Relationship window.

A Plea from Your Author—Spend Quality Time with Your Sample Database

Please take the time to peruse the other objects in this database when you have the chance. The Northwind database is very well-designed and should give you excellent insight into how you can build your own databases. And if it doesn't, no harm done—and you've looked like you were busy. And while you're at it, remember to treat this book with respect. Never let it leave your side. I don't want to find it on a table in a used bookstore.

Other Great Sample Databases

Access comes with two other sample databases: Orders and Solutions. Both these databases are highly automated and will show you some very good examples of typical database objects and advanced database objects such as macros and modules.

Closing a Database

When you finish with a database, it is quite easy to get rid of it. Click the **Close** button on the Database window. So, get rid of the Northwind database already!

Once you close a database, there's not a whole lot going on in the Access workspace. But there's no problem staying busy. You can either open an already existing database using the **Open** button on the Database toolbar, or if you would rather create a new database, you can click the **New** button.

There is a third alternative, of course. You can always exit Access.

Signing Off—Exiting Access

There will be times, I'm sad to say, when you're going to want to shut Access down completely and go off and neglect your database duties. But, hey, I guess it's not worth shedding tears over. I'll even show you how. Simply click the **File** menu, and then click **Exit**. If that's too much clicking for you, just click the Access window's **Close** button.

The Least You Need to Know

As you can plainly see (and hopefully saw in this chapter) Access is a powerful yet easy-to-use relational database package. And those sample databases—wow—they can really help you understand what kind of foundation a well-built database rests on.

➤ Launch Access via the **Start** button and the **Programs** group.

➤ All your database objects will reside in the Database window.

➤ Click the tab for the object type you want to work with.

➤ The Access toolbars are specific to the object type that you're currently working on.

➤ You can close a database, open an already existing database, or start a new database; you can find all the buttons necessary on the Database toolbar.

➤ Exiting Access using the **File** menu or the **Close** button shuts the application down.

Chapter 3

Help, I Need Someone

In This Chapter

➤ Use the Office Assistant for help when you get in a jam

➤ Look up information using the Access Help Contents and Index

➤ Get context-sensitive help with the *What's This?* Pointer

➤ Use Microsoft Online and surf the Web for Access Technical Support

Sometimes, things just don't seem to work the way they are supposed to, and computer software is no exception. No matter how hard you try (especially if you misplace this fantastic book under a pile of dirty laundry), there are going to be times when you throw your hands up in the air and holler for help. Access is great about throwing you the help lifeline when you're going down for the third time. And you'll find that there is more than one approach that you can use to get help in Access. It's all up to you.

Your Faithful Servant—The Office Assistant

You may be asking, "Who or what is the Office Assistant?" Well actually, whether it's a who or a what depends on you. The Office Assistant is a brand new Help feature that provides you with great tips, context-sensitive help, and the ability to search for help on a particular topic.

The Office Assistant uses Microsoft's IntelliSense technology, giving it the capability to almost anticipate your problems and help you out when you are stuck. It really makes other ways of getting help obsolete.

Techno Talk

Don't Forget the Office Assistant

When you install Access alone or as part of Microsoft Office (disks or CD-ROM) make sure that you install the Office Assistant. Otherwise, you will be missing out on an excellent avenue of help. For information on installing Access 97 and other Microsoft Office components, see Appendix A.

The Office Assistant appears as soon as you open Microsoft Access and resides in a small window that you can place anywhere in the Access workspace. If you don't see the Assistant, click the **Office Assistant** button on the Database toolbar (or the current toolbar).

The Office Assistant is always ready to help you.

The Office Assistant is kind of like the Shell Answer Man (sorry, person), but dresses better (boy did I date myself with that one). The great thing about the Assistant is that you can get help in several different ways. You can get *Suggested Help*, which gives you info on the task your currently tackling, or you can search for help by typing a question or topic in the *What would you like to do?* box. You can even grill the Assistant for clever tips about all sorts of Access features and commands by clicking on the *Tips* button. To take a look at all these great possibilities, click the **Office Assistant** (anywhere in the Assistant's window will do) and the Assistant's balloon will appear.

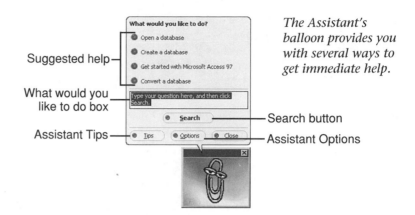

Suggested help

What would you like to do box

Assistant Tips

Search button

Assistant Options

The Assistant's balloon provides you with several ways to get immediate help.

Take a Guess—Suggested Help

The Assistant's balloon provides you with several different ways to get help. First, it provides you with a list of suggested Help topics that are germane (no, not Michael Jackson's brother, I mean *pertinent*) to the activity that you are currently dealing with in Access. For instance, when you start Access, you will want to open, create, or import a database; the list of Help topics that the Assistant provides address these database issues.

This type of help—Suggested Help—can be very timely; if you work on a table and get stuck, the Assistant provides you with a list of suggestions that help you troubleshoot your problem with tables—exactly what you're doing at the time. This type of immediate help can be, well, very helpful!

What Do You Want to Do?

"Nothing." That's the answer you always get from children under the age of 11; five minutes later, they're screaming that they are bored (offspring older than 11 won't even bother to answer… but I digress). Another great way to get help using the Assistant is the **What would you want to do?** box in the Assistant's balloon. All you have to do is click in the box and type a question. You can even type the question in English—no geekspeak necessary.

Say that you want information on creating a form. A question you might pose to the Assistant would be "How do I create a form?" Once you type in your question, click the **Search** button.

The Assistant will search the Help database for you and return a list of Suggested Help topics such as *create a form*, *create a form with a subform*, and other topics of this particular ilk. Just click the topic that best fits your need at the time.

Read All About It: Assistant Replaces Wizard

Techno Talk

The Assistant's What would you like to do? box replaces the Answer Wizard in Access 97.

Type in your question; then click the Search button.

Unsolicited Advice?

If you inadvertently click the Office Assistant while you are working in Access, click the **Close** button to close the Assistant balloon.

A Hot Tip

Another way to get help from the Assistant is by perusing the tip of the day. These tips give you advice on shortcuts and clever ways to get the job done smarter and faster when you work in Access.

To view the current tip, click the **Tips** button at the bottom of the Office Assistant Help balloon. The Tip of the Day will appear. These tips range from how to get the most out of the Office Assistant to fast ways to customize the toolbars that you find in Access. The Tips balloon also has **Back** and **Next** buttons that allow you to view previous tips or jump ahead to see new tips. When you finish reading the tip, click the **Close** button to close the Tip balloon.

A Cup of Coffee and the Tip of the Day

You can also set up the Tips so that the Tip of the Day automatically appears when you start Access. All you have to do is check the **Show the Tip of the Day** box in the Options dialog box of the Office Assistant.

Appearances Are Important

The Assistant can take on several different personalities, including Clipit, a paper clip; the Dot, a bouncing ball; and the Genius, an Albert Einstein look-alike. Choosing a particular assistant is quite easy; simply click the **Options** button and you are well on your way to customizing what the Assistant looks like and what kind of help it offers.

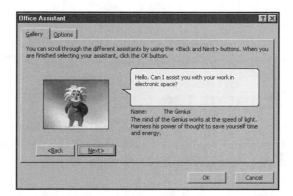

A ready-and-willing groups of assistants await your call.

Cheap Thrills!

If you are ever totally bored and your coworkers won't talk to you, put the mouse pointer on the Assistant and click. A shortcut menu appears. Click **Animate** and the Assistant will provide you with some cheap entertainment.

The Office Assistant's dialog box has two tabs: Gallery and Options. Use the Gallery tab to select the Assistant you want to work with. There are nine different Assistants, and I'm sure one will suit your personality and frame of mind. A set of **Back** and **Next** buttons make it easy for you to peruse the different possibilities. Once you make your selection, click **OK**.

What Are My Options?

The Options tab of the Office Assistant's dialog box allows you to decide how the Assistant interacts with you. You can decide on a number of options, including whether or not the F1 function key (the usual key for help) makes the Assistant appear; if the Assistant will help you when you work with the various Access wizards; or if the Assistant will guess at a list of Help topics when you run into trouble. All these features and a number of others are controlled by check boxes in this particular tab. Once you make your selections, click **OK**.

When You've Had Enough of the Assistant

There may be times when you don't want the Assistant in the Access workspace. Don't worry, the Assistant is well-adjusted enough to handle a little rejection. All you have to do is point at the Assistant with the mouse and right-click. A shortcut menu appears, and you can click **Hide Assistant** to remove the Assistant from view.

Feeling a little lonely? No problem. To get the Assistant back on-screen, click the Office Assistant button that resides on all the Access toolbars. You won't find a more loyal friend or anyone so willing to roll up her sleeves and give you a hand (unless you win the lottery, then you will have a lot of friends whether you want them or not).

Getting Help Without the Assistant

Although the Office Assistant may seem to be the answer to everyone's Access problems, there are other more conventional ways to get help. One of these is going directly to the Access help file and looking up information in a table of contents and index. Click the **Help** menu; then click **Contents and Index**. The Help Topics window that appears contains three tabs, each providing a different way to look up the help or information that you need.

The Help window allows you to look up information in the Access Help file.

The Contents tab supplies you with a list that will take you to major groupings of information such as what's new in access, an introduction to Access, and how to do specific tasks such as creating a database or creating a table.

Take a look at how the Contents tab supplies you with information on working with tables. Double-click **Creating, Importing, and Linking Tables**. The Help Book icon opens up and displays a sublist of more specific topics. Double-click **Creating Tables**.

The subject listing becomes even more specific. You've probably noticed that the Help topic icons for the table have now become sheets of paper. This means that when you double-click one of these choices, you will be taken directly to a window of information on that particular topic.

Say you want information on the actual steps for creating a table. Double-click **Create a table**. The Access Help system opens a window for the Create a table topic. A short paragraph at the top of the window provides you with general information on creating a table. Notice that the word *table* is in a different color (green is the default) and has a dashed line underneath it. Words presented in this fashion are *Glossary terms*. Clicking them gives you a definition of the word.

Give it a try. Click the word **table**. A definition box appears and defines table for you. When you finish viewing the definition, click anywhere in the Help window and the definition disappears (isn't this cool?).

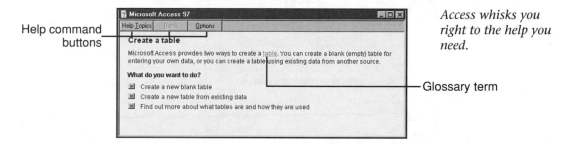

Help command buttons

Glossary term

Access whisks you right to the help you need.

By Your Command

There are also Help command buttons available in the Help window. Use the **Help Topics** button to return to the list of topics that you started with. The **Back** button takes you to the last screen. The **Options** button provides helpful features such as the ability to annotate, copy, print, change the font size, or keep the Help screen on the top of your application. Keeping the Help window on top is useful when you want to work with the database and view the suggestions that Help is making as you input or manipulate data.

The Help window asks you what you want to do next; do you want to create a new blank table, create a new table from existing data, or just find out more about tables in general? To see what Access has to say about creating a new blank table, click the button for this topic.

Just the Facts Ma'am

A new Help window opens up, chock-full of Glossary terms. Click a few of them for fun. Memorize some to impress your friends. You are also given information about the different ways to create a new blank table. Notice that another set of buttons is available that will take you to even more specific information on the subject. Click the **Creating a table using the Table Wizard** button.

You are taken to a window that lists the steps to create a new table using the Table Wizard. Go back to the window where all this started and look at some of the other ways to get help. Click the **Help Topics** button.

Using the Index

Another way to get to help from the Access Help Topics window is to do keyword searches in the Help system's index. For instance, say you want information on forms. Type **forms, creating** in the Index search text box. Did you notice that the Help system moved down through the Help index as soon as you started typing?

Type in indexed terms to get help in Access.

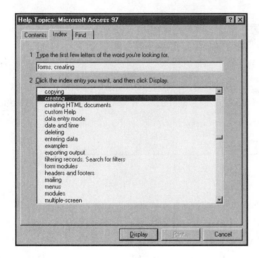

When you work with the index, you type in the main topic (the primary level of information you want to search for) followed by a comma and then any specific information; you did this when you included the word creating in the search. Double-click **creating** to see where you end up. A list of topics found by this keyword index search appears. You wanted information on creating a form and that is the first topic listed. Click the **Display** button to move to the next step.

A window appears that provides information on how to create a form. This is exactly the kind of window you ended up with when you used the **Contents** tab to locate help on the table topic. See, Help could not be more helpful!

Finding Your Way in Help

Click the **Help Topics** button to see what else this Help system has to offer. The third tab is **Find**. The Find feature allows you to search through the Help system by keywords. Give it a shot.

Type **field** in the **1 Type the word you want to find** box. A list of matching words and terms appears in the **2 Select some matching words to narrow your search** box. Click the second word **Field** in the matching words box. A list of possible topical matches appear in the **Click a topic** box. Click the seventh topic from the top: **Add a Field to a table in Design view**; then click the **Display** button. You are given help on how to add a field in the Form Design view. Pretty slick, huh?

Building a List
The first time that you use the Find tab, the Help system builds a list of keywords for the Help search engine to use.

When you finish with the Help Topics dialog box, click the **Close** button to remove it from the Access workspace. Now you're probably thinking, "Wow, Access really provides me great ways to get help." And you'd be right; but hold onto your mouse, Access newbie, because there's more!

What You See Is What Gets You Help

You may be one of those visually oriented people that like to pick up their cues from what they see around them. Well, this is your lucky day. You can actually use the mouse to click a part of the Access window and get help. All you have to do is click the **Help menu**, and then click **What's This?**

The What's This? menu selection turns your mouse into an informational help probe, sort of like those satellites we're always throwing at Mars and Venus; when they touch down, they gather information and beam it back to Earth. Well, that's how the mouse works when you activate the **Help** button. Boldly click where you've never clicked before (pretty much anywhere in the window), and Access provides you with some help on the item you selected.

Give it a try. Once you arm your mouse pointer with the **What's This?** question mark, click the Office Assistant. A box pops up and provides you with a sentence or two of help on the item you clicked. In this case, Access tells you that the Assistant provides you with help and tips to accomplish your Access tasks.

You can also use this little trick on the parts of the various windows that you work with in Access and on the buttons of the various toolbars found in Access. Click the **Help** menu. Click **What's This?** and then click the **Spelling** button on the toolbar. Access gives you information on what the Spelling button does.

Hey, this is great; a quick way to get simple information on a specific area of the Access workspace. You will find that these mouse-click Cliff notes are often just what you need to stay productive in Access.

Okay, take a deep breath because you're still not done exploring all the help possibilities in Access. Join me now in an exploration of Microsoft on the Web.

Getting Help on the Web

The Internet and particularly the World Wide Web have drastically changed the way we work using computers. The days of the isolated personal computer are over; we're now hooked into a giant network that spans the globe. You can take advantage of this fact by going directly to Microsoft for help, tips, and information on their software products.

Access and all the components of Microsoft Office 97 have Web pages that you can view. The great thing is that you can continue to work in Access while you check out the information these pages provide. This allows you to get in-depth help with Access that is updated regularly.

Access on the Web

To take advantage of this Access Help feature, make sure that you have Microsoft Internet Explorer 3.0 (or better) installed on your PC. Explorer serves as the Web browser and information gatherer. You will also need a modem and an Internet service provider.

A whole new world of help possibilities opens up when you're on the Web.

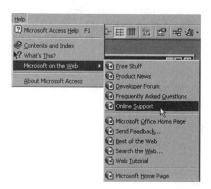

Connecting to Microsoft's Web pages is easy. Click the **Help menu**; then point at **Microsoft on the Web**. A list of possibilities opens up.

Surfing the Web with Bill

You can choose several different sites via the Microsoft on the Web menu choice. You can browse for free software, you can look at a list of frequently asked questions (FAQs) about using Access, or you can go directly to a Home Page for the Microsoft Office family of products. Once on the Office Home Page, you can easily connect to a specific page for Access.

Say you click the **Online Support** choice on the menu. If you aren't already connected to the Web, the Internet Explorer will open and hook you to the Access Support Page.

Technical Support Extraordinaire

Once on the Access Support page, you will notice that there is an incredible amount of information that you can use to help you get the most out of Access. You can view a

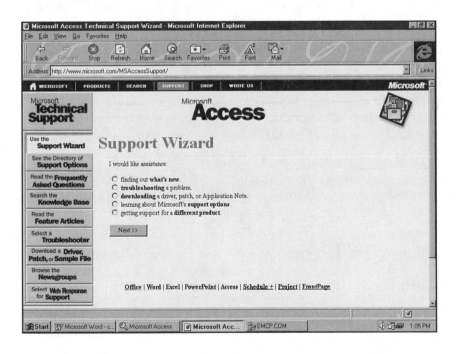

Microsoft on the Web offers you more Access help than you can shake a stick at!

Knowledge Base on Access, read feature articles, download drivers and sample files, even view Newsgroups that allow you to read and reply to posts made by Access users like yourself.

Access Support Is Just a Wizard Away

One of the most unique ways to gather information about Access via the Support Web page is the Support Wizard. You can find out what's new in Access, troubleshoot a particular problem, and learn more about the different support options that Microsoft offers for Access on the Web.

Suppose you would like help troubleshooting a particular problem; and I mean a serious problem. This type of help and support is geared toward actual software problems: bugs and other nasties that may be affecting Access performance. All you have to do is be on the Access Technical Support page; the rest is just a little bit of Web surfing. Click the **Troubleshooting a problem** option button, and then click the **Next** button.

A list of troubleshooters will appear. Select the one that best fits your need; then click the **Next** button. If none of the listed troubleshooters will do the job for you, click **None of the Above will help me**; but don't give up, move to the next screen anyhow.

A box appears on the next page where you can type in information or symptoms related to the problem that you are having. The next page will list technical articles and informational releases from Microsoft regarding the particular problem. When you have completed your Access research on the Web, click the Internet Explorer's **Close** button to close the application. If you plan on doing more Web browsing while you work in Access, click the Explorer's **Minimize** button and it will be ready the next time you need it.

As you can probably see, you can almost drown in all the information about Access that Microsoft on the Web can provide you. A good rule of thumb is to use the Help system and the Office Assistant first to solve problems and get answers on Access; then turn to the Web if you need more in-depth information or actual technical support.

The Least You Need to Know

Wow, there are really many ways to get help in Access. Don't be afraid or embarrassed to use it; better to pause for a moment and get some help than to create a database that doesn't really work for you. Besides, during those lonely nights when you are banging away at the keyboard entering data, help can be just like having a conversation with a good friend. You've learned a lot about Access Help in this chapter, but here are the highlights:

➤ The Office Assistant provides you with a one-stop shopping approach to getting help in Access. Simply click the Assistant and you'll get help on what you are currently working on.

➤ When you want to get an answer to a simple, plain English question, use the Assistant's **What do you want to do?** box. Then click **Search**.

➤ The Help menu is a good place to go for help if you like browsing a table of contents or viewing an index for the Access Help file.

➤ Use the **Contents** tab when you're not totally sure what you need help with; it divides the information into broad categories and lets you look up information by subject matter.

➤ When you know exactly what you're looking for, the Index and Find tabs are the way to go, letting you search for either indexed terms or keywords respectively. This is the fastest route to specific information.

➤ You can click up some quick help with the **What's This?** choice on the Help menu; it arms your mouse pointer with a Help icon that gets you help wherever you click.

➤ Microsoft on the Web offers you tons of technical support and information related to Microsoft Access. Surfing the various Web pages involving Access is a great way to build up your own mental database.

Part 2
Catching the Brass Ring: Creating Databases

So you're feeling a little crazed; you've got the database theory stuff under your belt, and you're ready to take a crack at actually building a database. But you're not real sure what you might end up with. It's kind of like being one of those mad scientists in the B movies; you have the best intentions when you throw that switch, but your creation turns out to be a real monster.

Bringing your database into being in Microsoft Access is much simpler than it sounds. In fact, you'll find that there is plenty of help along the way. There are even Wizards (a question and answer process for creating the various database elements) to help you build that ideal database. That's an advantage that Dr. Frankenstein could have used. Turn the page and create!

ROUGH COMPUTER CAFÉS.

Chapter 4

Database Creation: More Fun, Less Filling

In This Chapter

➤ Use the Database Wizard to create great databases

➤ Name a new database

➤ Specify or create a folder where you can save your databases

➤ View your new database and its objects.

Now that you've taken Access out for a test drive and have a good feel for what a database is and how to plan one, you can try your hand at actually building one. Remember, whenever you run into trouble, you can consult with the Office Assistant to get the help that you need.

Creating a New Database

For starters, you will create a simple database using the Access Database Wizard. The wizard will assist you in the building of the various objects—tables, queries, forms, and reports—that are found in a typical database. You can also choose to create a blank database, if you want to create all the Access objects from scratch.

Start Microsoft Access (a very important step). In the New Database window, click the **Database Wizard** option button (the little circle next to Database Wizard); then click **OK**. Hey, you're off to see the Wizard!

What's a Wizard?

Wizards are great productivity tools that guide you through a particular task (such as building a new database) via a set of screens. You are asked to respond to a question or make a particular choice from a list. The wizard will then move to the next step in the process based on your response. What could be easier?

Working with the Wizard

Dorothy really didn't get a whole lot out of her association with the Wizard. In fact, she found that everything she needed had been right in her own backyard. You'll find, however, that the Access Database Wizard is no humbug hiding behind a curtain. It will help you quickly build extremely user-friendly databases. Now click your heals together and repeat after me, "There's no database like Access, there's no database like Access…"

The Access New dialog box appears after you invoke the Database Wizard. This dialog box gives you access to a bunch of different database templates. A *template* is really nothing more than a blueprint for a database. It will contain ready-made database objects such as tables, forms, and queries.

The Access New dialog box is shown here.

Database templates

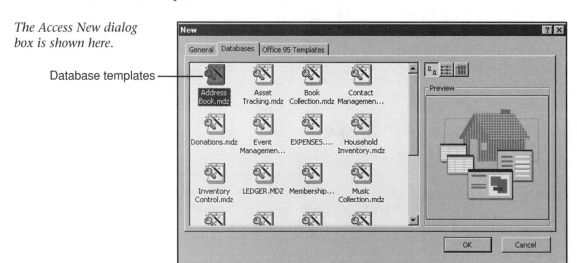

The New dialog box divides into three tabs: General (where the blank database template resides), Databases (where a large group of different types of database templates reside), and Office 95 Templates (where all the Access 97 templates reside).

The Database Wizard makes sure the Databases tab is selected and offers you a lot of different database possibilities. There are database templates for Event Management, Inventory Control, Recipes, Friends, even (gasp) a template for your Workouts.

Say you want to put together a database that will help you organize your huge music collection—this is a vinyl collection, scores of albums stuffed in over 40 orange crates, many warped beyond belief—not those wimpy little CDs that stack so easily and seem to last forever. You have Elvis, Buddy, Dolly, Bono (not Sonny), and a bunch of dogs that barked Christmas carols one season. Looking through the list of database templates, the best fit for your incredible record collection would be the Music Collection database.

Fine-Tune Your Databases
You will find that the sample databases can get you started, but you may have to fine-tune them to get the results that you need.

The Great thing about using one of the database templates is that it will create a number of database objects (remember, in Access objects are things like tables, queries, forms, and reports); this means that you will get ready-to-use tables, forms, and reports for your new database. All you will have to do is supply the data that will go into the object, such as a table or form.

The Assistant to the Rescue
Remember, you can always get instant help by clicking the Office Assistant.

Time to give this whole sample database thing a spin and see how a particular template can help you manage your record collection. Click the **Music Collection** database icon, and then click **OK**. The File New Database dialog box is where you name your database and designate where you are going to keep it on your computer (such as in your computer's hard disk or local drive).

Pick Your Spot

You can also save your files to drives other than your local drive or a floppy diskette. The File New Database gives you access to all network drives (where you have been assigned rights) as well as any File Transfer Protocol (FTP) sites you may be attached to via the Internet or your company's intranet. For more about Access on the Internet, see Chapter 23.

The File New Database dialog box lets you choose a name and a location for your new database.

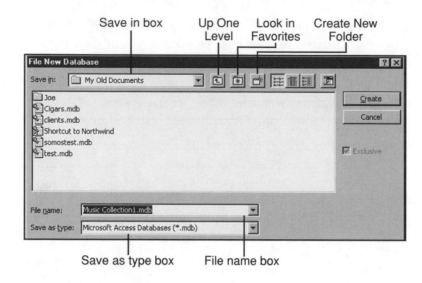

Save in box | Up One Level | Look in Favorites | Create New Folder

Save as type box | File name box

Press a Button—Any Button!

We have all been conditioned from early childhood to keep our mitts off of certain things—burning matches, nuclear isotopes, and buttons, especially red, blinking ones. You will find that Access 97 and Windows 95 provides you with all sorts of great buttons. And you know what? You can push 'em and not destroy the world.

All you need to do now is specify a location for the database file that you want to create. You can use a currently existing folder on your local drive, or you can use the New File dialog box to create a new folder.

Network Niceties

You may be working on a network and need to save your file somewhere other than your computer's local drive. You can specify and create file folders on a network drive using the **Commands and Settings** button. You can also use it to map network drives or set up FTP sites.

The File New Database dialog box provides you with seven buttons that make it easy to specify a location for your database file or view your file lists in different ways.

➤ **Up One Level**   Takes you to the parent directory of the directory that you are currently in.

➤ **Look in Favorites**   Takes you to a special subfolder or directory in the Windows directory.

➤ **Create New Folder**   Let's you create a brand-new folder to hold your files.

➤ **List**   Displays the files in the window in alphabetical order using small icons.

➤ **Details**   Shows a list of the files with additional information, such as when they were created or what type of file they are.

➤ **Properties**   Lists the files but also shows a property box that gives you information on the file size and when it was last modified.

➤ **Commands and Settings**   Sorts the file list by name, size, or type, and also to connect to network or Internet/intranet FTP sites.

Other important areas in the File New Database dialog box provide you with places to type the file name, designate where you want to save the file, and what file type you want to create.

➤ The Save in box is where you designate the place on your local, network, or FTP drive that you want to keep the file on.

➤ The file name box is where you type the file name.

➤ The Save as type box is where you specify the type of file that you want (since you are making a regular database, don't change the type).

ScreenTips Make It Easy   Whenever you want to find out the name and purpose of a particular button in your Microsoft Windows applications, place the mouse pointer on the button and a ScreenTip will appear giving you the needed information. Is this software great or what?

Now you have to give your database a name. Type **Classic Vinyl** in the **File name** box. Okay, your database has a name, now it needs a place to call its own on your local drive.

Long Live Long File Names!

Access is a Windows 32-bit application; this means that you can take advantage of long file names. You are no longer limited to a maximum of eight characters with an optional three-character extension—DOS naming conventions are dead. Windows 95 allows you to have file names of up to 250 characters. You can even put spaces in the names! Access, however, still reserves the three-character extension and tags each database file with the extension *.mdb* (it stands for Microsoft Access database).

Now push the envelope a little bit and actually create a new folder on the local drive to use as a repository for the databases you create.

1. Click the **Save in** box drop-down arrow, and select The **C:** drive or the letter of your computer's drive.

2. Click the **Create New Folder** button.

3. Type **My Databases** in the **New Folder** name box; then click **OK**.

4. Double-click the **My Databases Folder** in the New File dialog box to open it.

5. Click the **Create** button to begin the process of bringing your Classic Vinyl database into being.

It's very easy to create a new folder for your databases.

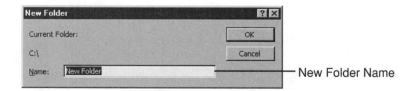

New Folder Name

Your computer will probably spin its wheels for a couple moments as the Database Wizard loads. You will even see a Database Explorer Window being built for your particular database (more on the Database Explorer later).

A Walk with the Wizard

Now the Database Wizard is in full-stride. It consists of a series of screens that walk you through the database creation process. This allows you to control certain aspects of the database, which is nice. The wizard does limit your control, however, basing many of the components that you will end up with on the original database template you selected. It's kind of like getting a haircut; you can tell the barber or stylist what you want, but once the scissors start to fly, the radical new doo you wanted may end up looking like every other haircut that walks out of the shop.

Notice that the wizard tells you what type of information it expects you to store in this particular database:

➤ Information about recording artists

➤ Recording information

➤ Track information

As you can see, this type of information may be perfect for your record collection database. However, you may be lacking the ambition to enter information on every track on every album. And besides, if you did, people would think you were nuts. So, you will find that all the database templates provide database objects (tables, forms, reports, and so on) that you may not use. You will also find that you may use a database template that does not include all the objects that you will want for your database. But do not despair, noble database neophyte, the Database Wizard is the starting point. It's not that hard to manipulate your databases once you've laid the ground work.

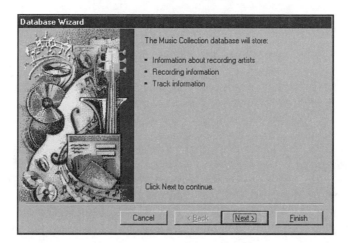

The Database Wizard walks you through the database creation process.

So, perhaps, you will be deleting some of the database objects (Track information) that are created by this sample database and perhaps creating other more useful ones from scratch (the multitudinous maneuvers to do this will be revealed later in this book).

Click the **Next** button to shift the Database Wizard into high gear.

Setting the Tables

You can view the tables that the Wizard creates and the fields that these tables will contain on the next screen. Again, remember, some of these tables will be useful; you can delete the ones that are not later.

Out in Left Field

At this point, you can also let Access know if there are any optional fields that you want to include in a specific database table. For instance, click **Recording information** in the **Tables in the database** list box.

Scroll down through the fields in the Table box. Notice that there is an optional field for year released. Now what would an album database be without the release year? Think about it, 1967, 1975, 1990; every year had its music and it's important to specify when each of the albums in your classic (if not somewhat monomaniacal) collection hit the record-store shelves.

41

You can select optional fields and even choose to have sample data placed in your database tables when you create a new database using the Database Wizard.

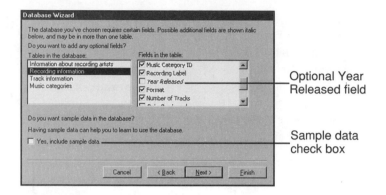

Optional Year Released field

Sample data check box

No Deletions Without a Sales Slip At this point in the database creation process, you can't delete any of the fields in the database tables. Later in this exciting text, you will learn how to delete fields, add fields, and much, much more.

To include the optional Year Released field click its check box.

Notice that there is a check box in the lower portion of the wizard screen labeled **Yes, include sample data**. You may as well take advantage of this feature since you will want some data to play with later when you really start manipulating the tables, forms, and reports in this database. Click the **Yes, include sample data** check box to select the option.

You can peruse the fields in the other tables in this database if you want; simply click a particular table name. When you are ready to move to the next step, click the **Next** button.

Sample a Little Data

Including sample data in a database created using the wizard is a great learning tool. Playing with the sample data can help you learn how to use the tables, forms, and reports included with each of the template.

You Gotta Have Style

The Database Wizard now gives you several different style options. So basically, it's up to you to choose what you want your different database screens to look like. This process is very much like wallpapering a room in your house. You are going to have to live with your choice for some time, so choose wisely.

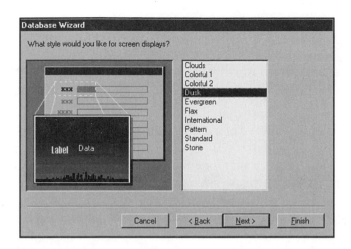

The Database Wizard lets you choose the look of your database screens.

Actually, Access is flexible about changing the style or look assigned to a particular database. In this case, since your database is just dripping with starry-eyed nostalgia, choose **Dusk**, by clicking it. The wizard gives you a preview of your new style, and this star-filled sky motif fits the music database perfectly (especially for Barry Manilow fans).

Click **Next** to continue.

You can also set up your reports using different styles and the wizard, a stickler for detail, wants to get a reading from you on how the reports you generate for this database should look. You have several choices. Since you are setting up a database for a home record collection and not a database of classified components for a giant corporation that manufactures spy satellites, you might as well adopt a casual style for your reports. Click **Casual** in the style box, and then click **Next** to continue.

What's in a Name?

Now that you've chosen the look for your database objects, the wizard wants you to give the database a name that it can put on all the reports that you create for the database. It makes sense to use a name that describes the database. You can use the same name that you gave to the database file when you saved it, but you don't necessarily have to.

Notice that Access automatically sticks the name of the template—music collection—that you used to generate the databases in the Title box. You, however, can let your creative juices flow and create a truly original name for this database; type **Record Collection** in the Title box.

Oh, well, I guess your creative abilities are just a little rusty—not unlike the Tin Man. "Oil can, oil can!"

Picture This

Access provides you a number of ways to create visually rich databases. In fact, the **Report** name screen also lets you decide whether or not to include a graphic (a company logo or photo) on the reports.

Pictures Are Always Nice!
The Select Picture dialog box is very much like the New File dialog box. To look in a particular folder, double-click it.

To include a picture, click the **yes include a picture** check box. Then click the **Picture** button. The Picture button allows you to peruse your local drive, network, or Internet FTP sites for graphic files. You can use a number of picture formats. Several pictures come with the Access software, and an entire collection of clip art comes with Microsoft Office. You can scan in Mick Jagger's pic if you want to.

You can select a picture that will appear on your database reports—a great way to include a company logo.

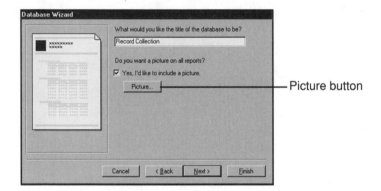

Picture button

The Checkered Flag

You are nearing the finish line; your database creation race is almost over. Let's recap the high points: You have chosen a sample database—music collection—that provides you with preset tables, forms, and reports; you have also selected a database style and a report style; you even opted to include a picture on your reports. Click **Next** to move to the final step in the database creation process.

The wizard wants to know if you'd like to start the database; a check box provides this **yes** or **no** possibility, with **yes** being the default answer. Starting the database means taking a look at your database. And, of course, you want to look at the database; that's why you created it. Click the **Finish** button.

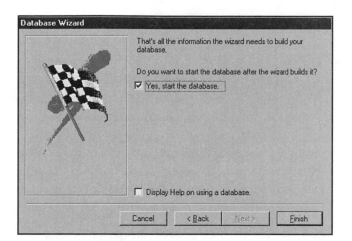

The Database Wizard gives you a choice.

A Little Help, Please

The final screen in the Database Wizard also gives you the choice of displaying Help while you work on your database. This is just one option for getting help as you work.

The wizard now does its stuff and creates the various objects (table, forms, and reports) that are part of this sample database.

Psyching Out the Switchboard

When you create a new database with the Database Wizard, Access assigns a special form—the Switchboard—to your new database. You can use the Switchboard to move around in your database, from one table to another, or to a report. The Switchboard is great for the novice user. For instance, say a friend who doesn't know Access wants to take a look at your record database.

No problem—a quick click in the right place and the Switchboard lets you take a look at your database tables and forms. Don't forget that when you built this database, you asked Access to provide sample data, providing a great way to learn about database objects, such as tables and forms.

The Switchboard provides an easy way to add or view data in your new database.

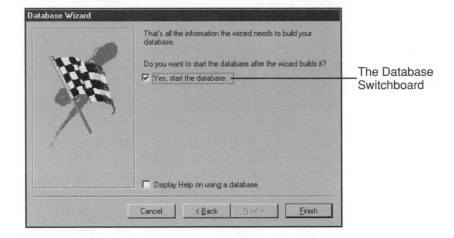

The Database Switchboard

You are given a couple of different choices concerning the type of information you can view or edit. The first choice on the Switchboard allows you to work with the recordings in your database. Let's say your friend would like to take a look at the Recording Artists you have listed in your database...

1. Click the **Enter/View Other Information** button. A second switchboard appears.

2. Click **Enter/View Recording Artists** button.

You are now looking at a form that the Database Wizard created for viewing or entering your recording artists' data. Notice that the form uses the background style that you picked during the database creation process. There is also data in the form that was supplied by the wizard. Notice that the data refers to only one Recording Group. This is how a form works; they show you one record at a time. To close this form and return to the database Switchboard, click the **Close** button in the upper-right corner. Now you can take a look at some of the other objects that were created with this database.

A Database with a View

You will more than likely use two very different views of your database as you enter and manipulate your data: the datasheet view and the form view. The datasheet gives you a view of the whole table. It's divided into rows and columns just like a spreadsheet program. Each row is a different record. The form, as you have seen, shows you the information for one record at a time. When you want to have a quick look at an entire table, the datasheet view is the way to go. For entering new records into a database, you will probably find that a form provides a format that is very easy on the eyes.

A report will give you a customized, polished view of your data. Reports have the ability to group your data in special ways and also to summarize your data. You will spend a lot of time working with and learning about reports in Chapters 13, 14, and 15.

The easiest way to switch between the different objects (which give you different views of your data) in your database is to use the Database window. This window is the container for all the objects that you build for a particular database. To see the Database window for your Classic Vinyl database, you have to get the Switchboard out of the way.

Click Switchboard's **Close** button (it's the button on the upper-right corner of the Switchboard with the **X** in it). The Database window has actually been on your desktop the whole time you have had this database open. However, when you create a database using a template, the Switchboard takes preeminence over the Database window as the method getting to the various objects.

Opening the Database Window

Once the Switchboard is gone, you will probably notice that the Database window is already on the desktop, although in a minimized fashion. You need to enlarge or open this window, so you can look at your database objects. Click the **Restore** button on the Database window.

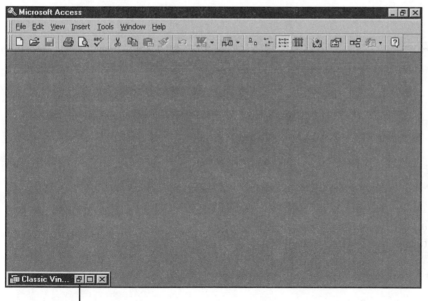

The minimized database window.

The Restore button

A Window on the Database World

The Database window is a holding tank for all the various objects that make up your database. Several views are available in the Database window (such as the small icons list or the file details list that you can use as you view each group of objects in the database).

Notice that the Database window has a tab for each of the different types of database objects: tables, queries, forms, reports, macros, and modules. Forms is the currently selected tab, and a list of the forms that were created with this sample database appears. Take a look at the tables that are in this database. Click the **Tables** tab.

Your friend and mine, the Database window.

The Database Window tabs

To take a look at a particular table, click the **Recordings** table icon, and then click the **Open** button. No surprises here; Access arranges the data in rows and columns. To close the table, click its **Close** button.

Switchboard Stuff

The Switchboard Items table and the Switchboard form are both associated with the Switchboard that appears when you open Classic Vinyl database. Neither are actual usable database objects, but together they make the Switchboard work.

To view one of the forms created for this database, click the **Forms** tab. Double-click the Albums form to open it. Notice that the form shows one record at a time. Close the form by clicking its **Close** button.

To view one of the reports created for this database, click the **Report** tab. Double-click the **Recordings by Artist** report. The report opens; notice its nice desktop-published format. It's kind of hard to see what is really on the report, however.

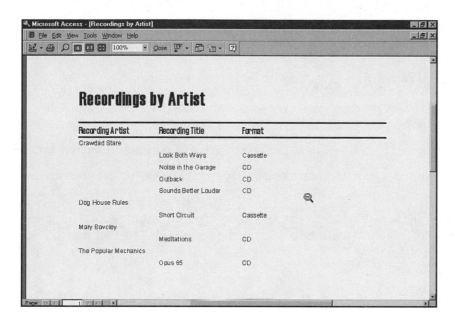

You can zoom in and out when you view the reports you create in Access.

Your mouse has turned into a magnifying glass; actually it's the Zoom tool. Click once and you zoom out getting an overall view of the report; click again and you zoom back in on the report. Zoom in and out on the report and then use the **Close** button to close the report.

Getting the Big Picture

Obviously the name of the game with databases is to enter data and then to manipulate it. Normally you will create a new database with the Database Wizard and then begin entering your data. Once you enter the data in your tables (either directly into the table datasheet view or into a form) you can manipulate the data and create objects like reports.

Our Classic Vinyl database has served its purpose. It shows how easily you can create a new database with the Wizard and how different database objects give you different views of your data. Since we are finished with the database you can close its window; click its **Close** button.

Give Yourself a Round of Applause

See, this database business isn't so tough. It's a lot better than trying to organize information on a bunch of dog-eared index cards or moldy file folders. Now that you have a feel for this whole database creation process and the different objects that go into a database, you can create a table of data in the next chapter.

The Least You Need to Know

➤ When you create a new database, you need to give the file a name and a place on your local drive or network to reside.

➤ The Database Wizard creates your new database based on a selected template.

➤ The Database templates contain premade tables, forms, and reports that you can use for your data.

➤ You can create your new database so that it already contains sample data. This gives you a chance to play around with the objects in the database before you start entering your own data.

Turning the Tables: Table Design

Okay, so you started Access, you used the Database Wizard, and you created a new database that held sample data. In the Classic Vinyl database that you created in Chapter 4, you had a chance to look at some of the various types of objects that are in a database—specifically tables, forms, and reports.

Lay Your Cards on the Table

Being an apprentice database wizard, you now know that the best place to enter data is in a table. Every row in the table is a discreet record. For instance, each row in a customer database is information regarding a specific customer.

Every record in the table divides into smaller, more precise bits of information. Yeah, you remember from earlier chapters, these items are *fields*. Again, a field may be a customer's phone number or his first name—a particular piece of information relating to that one person. The number of fields in the database table are dictated by the number of columns in the table.

It's the Wonder of New: New Tables for a New Database

Now that you know where the data needs to be, it's time to create a new table. Since the last database you created already contained data, start from scratch and create a new database container based on the blank database template. Once you have the new database, you can fill it with objects, such as tables. Create a database that will hold information relating to a cheese shop named *The Fromage Boutique* (fromage is the French word for cheese, get it?).

Bon, Allons! (I Mean, Let's Go)

You will find that since you have already created a new database once, the process will now be a real piece of cake, er…cheese.

In Access, click the **New** button on the Database toolbar and the New Database dialog box appears. You've dealt with this particular dialog box before. Make sure you have the **General** tab selected; then double-click the **Blank Database** template.

Start Your Engines

If Access is not running, start the software by selecting the **Start** button on the taskbar or the **Access** shortcut icon on your desktop. Once Access is up and running, the Database dialog box will appear. Click **Cancel** to close the dialog box and then follow the instructions on this page for creating a blank database.

In the File New Database dialog box that appears, double-click in the Filename box if the text in the back is not highlighted. Type **Fromage Boutique** as the database file name. Use the **Save In** drop-down arrow to select a place on your local drive or on a network drive if that's where you keep your information. Remember to click the **Create** button in the dialog box to conclude the database creation process.

You can store your new database in a current folder or create a new folder.

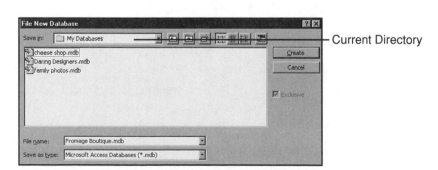

Current Directory

It's Alive, It's Alive!

Things are looking great; you are the proud owner of a brand, spanking-new database. Once you click the **Create** button, you return to the Access window; the Fromage Boutique database window sits right in front of you. This window, as you learned in Chapter 4, is kind of a command center for adding and manipulating the objects that you have in your database.

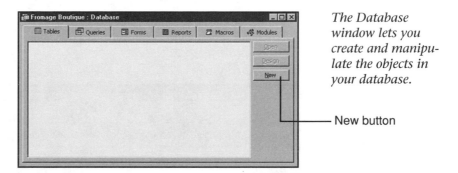

The Database window lets you create and manipulate the objects in your database.

— New button

Since you created the Fromage database from scratch (with the blank template), it does not contain any database objects. This makes your next move straightforward. The one-and-only choice is the **New** button, on the right of the window. Yeah, I know there are a bunch of tabs on the Database window, one for each of the various object types, but you have to trust me on this one; they are all empty. If you didn't trust me, and have been clicking around the object tabs in disbelief, make sure to select the **Tables** tab and then click the **New** button. The New Table dialog box appears offering you several possibilities. Two of the more straightforward methods of creating a new table are the Datasheet view and the Design view.

Déjà Vu Datasheet

The datasheet view looks a lot like a spreadsheet, meaning the table is divided into rows and columns. The heading on each of the columns will be the field names that you select for each field in the table.

53

The New Table dialog box lets you choose how to create your new table.

For simple tables such as the one you are going to create, the Design view gives you the most immediate input into how the fields in your table work. To enter the table Design view click **Design view** and then click **OK**.

The Table Design View lets you build a table with custom fields.

Table Design Toolbar

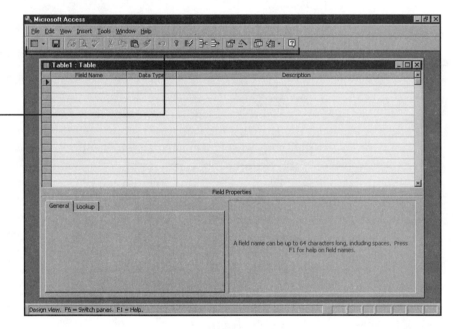

Your Table is Ready

The New Table dialog box offers you a number of different ways to build a new table. The *Datasheet view* allows you to set the table up like a spreadsheet. The *Design view* gives you complete control over the field parameters that go into the table. The *Table Wizard* lets you design your table based on a list of completed sample tables. The Import Table option imports data from other applications, such as Microsoft Excel, and places the information in an Access table. The *Link Table* option creates a table based on information that remains in another application, such as a spreadsheet program like Microsoft Excel.

The Table Design View Window

The Table Design view is where you build a table from scratch. All the tools that you need to do the job are available. You already know that each database object has a unique toolbar with a special group of buttons to assist you when you create or work with them; the Table Design Toolbar gives you one-click access to the features that you will use as you design your new table.

Fields of Dreams

Setting up the fields in the Design view is pretty straightforward; all you have to do is give each field a name and let Access know what kind of information you plan on putting in that field. Access provides you with a description area that allows you to attach descriptive text to a field. This text appears on the Access status bar whenever you are in that particular field during data entry.

Since you plan on placing customer information in this table, it makes sense to set up field names that request the type of data that you want for each person. Fields such as first name, last name, and address would be important to this type of table. Keep in mind that you have 64 characters (including spaces) for each field name that you create. It makes sense to keep your field names reasonably short and very descriptive. Then when you work with your table in the Datasheet view the field columns will not have to be super-wide to accommodate stupendously-long field names. Now, to create the fields:

Make sure the insertion point is in the first row of the field name column. Type **First Name**. Pretty easy so far; press **Enter**. This will move you to the Data type column.

Not My Type

It was no big deal coming up with a name for your field, but what in the world does Access want now? How do you come up with a field type? Field types refer to the kind of information you plan on putting in a particular field in the table. Letting Access know the data type makes it possible for special things to be done to that field, such as including the field data in a total sales figure, or placing an employee picture in a field from another application.

Sounds complicated, but don't worry; Access doesn't leave your data types to chance. It gives you a list of acceptable formats. All you have to do is step up to the plate (figuratively of course), choose from the list, and crack, you're off to the next field.

Click the **Data type** drop-down arrow in the current box. A list of data types appears.

A drop-down list provides you with all the different data types.

Data Type list ——

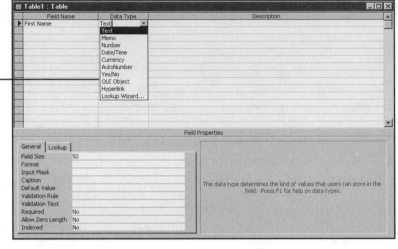

Data Type

Access provides you with ten different settings for data type:

Text—Text and numbers up to 255 characters

Memo—Lengthy text

Number—Numbers used in mathematical calculations

Date/Time—Date and time values

Currency—Numerical data used in calculations

AutoNumber—Sequentially numbers each new record

Yes/No—Lets you set up a field with a true/false data type

OLE (Object Linking and Embedding) Object—A picture, spreadsheet, or other item from another software program

Hyperlink–This field type lets you jump from the current field to information in another file

Lookup Wizard—The field chooses its values from another table

When you think about it, any fields that contain the names of people, places, or things will use the **Text** data type. After all, names are just a bunch of letters from the alphabet—text. Computer geeks like to call these *alphanumeric characters*.

So, the best field type for your first name field is text. Click **Text** in the Data Type list. Text is placed in the field type box. Press **Enter** to advance to the next column.

Description Optional

The Description column is where you can place a descriptive tag to accompany your field. Then, whenever you enter the field during data entry the description appears on the Access status bar.

The descriptions are totally optional. Their main purpose is to assist anyone who is doing data entry in a table and needs a reminder regarding what type of information should be placed in a particular field. The First Name field is self-descriptive; you put the first name in it. You can forgo the description on this particular field. Press **Enter** and you can set up your next field.

Farther a Field

You already have a field for the customer's first name, so you'll probably need one for their last name. Make sure that the insertion point is in the second row of the field name column. Type **Last Name** and press **Enter**. The field type is correct, it's a text field (which is the default field type in Access), so press **Enter** twice to advance to the next field (you can skip the description).

Now you can finish off the particulars regarding the customers, fields that contain information on where they live. Add the following field names to your table: Street, City, State, and ZIP. All the new fields will be text fields.

> **Check This Out...**
>
> ### You've Got the Moves
>
> It's easy to move from column to column or row to row in the Table Design view. You can use the Tab to move forward through the rows or Shift + Tab to move backward. The Arrow keys on the keyboard can also be used to move in their respective direction (for example the up arrow key moves up). If you are a mouse kind of person, just place the mouse I-beam in a particular row or column and then click to place the insertion point.

Text Puts the ZIP in Your Code

You may wonder why the ZIP code field is a text field rather than a numeric field. ZIP codes are designations rather than numbers with a numerical significance. When you assign the number type to a field, you want to make sure that it has some mathematical significance, such as the number of cases in stock or the amount of money you have in the bank.

The (Primary) Key to Success

Database tables can be tricky if you don't have some sort of scheme that uniquely identifies each of the records in the table. The Federal government (and, yes, the IRS) uses a unique social security number to identify each taxpayer. In a database table, a customer number field or a product catalog number field are both excellent ways to assign a unique number or designation that is particular to the record it contains. This special field is called the *primary key* or *key field*.

The Key to Your Database Table

The key to understanding the key field is that it must uniquely identify each record. You might think that the last name field will do the job. But what if there are a bunch of Smiths and Joneses in your database? When you determine the data that will go into your key field, remember that it must be different for every record; it can't repeat. This is why using a unique number such as a product code, or social security numbers, are your best bets when it comes to key field data.

Since you are working on a customer table, you will create a customer number field that designates as the primary key. Make sure that you are in the field name box below the ZIP code. Type **CustNo** (abbreviate to keep the size of the field name manageable). Press **Enter** to move to the Field type column.

Take a Number

You can handle the way that you determine the customer number for each of your customers a couple of different ways. You can type in a number for each of the customers during the data entry process, or you can let Access assign the numbers for you. Yes, that's right, Access will assign the numbers for you, saving you a lot of typing and ruling out the possibility of duplication.

So, where do you sign up for this automatic numbering option? You designate the Field type for the CustNo field as **AutoNumber**; it's that easy. Click the **Field Type** drop-down arrow and then click **AutoNumber**.

The CustNo field probably could use a description. That way, if you have someone doing data entry who isn't familiar with AutoNumber, she won't have a nervous breakdown when Access won't let her enter anything into the field. Press **Enter** and type **This field will AutoNumber each customer**.

Super! You have the Customer Number field set up. Now you all you have to do is assign it the key field designation.

Access makes it very easy to designate the CustNo field (or any field) as the key for the table. Make sure that the insertion point is currently in the **CustNo** row. Click the **Primary Key** button on the Table Design toolbar. Notice that a key appears to the left of the CustNo field.

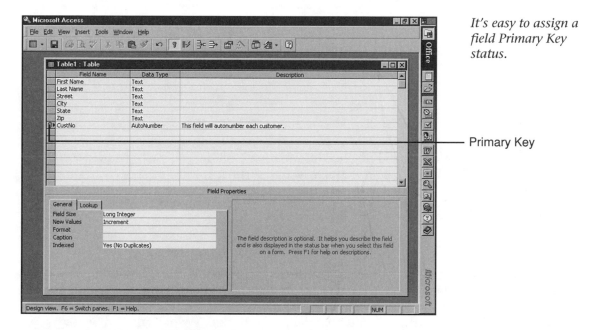

It's easy to assign a field Primary Key status.

Primary Key

Better Save Than Sorry

A fair amount of work has gone into the designing of this table, and you don't want to lose it. So, save it already.

Click the **Save** button. The Save As dialog box appears asking you for a name for the table. Type **Customers** in the **Name** box. Click **OK** to make the saving of your table a done deal. Notice that the name of your table, **Customers**, now appears in the upper-left of the table design window.

Done in Front—Moving Your Field

As you set up your field names in each of the field rows, you may want to rearrange their order. For example, it would make sense to make the key field the first field in the new Customer table that you've been working with; so you need to move the CustNo field.

Access makes it very easy for you to move a particular field and its parameters in the Design window. All you have to do is place the mouse pointer on the gray button (it looks like a box) just to the left of the field name. The mouse pointer becomes a right pointing arrow. Clicking the **Row** button will then select the entire field row. To move the CustNo field, all you have to do is select that field's row by clicking the **Row** button.

Click the Row button to select the Field row.

These gray boxes are Row buttons.

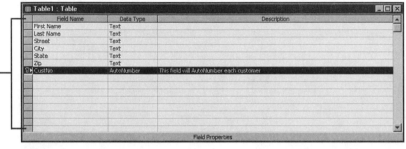

Field Name	Data Type	Description
First Name	Text	
Last Name	Text	
Street	Text	
City	Text	
State	Text	
Zip	Text	
CustNo	AutoNumber	This field will AutoNumber each customer

To actually move the row and the field information in it, drag the selected field row to the new location, which in your example would be the first row of the table. Good job—your dragging technique is quite impressive.

Drag and Drop: The Untold Story

Moving field rows in the Table Design view and moving field columns in the Table Datasheet view share a common technique—Drag and Drop. To move a field row, select it by clicking on its row button. Then click on the row and hold the mouse button down. Drag the row to its new location and then release the mouse button. This is called *dragging*. To move Field columns in the Datasheet view, click on the column name and then drag the item to its new location. Then give your mouse a rest!

Save Your Changes!

Whenever you make changes to the structure of your Access table, make sure to save the table. You don't want to lose any of your hard work.

You're just flying now; you've saved your table design, designated the primary key, and even moved a field. Now you can venture into a strange, new world: the world of masked fields (for greater effect, read that last sentence out loud in your best Rod Serling, *Twilight Zone* voice).

Who Is That Masked Field?

From out of the West, on a white horse, rode a masked man known as the Lone Data Arranger. Sorry, I couldn't resist the pun. The next step in designing a new table is to set up fields that really make data entry easy. This is done by putting an input mask on the field. An *input mask* is used to format the data you enter in the field (such as formatting numbers as currency) and to limit the number of characters that can be entered. Input masks are also great at placing items in the field for you, such as the parentheses around the area code in a phone number or the dashes in a social security number. The big question is where do you create input masks?

As you've created the fields for your table, you may have noticed that the lower-half of the Table design window is taken up by a tabbed area called *Field Properties*. Although you may think this area has something to do with agricultural real estate, the Field Properties are actually a set of parameters that you assign to a field to control how Access stores, handles, or displays the data.

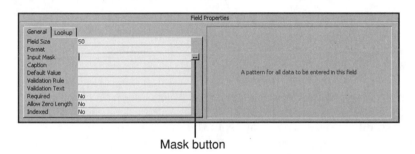

The Field Properties area in the Design window allows you to control how the data will work in a particular field.

Mask button

It is in this Field Properties area that you define your Input Mask for a particular field. For example, you have a field that will hold the ZIP code for each of the records in your table. It makes sense to set up the ZIP code field so that it will allow the entry of five characters, then automatically insert a dash, and then allow the entry of four more characters (this is the format for the new ZIP codes; are these four new numbers the reason they keep raising the price of stamps?). Masking a field is quite easy; you merely invoke the Input Mask Wizard.

Riding with the Input Mask Wizard

Now we can get down to business and actually use an input mask to control how data is entered into the ZIP code field. in the Table Design window click in the **ZIP Code** field row. The Field Properties that you set now will be assigned to this particular field. In the Field Properties box, click in the **Input Mask** entry box. A button with an ellipsis appears in the far-right of the Input Mask entry box. This button is the Mask button.

Click the **Mask** button. The Input Mask Wizard appears. The Input Mask Wizard contains a whole bunch of input masks for your data: ZIP Code, Social Security Number, Phone Number, and so on—and even gives you an opportunity to try out a mask before you apply it to your data.

*The Data Look
column shows you the
pattern that your data
will take as you enter
it in the masked field.*

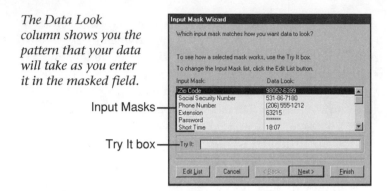

Input Masks

Try It box

To apply an input mask to the ZIP Code field, click the **Zip Code** input mask if it isn't already selected. Before you do anything drastic, you'll want to test drive this mask. To do so, press the **Tab** key; the insertion point moves into the Try It box. Type **443405555** and watch what happens. The wizard inserts the dash after the first five characters. Try to enter additional characters and the wizard just beeps at you. The mask limits the number of characters to nine.

Looks to me like this mask thing is going to work out just fine. Click **Next**. The wizard even gives you the option of modifying the way the mask is set up. Click **Next** again. Now the wizard asks you if you want the symbols in the mask (in this case the dash) to be stored with the data; sure, a few stored symbols will not really affect the size of your database file (in the case of very complex masks that enter a large number of symbols you might decide not to store them with the data). Click **Next** to move to the last screen in the Input Mask Wizard.

Well, you made it. Just click **Finish** to assign this mask to your field. Now the mask pattern appears in the Input Mask box. Hi ho, Silver!

*The Input Mask box
holds the input mask
that you've created
for your field.*

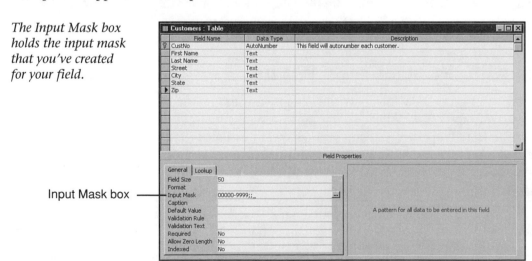

Input Mask box

62

Congratulations, your customer table looks great. You created several fields, set up an autonumbering customer number field, and masked the ZIP Code field. Now you should make sure to save your work. Click the **Save** button on the toolbar.

Changing Your View Point

It makes sense to take a peek at this new table in the Datasheet view: the view that you will actually be using for data entry. Again, the best place to go to change your view quickly and easily is the toolbar.

The very first button on the left side of the toolbar—The Table View button—allows you to switch between the table Design and Datasheet views. Click the button. Shazam! You're in the Datasheet view. The Datasheet is made up of rows and columns; each column has a heading that directly relates to the fields that you designed. Once you start doing your data entry you will find that each record will appear in the datasheet as a separate row. Switching between the Datasheet view and the Design view will become second nature to you as you work with your Access tables. When you want to input or view data go to the Datasheet view. When you need to add or edit a field (like putting an input mask on a field), you use the Design view. Let's return to the Design view.

Click Table view again, and you are whisked back to the Design view. Now you could bounce back and forth between these two views all day, and maybe even take the time to enter a little data, but your table design chores are not quite over. Remember, Access is a relational database, meaning your database will be made up of more than one table. Each table will contain a discrete body of information.

For instance, customer information will be in one table, product information in another, and then order information in a third. The key fields in these tables will be used to relate the information—a record in the orders table will contain the customer's number who ordered the product and a product number for the item that was ordered (you will get a lot more information on relating database tables in Chapter 8).

You have a table that you can use for customer data; but you will also eventually need tables for your products, your orders or sales, and your suppliers. I mean, you are trying to run a cheese shop here, and you can't let poor database management curdle your profits.

Return to the Design view of your table and click the **Close** button to close the Design window. Notice that your Customers table now appears in the Database Explorer for the Fromage Boutique database. Continue on your table design course and set up a table for your cheese products.

Using the Table Wizard to Design Your Database

You are probably starting to get the feel for the different routes that you can take in Access to design your databases and the objects they contain. To boil it all down in the simplest terms, you have a choice between using a wizard or not. The wizards are great if you need to build a complex table and don't want to have to create all the fields from scratch and deal with a bunch of input masks. For simple tables, it is probably faster to design them from scratch. Using these two different paths wisely will allow you to build really great and very usable tables. You already designed a table from scratch; now see what the Table Wizard has to offer as you create a second table for your database.

A Little of This, a Little of That: Selecting Fields from the Sample Table

Make sure that you have selected the **Tables** tab in the Database window, and then click the **New** button. Double-click the **Table Wizard** in the New Table dialog box. On the left side of the Table Wizard window, you see a list of **Sample Tables**. You can use one of these tables as the framework for the table you're building. The Sample Fields list box displays the fields available in the currently selected Sample Table. You use this wizard by selecting a Sample Table, then selecting individual fields from that table and inserting them into your new table. The Sample Fields you select for insertion into your table appear in the Fields in my new table list box, on the right side of the Table Wizard window. Many of these sample fields already contain input masks.

Let's build our new table using some of the fields from the sample database. In the Sample Tables list box, scroll down until you find the **Products** sample table; then click it. The Sample Fields list box changes to contain the names of all the fields available for that sample table.

The Table Wizard let's you borrow fields from sample tables.

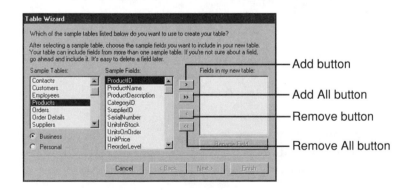

64

In the **Sample Fields** list, you can select the fields that you want to purloin from the sample table and include them in your own table. The first sample field available is ProductID, and it's a good one for you to put in your table. This field will serve the same purpose as the CustNo field that you put in your customer database. ProductID will autonumber each of the products you enter in the table, and the field will serve as the primary key for the table.

A set of buttons are available for inserting or removing sample fields from your table. Make sure to select the **ProductID** sample field and then click the **Insert** button (the single, right-pointing chevron) to include the field in your table.

Use the **Insert** button to place the following additional sample fields in your table in the order they appear (remember you must select the field before clicking the **Insert** button): ProductName, SupplierID, UnitsInStock, UnitsOnOrder, and UnitPrice.

> **Check This Out...**
>
> **Put Them in Or Take Them Out**   Use the **Add All** button (the right-pointing, double chevrons) to insert all the sample fields, the **Remove** button (left-pointing, single chevron) to remove unwanted fields, and the **Remove All** button (left-pointing, double chevron) to remove all the sample fields. Whether you are adding or removing fields, make sure that you click on the field to select it before clicking on Add or Remove.

And Now for Something Completely Different

Not really, but I didn't want your enthusiasm to wane. Now that you have selected the fields for your table, you can move to the next step. Click **Next**. The wizard wants to know what you want to name the table and if you want it to automatically assign a primary key field to the table.

The wizard has already assigned a name for the table—Products—that is fine. It also makes sense to let the wizard assign the primary key. If you think back to the fields that you included in this table, the most likely key to assign as the primary key is the ProductID field. If the wizard doesn't choose the right key field, you can always change it later in the table Design view. Click **Next**.

The Table Wizard wants to know if there is any kind of relationship between the existing tables in your database. For now, to keep things simple, and to put off the discussion of table relations until later, just say that these tables are not related. Click **Next**.

The Table Wizard has completed the design of your new table and wants to know if you want to start entering data in the Datasheet view or take a look at the table in the Design view. Since you worked in the Design view before, take a look at how this thing is set up. Click the **Modify the table design** option button. Click **Finish**.

Your finished table in the Design view.

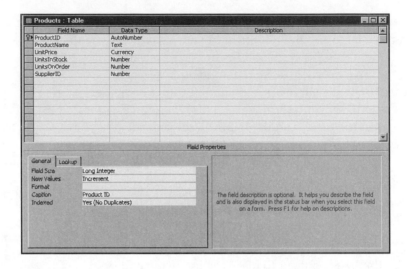

You finished the table! As predicted, the ProductID field was designated the primary key. Peruse the other fields and notice that some are set up as text fields and other as number fields. If you ponder the purpose of each of the fields, I think you will agree that the Table Wizard did a pretty good job setting up the fields and their properties. Click **Save** on the toolbar to make this whole thing a done deal. Click **Close** to close the design window.

Now you have two well-designed tables and are ready for the next step in building a database: data entry. Rest those fingers now; there's data input to do in Chapter 7.

The Least You Need to Know

> ➤ You can create a new table from scratch and manually define the fields in the table.

> ➤ The Table Design view is where you define your field and their properties.

> ➤ Selecting a field in the Design view makes it easy to move the field row.

> ➤ You can set up fields such as a customer number that will automatically number (autonumber) the records in the table.

> ➤ You can assign input masks to fields. These masks can limit the number of characters in an entry as well as control the look of the entry in the field.

> ➤ You can also create tables using the Table Wizard. The wizard allows you to copy fields from sample tables, and these fields already have been assigned appropriate field types and input masks.

Chapter 6

Going On Record: Adding and Editing Data

In This Chapter

➤ Enter and edit data in the table Datasheet view

➤ Move around your table with the greatest of ease

➤ Change column widths

➤ Move a Field Column from one place to another

➤ Add and delete fields in your table

➤ Use an AutoForm for easy data entry

You put your new data in, you take your old data out; you do the hokey pokey and you shake it all about. Oh, sorry, I was just killing time until you turned to this page. Now that you know how to construct databases and have worked through the table creation process, it's time to learn how you enter and manipulate data in a table.

Working in the Datasheet View

In the last chapter you saw that you can work on your tables in two different views: the Design view and the Datasheet view. The purpose of the Design view is to set up the fields in the table, which determines the structure of the table.

It's the Datasheet view that you use when you want to enter and edit the data that goes into the table. We will be spending most of this chapter in the Datasheet view. So, get comfortable in your chair, place your hands on home row, and let's go for it.

Entering Your Data

Data, the information you put in your tables, is by far the most important component of this whole database thing. Empires are built and lost because of data, so it is important for you to get it in your database and get it organized.

Let's start by putting together a simple customer table. In fact, we can enter our data in the Customers table that you created for the Fromage Boutique database in the last chapter. Make sure that you have the Database window for the Fromage database open on your desktop (or any other database). Activate the **Tables tab** with a click and then double-click the **Customers** table (or any table) to open it.

Once your table is open in the Datasheet view, it's ready for data entry.

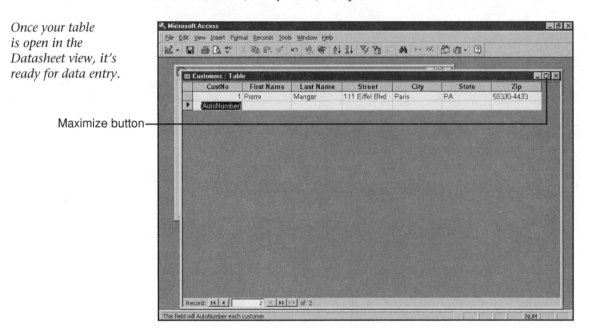

Maximize button

You have the Customers table open and things look like they should; the table is divided into rows (records) and columns (fields). You're probably thinking that a table in the Datasheet view looks a lot like a spreadsheet (in Excel for instance). So that you can see as much of the data entry area as possible, click the **Maximize** button on the table window.

It's time to type in our first customer's data. The First Name field is where you want to do your typing, so press the **Enter** key to move from the CustNo field (it's an autonumber field so you don't have to type anything in it) to the First Name field. Type **Pierre** and then press the **Enter** key. Hurrah! You've entered data and advanced to the next field.

If you make a mistake when you are typing in a field, you can press the **Backspace** key to delete the typo. Then just key in the appropriate text. What's that you say? you've already moved to the next field and now you see the typo? No problem, just use the mouse pointer (I-beam) to place the insertion point back into any of your fields with a quick click.

Fill in the rest of Pierre's record as follows (remember to press the **Enter** key at the end of each entry):

Last Name:	Manger
Street:	111 Eiffel Blvd.
City:	Paris
State:	PA
Zip:	55330-4433

Check This Out...

You Asked For It!

When you entered the ZIP code, Access automatically placed the dash in the entry. This is all due to the field mask that you set up when you designed the table. You also may have noticed that when you pressed Enter after typing the ZIP code, that a customer number (1) was automatically assigned to Pierre. The autonumber field type is doing its job, assigning sequential numbers to your customers as you enter their data. For more information on field types, take a look at Chapter 5.

Press **Enter** again and you will move to the First Name field for your next customer. There is still a little more typing to do; Enter the customer information found below.

Janet	Dugong	12 Coastal Way	Waterford	OH	44240-5567
Bob	Jones	1340 America Dr.	Crystal	PA	65012-6894
Alice	Barney	4443 Maine Ave.	Spokane	PA	65437-1234
Kim	Reech	55 Platinum St.	Lost Angeles	OH	44240-9354

The Table window displays your data and provides you with all the tools you need to add and edit records.

Select All   Field Names   Record Selectors

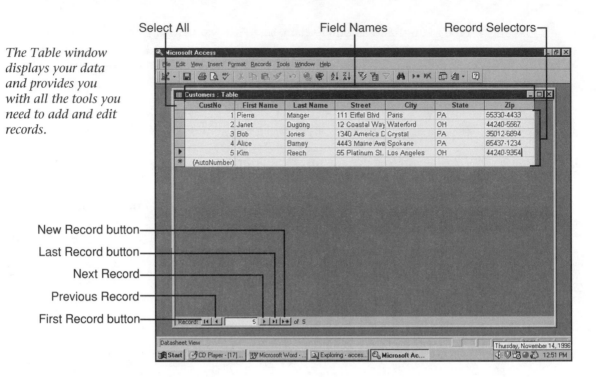

New Record button
Last Record button
Next Record
Previous Record
First Record button

Editing Your Table

Editing records is every bit as easy as entering new records. Let's say that Alice Barney dropped by your cheese shop this morning and bought an impressive amount of curd, over three pounds of brie and seven pounds of cheddar. When she paid for her purchase by check, you noticed that she had a new home address (she purchased the cheese for a house-warming party). As soon as she departs, you rush to your computer. You're excited, not because she bought so much cheese, but because you get to edit one of the records in your database.

Changing Field Data

Alice is still going to reside in the beautiful garden state of Pennsylvania, but her Street, City, and ZIP have changed. Place the mouse pointer on the very left edge of Alice's Street field. The mouse pointer will turn into a cell pointer. Click once and all the data in the field will be selected.

Now, all you have to do is type the new data. Type **1420 Mineshaft Street**. The new data replaces the currently selected old data. Use the mouse pointer (as the cell pointer) to select the data in the City field. Replace Spokane with **Big City**. We also need to edit Alice's Zip, but only the last four digits have changed. Place the mouse pointer (it becomes an I-beam inside the field) just before the first number in the ZIP's last four. Hold down the left mouse button and drag the I-beam across the four numbers to select them. Now you can type the new last four; type **8765**. The new numbers replace the selected old numbers.

Selection Election

When a single word or number appears in a particular field you can select the item with a quick double-click. In entries that are made up of multiple words or items separated by spaces or other delimiters such as hyphens (like *Kansas City or a ZIP code–44240-5555*) a double-click will only select the portion of the entry that the I-beam rests on. For those of you that shun the mouse totally when selecting items you can use the Shift + the right arrow key to select items in a field (a character at a time) once you have placed the insertion point in that field.

Navigating the Tossing Sea of Your Table

As you enter data into your table, or edit records that are already there, it makes sense to know how to easily navigate around the table. An important area of navigational interest is just to the left of the horizontal scroll bar at the bottom of the maximized Table window; this area contains the Datasheet navigation buttons. These buttons let you move one record forward or back and to the beginning or end of your records.

Click the **First Record** button (it's the first button on the left). The record selector moves to Pierre's record. Notice that it selects the text in a particular field. The field that is selected will be in the same column that you left the insertion point in after your last round of data entry. Click the **Next Record** button. The indicator moves to Janet's record. Click the **Last Record button** and the indicator moves to Carol's record. Click the **Previous Record** button and the indicator moves to Alice's record.

Another phenomenon that you will face in Access, is that the mouse pointer takes on a variety of shapes depending on where you've placed it. For instance, when you place it at the top of a column, you get a down pointing column selection tool. When you place the mouse pointer on a particular field in a particular record, you get a cross-like pointer called a cell pointer. You can use it to select one field in a record.

The best way to get familiar with the various mouse shapes is to move the mouse pointer around the table and see what happens. So, go on, what are you waiting for?

A Keyboard Sonata (Or a Movement in the Key of Board)

The keyboard also offers you several different avenues for moving around the fields in your table. Some of the movements only require one key to get the job done, like the Tab key (it moves you forward through the fields). In other cases you need to press two keys simultaneously like the Shift + Tab (this moves you backwards through the fields). Take a look at some of the other keyboard movements in the list below:

Check This Out...

Sound Practices
When you use the mouse to move around a table the placement of the insertion point is as easy as one click. However, when you are typing data it makes sense to keep your hands on the keyboard and use the keys for movement in the table.

Tab	One field forward
Shift + Tab	One field back
Up Arrow	One field up
Down Arrow	One field down
Home	first field in a record
End	last field in a record
Page Up	Up one screen of records
Page Down	Down one screen of records
Ctrl + Home	First field in the first record
Ctrl + End	Last field in the last record

Try out some of the keystrokes. Once you've tried both the mouse and the keyboard, you can decide which way of moving through the table you prefer.

Manipulating the Columns

The default column width for the Datasheet view of your tables is one inch. This means that you may type data into a field that is not accommodated by the field's column width. You have probably noticed that some of the customers' street addresses that we've placed in the Address field are being cut off because of the narrow column width.

Changing column widths is extremely simple. Place your mouse pointer on the dividing line between the Street column heading and the City column heading. The mouse pointer becomes a column sizing tool. Click and hold the left mouse button. Using the column sizing tool, drag the column border to the right until the Street column is wide enough to accommodate all your entries.

Column Sizing Tool

CustNo	First Name	Last Name	Street	City	State	Zip
1	Pierre	Manger	111 Eiffel Blvd	Paris	PA	55330-4433
2	Janet	Dugong	12 Coastal Way	Waterford	OH	44240-5567
3	Bob	Jones	1340 America D	Crystal	PA	35012-6894
4	Alice	Barney	4443 Maine Ave	Spokane	PA	65437-1234
5	Kim	Reech	55 Platinum St.	Los Angeles	OH	44240-9354
(AutoNumber)						

The Column Sizing Tool lets you change the width of your columns.

Fit to be Tried

Now you know that you can increase or decrease a column width by dragging the column dividers. There is another way to quickly change a column width: Place the mouse pointer on the column divider between the Street and City fields. When the column width tool appears, double-click. That's right, just double-click. The column widens to accommodate the truncated entry.

This little trick is called *best fit*. Whenever you want a field column to automatically accommodate the longest entry in it, just move to the column divider and double-click.

Saving Your Work

When you work in other Microsoft programs (such as Word or Excel) you have to save all the information you enter, or you can lose it when you close the application. Saving the data in Access tables is different; the data that you enter is saved to the table as soon as you place it in the field. If you inadvertently exit Access without clicking Save for instance, you will find that all the data you entered is in your table even though you didn't save it. This is one of the (beautiful) enigmas of Access.

Make Those Columns Bigger You can change the default setting for the columns in your new table's Datasheet view. Click the **Tools menu**, then click **Options**. Click the **Datasheet tab** and then put the new column width in the Default column width box. Changing this setting will not override changes that you make to individual field columns in your tables using the mouse.

Access Warnings! You will find that if you try to exit a table that you have made structural changes to (such as field column width changes or field deletions), Access will let you know that you need to save the table.

You do, however, have to save your work whenever you make design changes to the table, such as adding a field, deleting a field or widening or narrowing a column. So, if you change the structure of the table, save it or lose it.

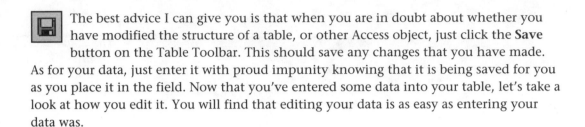

The best advice I can give you is that when you are in doubt about whether you have modified the structure of a table, or other Access object, just click the **Save** button on the Table Toolbar. This should save any changes that you have made. As for your data, just enter it with proud impunity knowing that it is being saved for you as you place it in the field. Now that you've entered some data into your table, let's take a look at how you edit it. You will find that editing your data is as easy as entering your data was.

Selecting Rows and Columns

There will be times when it is advantageous to select an entire record, or a field column in your table (such as moving a column or deleting a record). You can click headings (field names) to select an entire column and you can click a gray row button (record selectors) to select a record. To select all the records in your datasheet, you can click the **Select All** button which is the gray square just to the left of your first field.

Access makes it easy for you to select your records and field columns.

Moving a Column

Being able to select an entire record or field column makes it very easy to move these items. For instance, it may make more sense to have the table fields arranged so that the Last Name field appears before the First Name field. Place the mouse pointer at the top of the Last Name field heading (the column heading). The mouse pointer turns into a down pointing arrow, a field selection tool. Click once and the entire Last Name column will be selected. Now comes the hard part. Press the left mouse button down and drag the entire Last Name column to the left one column. In effect you are dropping the Last Name column on top of the First Name column.

Moving a field column in the Datasheet view is just a click and a drag away.

Don't let go of the mouse button until you have the column in the right place. A dark black line will appear along the border of the column you are moving the column to. Let go of the mouse button and the column drops into its new position. Click anywhere in the table to deselect the column.

Way to go! You've just become familiar with *drag and drop*. You can use this feature to move columns, fields, texts, even graphics. Drag and drop is the easiest way to move or copy a selection a short distance.

Broken Record (Deleting a Record)

Life has a way of raising you up one moment, and then dashing you down the next; you just get done making all these improvements to your database table when the phone rings. An entrepreneurial colleague down the street who runs a bakery calls to let you know that one of your best customers, Janet Dugong, has moved out of town. After hanging up the phone, you sit down, wondering what you'll do with all that Stilton that you keep on stock for her. (What you'll do is fill out your Products table and keep better track of your inventory using Access). You should probably delete Janet's record. Click the selector button for Janet's record (the mouse turns to a right pointing arrow). Janet's entire record is selected.

 Now all you have to do is delete Janet's record. Courage, I know this is tough. Take the mouse and click the **Delete Record** button on the Table toolbar.

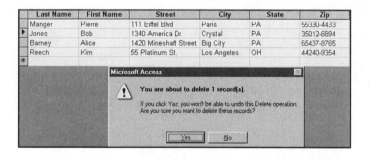

Janet leaves the Table.

Access is pretty smart. It knows that you are about to delete a record. It wants to make sure that you really want to do this. You have the option of deleting the record forever (the **Yes** choice), or letting Janet's record live to see another day (the **No** choice). You really don't need this record any longer, so click **Yes**. Janet is gone.

Adding a Field to Your Table

Check This Out...

Deleting a field is just as easy as inserting a new field Select the column (and field) that you wish to delete and then click **Cut**. When you delete a field, you are probably also deleting some data. Access takes this into account and will ask you if you truly wish to remove the field from the table. Just keep in mind that you can't have it both ways: no field no data. It's that simple.

Although you are traumatized over the deletion of Janet's record, you realize that your colleague's phone call has given you a sudden spark of inspiration. Your table does not include the phone numbers of your customers. You realize that if you had their phone numbers, you could keep in better touch with them, maybe even become their friend. And then they won't move away like Janet.

Your course is decided; you must add a telephone field to your table. Adding a field to a table is just a matter of adding a new column. Access will add the column to the left of any column you select. In this case, you want the telephone number to go to the left of the Street address. Select the Street field column and then click **Column** is a choice in the Insert menu so click it. A new column is placed in your table to the left of the Street column.

A Name Is Just a Name

Techno Talk

Fields Fields can also be added, deleted, and moved in the design view. Any changes you make to the tables design (such as adding or deleting a field) will be reflected in the table's Datasheet view.

You will obviously want to name the new field that you've placed in your table because the name that Access automatically sticks in there, **Field1**, probably isn't going to do the job for you. To replace this field name, double-click the column heading (Field1). This selects the text. Now you can type your own field name, such as **Phone**. Click anywhere in the table, and your new field name is centered and you're good to go.

No Fuss Field

Now that you've added a new field column to the table and named it, all you have to do is switch to the Design view and determine the field type. Then add an input mask if you wish. Since this is going to be a field for telephone numbers it would be nice to mask the field so that the parentheses around the area code and the dash after the first three digits are automatically placed in your entries.

Click the **Table view** button on the toolbar. This switches you to the Design view. Notice that the new field has already been placed in the table design; it appears just below First Name. Click in the new field's **Field Type** box.

Since we will be dealing with phone numbers (which aren't really numbers of numerical significance), the field type can remain text. We do, however, want to mask the field to make the data entry easier. Click in the **Input Mask** box in the **Field Properties** area. Click the **Input Mask** button to invoke the Input Mask Wizard.

The third mask type on the wizard's screen is for phone numbers. Select it with the mouse and then you can move through each of the screens as you did for the ZIP Code mask. However, since the phone number mask is exactly what we are after, you can click **Finish** (again, this button has no relation to any European countries or the body parts of fish) to complete the masking process.

 The mask is placed exactly where we want it. Save your table design using the **Save** button and then use the **Table view** button to return to the Datasheet view. Now you can enter the phone numbers for your customers. Start at the top of the column and then press the down arrow key after each entry. You may also wish to widen the column to accommodate your entries (remember, you don't have to enter the parentheses or the dash).

Customer Phone Numbers:

Pierre	(216)555-1234
Bob	(216)555-5436
Alice	216)555-7777
Kim	(512)555-3643

Phone
(216) 555-1234
(216) 555-5436
(216) 555-7777
(512) 555-3643

A nice column of phone numbers.

Saved!

You will be asked to save the table when you manipulate your fields and then switch back to the Table view or call up one of the wizards. Any changes made to the structure of the table must be saved!

Adding A New Record to a Table

A new customer drops by your shop and is incredibly excited to find such a wide variety of cheeses. This person is so excited, in fact, that they want to make sure they are in your database. They want to be notified of any special sales or rare acquisitions, such as the Pacific rim favorite, or Hawaiian Coconut Curd (okay, so I made it up, just wanted to see if you were still paying attention).

Time to enter the new customer's data into the database. You have probably noticed that working in the Datasheet view can be distracting; it's hard to concentrate on just one record when you can see the entire table. There is a quick and easy way to isolate records for data input and editing, the AutoForm.

Creating a Quick Form for Data Entry

You just want a quick and dirty form that shows all the fields in the table and lets you work on one record at a time; this is the basically the definition of an AutoForm. The AutoForm option lets you create a new object such as a form or report without going through a long design process.

To use the AutoForm option, click the **New Object** drop-down **arrow** button on the Table toolbar. A list of possible new objects is displayed. Next, click the **AutoForm** choice on the **New Object** menu. Voilà! Your AutoForm is created. Your form has incorporated all the fields from your table.

The New Object menu is a quick-fix solution to creating a data-entry forms.

Working in the Data Entry AutoForm

Pierre's was the first record in your table and appears in the newly created form. You may have to scroll down a little, but this form has a set of navigation buttons just like the datasheet.

The AutoForm uses the fields that were in your table.

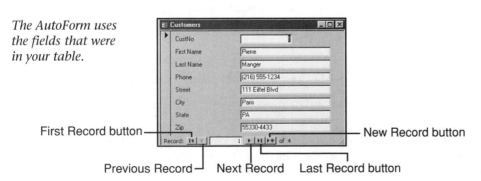

First Record button — Previous Record — Next Record — Last Record button — New Record button

Click the **Next record** button. You have moved to the second record in the table, Bob Jones. It's nice being able to see each of the records in this isolated manner, but we want to enter data for a brand new customer. Click the **New record** button (it's the button with the asterisk).

Now we have a blank record. Press the **Enter** key and fill in the information that follows (remember to hit the **Enter** key after each field entry):

Last Name	Curly-Moe
First Name	Larry
Phone Number	(216) 555-8444
Street	3 Stooges Lane
City	Hollywood
State	OH
Zip	44240-3210

Way to go! You've added another record to your table. AutoForms are usually used for quick data entry and then discarded without saving. Click the **Close** button on the AutoForm. Now let's take a look at the table and see what the record looks like in the Datasheet view.

Check This Out...

Form your own opinion Forms can include all or just some of the fields found in a table. Forms can also be designed that include fields from more than one table. You will learn about forms that use fields from multiple tables later in the book.

Where's My Record? Viewing Your Table Updates

Mr. Curly-Moe's record does not appear in our table; what gives? Actually, nothing bad has happened. All you have to do update the data in the table. Click anywhere in the table. Hold down the **Shift** key and press the **F9** function key. Ah, there we go. All the records now show in the table. Now you can continue to enter data, add fields, or even delete fields in the Datasheet view. You can also switch to the Design view and work on the fields and field types in the table. Just a click back on the **AutoForm** allows you to continue to enter information into the table. When you are finished with the AutoForm, you can save it or close it without saving it. It's your choice.

Check This Out...

Moving the form If you have to move the AutoForm out of the way, grab it by its title bar and drag it away from the table.

The Least You Need to Know

Wow, you sure put that table through its paces. As you can see, the table offers the perfect holding tank for your data. Its datasheet construction makes it easy for you to see your fields and records in a very simple and easy-to-use format.

➤ The Datasheet view provides you with a spreadsheet-like view of the information in your table. You can add, delete, or edit records in the Datasheet view.

➤ The Navigation buttons provide you with a way to move from record to record in the Datasheet view or in the AutoForm view.

➤ You can select a Field Column and drag it to a new location using drag and drop.

➤ You can add fields to the Table in the Datasheet view.

➤ After you enter data into an AutoForm click in the table and make sure to press **Shift + F9** to update the records in the table.

Chapter 7

Being Manipulative: Different Ways to View Your Records

In This Chapter

➤ Sort your records like a pro

➤ Freeze fields for easy scrolling

➤ Use the Find feature to search out data

➤ Filter records by example

➤ Filter records by form

➤ Hide fields and then find them again

Okay, so you got your feet wet with tables and learned how to enter, edit, and delete records. Your first table was a real light-weight. However, now you need a stiff dose of database reality—the potentially large size that your tables can take on. Dive in.

In most cases, especially if you use Access to manage business data (a mailing list or a product table), the number of records in a table can be staggering. No reason to panic, however, (unless you like to panic; if you do, hyperventilate now) Access provides several clever tools for dealing with massive amounts of data in your tables.

Out of Sorts

You now know (much to your chagrin) tables can potentially amass hundreds, even thousands of records. Obviously, you cannot view a table this size in its entirety in the Access window. Not being able to view the records easily increases the chances of data-entry mistakes, even missing field data. You can scroll up and down through the table records, you can even try out an AutoForm to view each record alone, but when you're dealing with a lot of records, you need other strategies to insure accuracy.

One way to manipulate and re-order your records is with the Sort feature. Access makes sorting very easy; you can sort by any field and either sort ascending (a to z) or descending (z to a).

Basic Sorts of the Big Kahuna—Northwind

Obviously, if I'm going to convince you of the need for sorting your records, I need to show you a big database table. Use the Northwind Trader's database in Chapter 2, in the sample folder inside the Access software folder.

The Northwind Database window.

In the Northwind Database window, open the **Products** table (double-click on its icon). This table has 77 records—a good number to play around with.

Going Down, Please (Descending Sort)

This whole sorting thing is not difficult. All you have to do is select the field and click one of the Sort buttons on the toolbar. For example, you may be in a situation where you are horribly overstocked; your warehouse is filled to the ceiling with products. Now you can either a) burn down the warehouse and collect the insurance money (and probably go directly to jail), or b) sell some of your merchandise. And why not start with the products that you have the most of?

The Northwind Products table has a Units In Stock field. You can use this field to sort the records in the table in descending order. This will give a list that places the products with the greatest number in stock at the top of your list.

Z↓A▼ Click the **Units In Stock** field heading to select the entire column of data. The field column for Units In Stock becomes highlighted. To sort the data from large to small (descending) click the **Sort Descending** button on the toolbar. As soon as you click on the Sort Descending button the records are re-arranged by Units In Stock from large to small—descending!

Techno Talk

Filters are Fine, but Queries really Quake You will find that sorting, filtering, and finding data works fine when you only want to manipulate the records in one table. For a more advanced way of sorting and filtering data, use the query. You can design queries for one table or multiple, related tables. You will work with queries in Chapter 10.

Category	Quantity Per Unit	Unit Price	Units In Stock	Units On Order	Reorder Level	Discontinued
Beverages	24 - 0.5 l bottles	$7.75	125	0	25	☐
Seafood	24 - 4 oz tins	$18.40	123	0	30	☐
Condiments	12 - 8 oz jars	$25.00	120	0	25	☐
Meat/Poultry	24 boxes x 2 pies	$24.00	115	0	20	☐
Condiments	24 - 500 ml bottles	$28.50	113	0	25	☐
Dairy Products	500 g	$2.50	112	0	20	☐
Seafood	24 - 250 g jars	$19.00	112	0	20	☐
Beverages	24 - 12 oz bottles	$14.00	111	0	15	☐
Grains/Cereals	24 - 500 g pkgs.	$21.00	104	0	25	☐
Seafood	24 - 150 g jars	$15.00	101	0	5	☐
Seafood	4 - 450 g glasses	$12.00	95	0	0	☐
Dairy Products	10 - 500 g pkgs.	$38.00	86	0	0	☐
Seafood	12 - 12 oz cans	$9.65	85	0	10	☐
Dairy Products	5 kg pkg.	$55.00	79	0	0	☐
Confections	20 - 450 g glasses	$14.00	76	0	30	☐
Condiments	32 - 8 oz bottles	$21.05	76	0	0	☐
Beverages	750 cc per bottle	$18.00	69	0	5	☐
Confections	12 - 100 g bars	$16.25	65	0	30	☐
Seafood	24 pieces	$13.25	62	0	20	☐
Grains/Cereals	12 - 250 g pkgs.	$9.00	61	0	25	☐
Beverages	500 ml	$18.00	57	0	20	☐
Condiments	48 - 6 oz jars	$22.00	53	0	0	☐
Beverages	24 - 12 oz bottles	$14.00	52	0	10	☐
Confections	100 - 100 g pieces	$43.90	49	0	30	☐
Seafood	16 kg pkg.	$62.50	42	0	0	☐

The results of your sort!

Now you have the data sorted in descending order, which is great. You can see that you have 125 units of something in stock (the item at the top of the sorted **Units in Stock** column), and you can probably also see that it is in the **Beverages** category (in the **Category** field) What you can't see, however, is the name of the item—the **Product Name** column is off to the right of the screen. For you to see the name and the units in stock at the same time, you need to scroll back and forth using the horizontal scroll bar. But hold on just a minute; don't scroll yet. There is a way to remedy this little problem so you can see the name and the units at the same time.

Freezing Columns (Is It Cold in Here, or Is It Me?)

It would be great if you could somehow trick the Product Name field into staying on the screen when you scroll to the Units In Stock column. And you know, if you've been reading this book carefully, that there is certainly a way to do this, or I wouldn't bring it up. Freezing columns——that's how you can get the Product Name and Units in Stock on the screen at the same time.

Check This Out...

Putting the Freeze on Multiple Fields

To freeze a field (remember, fields are columns in the datasheet view) select the field or make sure that the insertion point is present somewhere in the field column. Then click on the Format menu and then click on Freeze Frames. To freeze multiple field columns, click the first field name (the column heading); then hold down the **Shift** key and click the last field name that you intend to freeze.

So, freeze a column (my teeth are chattering). Click the column heading in the **Product Name** data column. This selects the entire column of data.

Click the **Format** menu; then click **Freeze Columns** (in this case, it's one column—Product Name). If you did this right, the Product Name column moves over to the first field position in the table. Click anywhere in the table to deselect the field column.

Now see if this whole freeze action actually worked. (The last time I tried this kind of thing, I ended up with some Popsicle sticks slumped over in some half-frozen yogurt, but that's another story.) Use the right scroll button on the horizontal scroll bar to scroll toward the **Units in Stock** column. Notice that as you scroll, the Product Name stays put—that's the frozen column.

Wow! You can scroll horizontally until the Units In Stock column is right next to the Product Name column. The thing that you had 125 units of is Rhönbräu Klosterbier (whatever that is, some kind of German beer, I guess. Oops, this was supposed to be a nonalcoholic-beverage-only book).

You can freeze columns and then scroll to view columns of data that were many fields apart.

Product Name	Units In Stock	Units On Order	Reorder Level	Discontinued
Rhönbräu Klosterbier	125	0	25	☐
Boston Crab Meat	123	0	30	☐
Grandma's Boysenberry Spread	120	0	25	☐
Pâté chinois	115	0	20	☐
Sirop d'érable	113	0	25	☐
Geitost	112	0	20	☐
Inlagd Sill	112	0	20	☐
Sasquatch Ale	111	0	15	☐
Gustaf's Knäckebröd	104	0	25	☐
Röd Kaviar	101	0	5	☐
Spegesild	95	0	0	☐
Queso Manchego La Pastora	86	0	0	☐
Jack's New England Clam Chowder	85	0	10	☐
Raclette Courdavault	79	0	0	☐
NuNuCa Nuß-Nougat-Creme	76	0	30	☐
Louisiana Fiery Hot Pepper Sauce	76	0	0	☐
Chartreuse verte	69	0	5	☐
Valkoinen suklaa	65	0	30	☐
Escargots de Bourgogne	62	0	20	☐
Tunnbröd	61	0	25	☐
Lakkalikööri	57	0	20	☐
Chef Anton's Cajun Seasoning	53	0	0	☐
Laughing Lumberjack Lager	52	0	10	☐
Schoggi Schokolade	49	0	30	☐
Carnarvon Tigers	42	0	0	☐

Record: ◄◄ ◄ 24 ► ►► ►* of 77 ◄

Now you know what items to place on blue-light special in your store to get the inventory down. Notice that the second highest stocked item is crab meat. I guess you need to sell your customers on the idea that crab meat and German beer really go well together—yum, yum.

Spring Thaw: Unfreeze Those Columns

It's easy to unfreeze the columns that you put the freeze on. Just click the **Format** menu, and then click **Unfreeze All Columns**. Now when you scroll to the right in your table, the Product Name column does not remain (frozen) in the table datasheet.

Going Up, Please (Ascending Sort)

You've already done a great job with a descending sort, so you probably won't have any problem at all with an ascending sort. Say that you would like to put the records back in their original order, based on their Product ID.

Select the **Product ID** column, and then click the **Sort Ascending** button on the toolbar. Now the records are back in their original order. As you can see, the Sort buttons are somewhat limited; you can sort by one field in either an ascending or a descending direction.

Sorting Out the Details (Advanced Sorts)

As you can see, the Sort command kind of leaves you high and dry if you need to sort a table by more than one field, especially if the fields are not adjacent in the table. Not a problem; you just need to conduct a sort based on multiple fields—which in Access lingo is an *advanced sort*. With an advanced sort, you can sort by as many as 15 fields—if you REALLY want to.

The advanced sort feature is accessed by clicking on **Filter** on the Records menu. A *filter* is a list of certain criteria (such as customers in Germany) that will give you a subset of the records in your table. Since filtering and sorting are different ways to manipulate your records, they are found in the same menu: Records. We will talk about filters shortly; for now, we'll take a look at an advanced sort using more than one field.

> **Check This Out...**
>
> **Field Position**
> You probably noticed that the Product Name column remained in the first position. If you want to put the Product ID back in its original place, select that column and drag it.

> **Techno Talk**
>
> **Check Under the Autonumbering Hood** The number in the Product ID field shows the order in which the records were input into the table. To check a field in a database for autonumbering, you can switch to the Table Design view using the toolbar, and then check the field type of the particular field.

85

Let's say that you run a company that sells products to other businesses. These businesses would be listed in your Customers table. The catch is that these customers are located all over the world and you would like to see the records in the table sorted by country. Since you have more than one customer in each country, you would also like the cities that these businesses are located in sorted alphabetically as well.

Sort Adjacent Columns

You can sort by more than one field using the Sort buttons if the two fields are adjacent and the fields are in the order that you want to sort the records by. Just drag to select the two adjacent columns and then click on either of the Sort buttons on the Table toolbar.

When you sort by more than one field, you need to assign a primary sort field (in this example, Country) and at least a secondary sort field (in this case, the City field) and determine which direction (ascending or descending) you want the sort to follow. When you give Access all these instructions for your advanced sort, you're setting up the *sort parameters*. Setting these parameters is the first step in conducting an advanced sort.

Well, almost the first step. You can't do any kind of sort if you don't have a database table open in Access. The Northwind database provides a Customers table that lists companies. The fields in the table include a field for Country and a field for City. So, to play out the scenario described above, open the NorthWind Database and then double click on the **Customers** table to open it. Now you have the raw material that you need (a database table) and you can set your sort parameters.

Setting Your Sort Parameters

The first step in conducting an advanced sort is to enter your sort parameters. You do that in the Filter window. To get there, click the **Records** menu, and then click **Filter**. Click **Advanced Filter/Sort** to enter the Filter window.

The Filter window has two parts: the upper-half of the window shows the current table and the fields that it contains. The lower-half of the window is where you really get the job done. The area is divided in several rows and columns. The two rows that are important are the ones marked **Field** and the one below it marked **Sort**.

When you sort by more than one field, you should place the field names in the Filter window in the order that you want the sort to take place. So, click in the first field column next to **Field**; a drop-down arrow appears. Click the drop-down arrow, and wonder of wonders, a list of the fields in the table appears. All you have to do is choose the primary field that you want to sort the table by. In this case, choose the **Country** field. Then click in the **Sort** box and choose **Ascending** from the drop-down list.

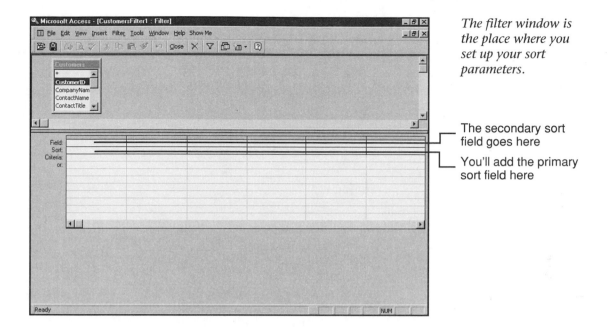

The filter window is the place where you set up your sort parameters.

The secondary sort field goes here

You'll add the primary sort field here

Add Fields to the Filter Window with a Double-Click

You can also add fields to the field columns in the Filter window via the Field Name box that appears in the top-half of the Filter window. Click in the field column you wish to place the field in, then double-click on the field name in the Field Name box.

Now it's time to add your secondary sort field. Click in the second column across from the **Field** row heading; Access again supplies a drop-down list of the fields in the table. Choose **City**; then move to the **Sort** box and use the same technique you used before to set the direction of the sort for this field as **Ascending**.

Super Sorts and Brain Teasers

As I said earlier, in an advanced sort, you can sort by as many as 15 fields, and sort some of the fields in an ascending direction, and others in a descending direction. It would be a challenge (and people would probably think you pretty odd) trying to come up with a multidirectional sort that involved more than three or four fields. Oh, and you can also save advance sorts as queries by clicking the **Save** button, but more about queries later.

You can quickly set up your sort parameters in the Filter window.

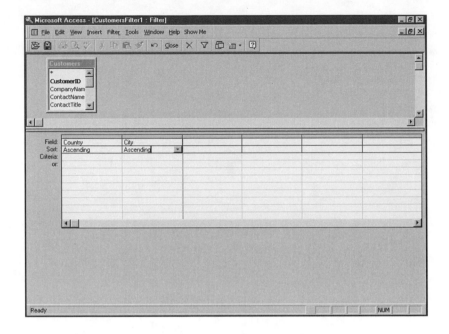

Now, Sort!

 You've supplied sort parameters to your table; now there must be a button somewhere that will make this a done deal. Aha, there it is, on the toolbar: the Apply Filter button. If you've been playing along, click the **Apply Filter** button. Access looks in the Filter window and sorts your data by each of the fields you selected (moving from left to right in the Filter window). The records in the table are sorted first (ascending alphabetically) by the Country field and then by the City field.

A Toolbar for Every Occasion!

If you haven't noticed already, each of the different views (Table view, Design view, Filter view, Form view, and many others) that you use to work on your database has its own toolbar. Since you are in the Filter window, the currently displayed toolbar is the Filter/Sort toolbar.

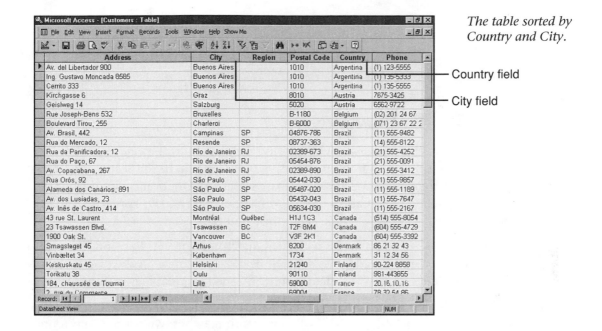

The table sorted by Country and City.

— Country field

— City field

Using Find (I'm Lost!)

There will be times when you want to quickly find a specific record in a table, or take a look at a group of records that have the data in a particular field in common. Well, look no further, your answer is found; I mean *find*. The Find feature is a quick way of tracking down records that meet a particular search criteria.

Say you have a table of suppliers (just like the Suppliers table in the Northwind database) and these companies are all over the world, making it hard for you to drop by and check up on their operations. So you happen to be taking a vacation to Canada, and you're sure that you have at least one supplier in that country. And even though everyone warns you about mixing business with pleasure, you pull your Suppliers table up in the Access window to search for your Canadian suppliers.

Piece of cake; scroll to the Country field column. Click in the very first record's Country field (this would be the first field in the Country field column.) Then click the **Find** button on the Table toolbar (it looks like a little pair of binoculars. I mean little compared to real binoculars.) As soon as you click the **Find** button, a Find dialog box pops up. This is where you tell Access what you want it to search for; as in sorting, these instructions are called *parameters*. The Find dialog box offers all the options you need to set your search parameters.

If you're lost, use the Find feature and be found.

Setting Your Search Parameters

Let's take a gander at the various areas of the Find dialog box. In the *Find What* box, type the item that you want to search for. In this case, type **Canada**. In the Search drop-down list, specify whether you want the entire database searched (**All**), or just **Up** or **Down** from the selected field. There is also a drop-down box marked *Match*. This box contains three choices: Any Part of Field, Whole Field (the default), or Start of Field.

If you choose Any Part of Field, Access will try to match the entry in the Find What box with any part of the data entered in the selected field. For instance, in the case of Canada, Access would consider Canada, Canadian, and U.S./Canada all matches in your search.

Whole Field, on the other hand, would return matches where only Canada is found—the whole word only. Finally, Start of Field will only return matches where Canada is found at the beginning of the field entry. In this case Canada and Canadian would both be considered matches because the characters *Canada* come at the beginning of the field data.

Once you have typed in your search string in the Find What box and chosen how you want Access to return the matches in the Match box, there are a couple of check boxes that you have to deal with: Match Case, Search Fields as Formatted, and Search Only Current Field.

The **Match Case** check box allows you to find text that has the same pattern of upper- and lowercase characters as the entry you placed in the Find What box. This allows you to search for data that has been entered in a particular way, for instance. The **Search Fields As Formatted** box (when selected) searches for items as they appear in the field; an example of this is a number entered as **52000** but that appears in the field as **$52,000.00**. You would check the box and do your search for the **$52,000.00**. This search parameter is also important for dates; you may have entered a date as a numerical entry (**9/12/60**) but it appears in a different format (**September 12, 1960**). The **Search Only Current Field** check box is straightforward; if you select it, the find feature will only search the field column that the insertion point is currently in.

In the case of this search, you only want to look for **Canada** in the Country field, so leave this check box selected.

Going Wild With Wild Cards

When you set up the search for Canada in the Country field, you typed in a complete text string—Canada—in the Find What box. There may be times when you want Access to search for parts of words or a particular pattern of alphanumeric characters (letters of the alphabet); you can do this using *wild-card characters* as placeholders. Wild cards can represent one character, several characters, a list of characters, or even a numeric character (you know, a number). Some of the most commonly used wild-card characters and their usage follow:

* This character can take the place of any number of characters. You can use it at the beginning, middle, or end of a character string. An example would be C*a. A search for this text string in a field column of countries would return countries that begin with a capital C and end with the letter a such as Canada and Cambodia. The number of characters represented by the asterisk can vary.

? The question mark can be used anywhere in your search string to represent a single alphanumeric character. Let's say you use the Find feature to search for the text string f?ll. Some of the possible matches you could get in a search like this would be words that differ by just one character such as fill, fall, full, and fell.

[ ] The brackets are used to specify a list of possible matches for a single character found in the items you are searching for. For instance you could set up the Find feature to look for the text string Jo[ah]n. Matches to this text string would be limited to Joan and John.

The number sign is used to represent a single numeric character in a search string. It works very much like the question mark wild card. Let's say that you have a Product number field that contains data in the form of three digit codes (such as 142 or 333). Your supplier calls and tells you all the products ending in 22 are going to be discontinued. No problem, you can do a search using #22 to find them.

Wild cards can be a big help when you need to use the Find feature, and want your matches to consist of items that you just can't get by typing in a whole word (such as Canada). Always take a moment to think about what exactly you would like the Find feature to dig up for you; chances are you can use a wild card to get the right results.

Click and You Shall Find

Once you set all the parameters in the Find dialog box, it's just a matter of clicking the **Find First** button to make things happen. You were looking for **Canada** and that's what Access found; the Find feature takes you to the first record that has the word **Canada** as a field value.

To find the next record that matches the search parameters, click the **Find Next** button. Access finds the next record that contains the Canada field value. When you have exhausted all the possible matches, you get a message that Access has finished searching the records and the search item was not found.

As you can see, Find allows you to move to records in the table that match your search parameters. If you needed to edit or compare a lot of records that share common field values, the Find feature might not be up to the task. It has no capability to group the matching records together, or preclude records from your view that don't match the search parameters. But don't despair, Access has you covered. You can use a *filter*.

Regular or Filter?

The obvious cigarette reference above isn't exactly PC (*politically correct* not *personal computer*), but this filter is healthy for your database. You can handle this next topic so you're not doing much mental huffing and puffing. A filter is a list of criteria that will give you a subset of the records in your table and filtering tables is easy! There are two ways of filtering tables so you can view a subset of your records: Filter by Example and Filter by Form. You get the same results no matter which of the two filter types you pick. It's kind of like the same camel with two different humps.

A word about the Find feature and filters: You already know that the Find feature can be used to move through a table and locate records that meet your search criteria. However, all the records, even those that don't match your criteria, still appear in the table, making things rather busy.

Filters also use criteria to operate. However, filters are superior to the Find feature in that they only show you the records that match the filter criteria. The other records in the table are hidden. This makes working with the records easier. Use find to quickly locate records that have a field matching certain criteria. Use filters when you really need to take a hard look at a subset of your table—the records matching the filter criteria.

Filtering by Example

An incredibly straightforward way to filter records is filtering by selection. All you have to do is show Access an example of the data you want to work with and it will show you the records that match. For example, in the Northwind Products table, the records in the table each contain a field for suppliers. So if you would like to see the products supplied by just one of your suppliers, you filter the records.

Give this a try. First, select the field data that you want Access to use for the filter. In the Products table, scroll down until you can see the first record that contains **Pavlova, Ltd.** in the Supplier column. Click-and-drag to select the field text (**Pavlova, Ltd.**). Now all you have to do is have Access perform the actual filtering. Click the **Filter by Selection** button on the Table toolbar.

Product ID	Product Name	Supplier	Category
16	Pavlova	Pavlova, Ltd.	Confections
17	Alice Mutton	Pavlova, Ltd.	Meat/Poultry
18	Carnarvon Tigers	Pavlova, Ltd.	Seafood
63	Vegie-spread	Pavlova, Ltd.	Condiments
70	Outback Lager	Pavlova, Ltd.	Beverages
*	(AutoNumber)		

Filtering by selection: select the field data and you are on your way.

Access displays only the records that match the filter criteria, in this case, **Pavlova, Ltd.** in the Supplier field. Now you can edit these records if you want to, and you are not lost in the fog of a huge table with massive amount of records.

Give Me My Records Back!

My sister used to say that about her Partridge Family albums. I'd answer, "What records?" Little did she know that the kid next door and I used them as Frisbees (David Cassidy would not be amused). Anyhow, when you finish using the filtered records, you are certainly going to want to put the table back the way that it was—complete with all the records you had available before. To do this, all you have to do is remove the filter. To remove the current filter, click the **Records** menu, and then click **Remove Filter/Sort**. All your records reappear in their original order. Even though filtering by example seems like the end-all way to set up a filter, Access does provide you with an alternative: Filter by Form.

Filtering by Form, Anyone?

When you Filter by Form a blank datasheet appears with all the appropriate Field columns found in your table. Then all you have to do pick the field or fields you want involved in the filtering. A drop-down arrow appears in each of the field boxes and all you have to do is click on it and select the data that will serve as the filter criteria.

The major difference between Filtering by Form and Filtering by Example is the number of criteria that you

Techno Talk

A Form for Filtering If you are in the Form view and want to Filter by Form, Access provides you with a form view of a blank record rather than the blank datasheet record that you get when you filter by form in the Datasheet view.

can set. Filtering by form allows you to set criteria in multiple fields. When you filter by example you can only select one criteria in one field (such as highlighting Canada in the Country field). Click the **Filter By Form** button to get a bird's-eye view of how this filtering technique operates.

You are looking at a table datasheet with a blank record that contains all the fields used in your table. You can either click in a particular field and select your criteria from a data list or type in the field data that you want the table to be filtered by (allowing you to use wild cards). Say you want to filter the products in the Products table by a certain entry in the Category field. For instance, you just want to see the records that are for Beverages.

Click in the empty **Category** field in the blank filter record. A drop-down arrow appears. Click the drop-down arrow and select the field data from the list—in this case, **Beverages**.

 Once you select your filter data in a specific field, click the **Apply Filter** button on the toolbar to see the results of the filtering.

Filtering by Form allows you to quickly select your filter parameters.

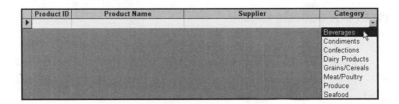

Clearing the Field with Delete

To clear field data already appearing in the Filter By Form record, select the entry and press the **Delete** key to remove it. You can use the Filter By Form method to filter a table by more than one field parameter at a time. Your need for these complex filters, however, may be better served by queries. *Queries* (an upcoming subject in this book) allow you to create new tables that hold the results of the filtering that you do, making queries ultimately more useful than filters.

Access shows the records that have an entry in the Category field that matches your filter selection such as Beverages. Now you can do what you want to these particular records without the distraction of the entire table information. To return the table to normal, use the **Remove Filter/Sort** command under the **Records** menu.

When you want to filter by more than one field just select a filter criteria in each of fields involved. For instance, you may want to filter the Products table so that you only see a list of the beverages you buy from a particular supplier, Bigfoot Breweries. To set up this filter in a Filter by Form situation, you would select Beverages in the Category field and then select Bigfoot Breweries in the Supplier field. The records filtered would then have fields that match both of your filter criteria. Pretty cool, huh?

Hiding Out (Hiding Fields in a Table)

You've spent a number of pages finding (and filtering records) using field information, but what if you want to lose a field—hide it from view? For example, you have an employee table that has salary information in it and you want to hide that column (it's not a good idea to let employees find out what their coworkers make; it usually leads to a lot of pounding on the boss' door).

Now You See It, Now You Don't

Hiding fields only requires that you specify the field that you want to hide and then let Access know that you are ready to hide it. In the Products table, say that you want to hide the Unit Price field. Click the Field heading (**Unit Price**) to select the entire column of data. Then click the **Format** menu and select **Hide Columns**. The Unit Price field is gone, hidden from view. Now, what if you want to get that column back?

> *Techno Talk*
>
> **Hiding Multiple Fields** You can hide more than one field at a time. Select each of the fields and follow the steps for hiding the column.

They're Back

Did they wipe their feet when they came into the house? While making fields disappear may seem a little scary at first, you'll find that it's really no big deal. Restoring the field column to the Datasheet view is even simpler than hiding the column in the first place.

To Unhide (what is happening to the English language?) the Unit Price column (or any column), click the **Format** menu. Then click **Unhide Columns**.

The Unhide Columns dialog box appears. The dialog box lists all the fields that appear in the table. A check box precedes each field name. If the check box is empty (not selected), the field is currently hidden. To unhide the field, click in its check box. Select the **Unit Price** check box to unhide the field. To return to the table, click the **Close** button.

You did a great job making those columns disappear and appear! You probably expect me to ask you to pull

> *Check This Out...*
>
> **Hiding Multiple Columns Couldn't Be Easier!** You can use the Unhide Columns dialog box to hide or unhide columns. To hide a column listed, simply remove the check-mark from the check box by clicking it.

a rabbit out of a hat next. Maybe later; for now, just recap some of the important Access features that you worked with in this chapter.

The Least You Need to Know

➤ You can sort your tables by specific field columns in either an ascending or descending order.

➤ In tables that contain a large number of columns, you can freeze fields so they remain in the Table window as you scroll.

➤ Use the **Find** command when you want to find records that contain specific information in a specific field.

➤ Use the **Filter** command when you want to select a subset of the records in your table by a specific entry in a certain field.

➤ You can find most of the commands for Sort, Find, and Filter on the Table toolbar.

➤ The **Remove Filter/Sort** command on the Record menu puts your table back the way it was before the sort or filter.

➤ You can hide one or a number of field columns in a table using the **Hide Columns** command.

Chapter 8

Between You and Me and Access: Table Relationships

In This Chapter

➤ Understand database relationships

➤ Define relationships between the tables in your databases

➤ Grasp the differences between the different types of table relationships

➤ Delete tables and other objects from your databases

"They're creepy and they're kooky, mysterious and spooky; they're all together ooky…" Hey, that could be my family! Dealing with database relationships can be every bit as taxing (and as fun) as dealing with personal relations (meaning family members). After all, people are just people and databases are just databases (or is that data?). So having good relationships between your data tables is the key to good database management.

You may remember that earlier in this book (so early that it may seem like two books ago), I mentioned that one of the strengths of Access (a relational database) is its capability to relate the data in different tables together via a common field. For instance, you may have a Customer Table that contains all the information on your customers, including a separate customer number for each record (this customer number would also be the key field for this table).

You also have a second table, an Orders Table, that details every order that you've taken. The Orders Table would obviously need to reference which customer made the order. This would be done by entering the customer number in the Orders Table. The data in these two example tables then would be linked (that is, related) by their common field: the customer number.

This link is just one relationship within this database

The Customers and the Orders Tables share a common field: CustNo.

Why Are You Telling Me This?

You are probably wondering what's the point of all this relationship stuff; well it's quite straightforward. You design simple self-contained tables that hold subsets of the complete data (all the information) that makes up the database. Then by linking the various tables by their common fields, you can integrate the information in the different tables together in queries, forms, and reports.

As you design your tables, you should keep possible relationships in mind. Well-designed and well-related tables allow you to treat all the data in the separate tables like one big happy family, so you can get the most use (and information) from the data you stored in the database. I feel a group hug coming on.

Creating Table Relationships

Take a look at how you and Access create these relationships between the various tables in a database. First, you need at least two tables to create a relationship; I happen to have three. Two of them you may be familiar with: the Customers and Products tables created when we discussed tables in Chapter 5 (Remember the Fromage Boutique database?). There is a third table—Orders—that is also important to this discussion.

Access makes it easy to initiate the relationship creation process; make sure you have the database open that you want to work with. Then click **Relationships** on the Database toolbar. The Relationship window appears.

Ready-Made Relationships

When you use the Table Wizard, the tables you create with the sample fields will often have shared fields. Access knows that you will want to relate the tables eventually, so the sample fields overlap between the different sample table types. The Table Wizard even offers you the option of relating the table that you are making to any of the current tables in the database during the creation process. It asks you if there is a shared field. What could be easier?

Now Appearing—Your Tables!

In the Relationships window, the Show Table dialog box appears. This provides you with a list of the tables that are in your database.

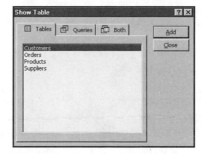

Select the table you want in the Relation-ships window and click Add.

Need Another Table?

If you inadvertently close the Show Table box or have already created some relationships between tables and want to add more, you can open the Show Table dialog box by clicking the **Show Table** button on the Relationship toolbar.

Since you want to establish a relationship between the Customers Table and the Orders Table, you need to get both of them into the Relationship windows. Click **Customers** Table and then click **Add**. Repeat this procedure to add the **Orders** Table to the window.

It makes sense to get rid of the Show Table dialog box when you are finished with it. Click **Close** to shut it down. Now you are resting comfortably in the Relationship window and are ready to establish a relationship between the two tables that you placed there.

Database Matchmaker: Using the Relationship Dialog Box

Establishing a relationship between two tables is easier than it sounds. I know I've said this before but, the tables must have a field in common for this to work. This field should be the primary key for one of the tables (this identifies each of the records in that table uniquely). The two tables you created earlier satisfy these conditions. Now comes the fun part.

Drag the **CustNo** field from the **Customers** table and drop it on the **CustNo** field in the **Orders** table. Wow, something's happening; the Relationships dialog box appears.

The Relationship dialog box verifies the relationship that you created.

Click CustNo here...

...then drag-and-drop it here

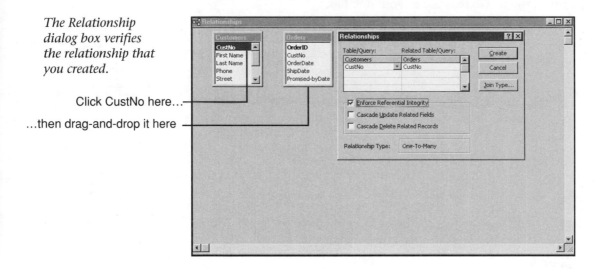

The Relationships dialog box shows the two tables that you are attempting to relate—in this example, Customers and Orders. Notice that the field that forms the relationship appears under each of the table names.

Right in the middle of the dialog box is a check box labeled **Enforce Referential Integrity**; sounds like something you'd never get a politician to agree to, but it actually means that you want Access to be certain that any CustNo values found in the Orders table must match CustNo values found in the Customers table. From a data entry standpoint, this is a good thing. If you enter a CustNo in the Orders table that does not exist in the Customers table, Access won't let you leave the table until you enter a valid number. Pretty neat, huh?

Join Types Often Need No Adjustment

On the right side of the Relationships dialog box, notice the Join Type button. Join types allow you to define how the data in the two joined tables relates. This is important when you run a query on the table. The default join type is set so that a query will select equivalent records only, meaning the values must be the same in the joined field. If you enforce referential integrity, the values must be the same in shared fields. Now this may seem confusing, however 99 percent of the time the default join type is the way to go; no adjustments are necessary.

You'll find another important item at the bottom of the dialog box, the Relationship Type information. Relationship types deserve their own discussion, so you'll get to them in just a minute. But for now, put this topic aside, so that you can complete the steps that actually form the relationship.

Click the **Enforce Referential Integrity** check box. Click **Create** to make this relationship a done deal. Your table relationship shows a line joining the two tables.

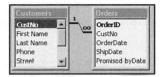

Your first relationship!

Notice that a **1** marks the portion of the line attached to the Customers Table and that an infinity sign (∞) marks the portion of the line attached to the Orders Table. These two little symbols actually say a lot about this table relationship. Speaking of which, it's time for that little discussion about relationships that I've been meaning to have with you...

The Types of Relationships

While you don't want to get too bogged down in detail, it wouldn't be a bad idea to take a minute and define the types of relationships you can have between your database tables. You've probably already made up your mind that there are only two kinds of relationships: good and bad. Well, you get an added bonus in Access; you can have three different types of relationships between your tables: One-To-Many, Many-To-Many, and One-To-One.

One-To-Many (Which Is Not the Same as One Too Many)

Let's start with the *One-To-Many relationship*. This is the type of relationship that you have between the Customers Table and the Orders Table. A unique customer number identifies each customer. This uniquely identified customer can make many orders of your fine cheese products. So Access can match each of the records in Customers (one) to an infinite number of records (many) in the Orders Table. You established this relationship by including the CustNo field in the Orders Table.

You now can also see the significance of the little symbols (the 1 and the infinity symbol) that Access stuck on the ends of the relationship line; they define the relationship type for you. One-To-Many relationships are probably the most common of the three relationship types; however, don't neglect the other two.

...And Then There's One-To-One

Another possibility is a *One-To-One relationship*. In this case, a record in one table would have only one possible matching record in the second table. An example would be a publishing company that only lets it authors write one book and one book only (hopefully, there is no such publisher in this fine country of ours). If you had an author table and a book table for the situation described, sharing the common author number field, you would have a One-To-One relationship. Each author record would match one book record.

But Don't Forget Many-To-Many

The third type is the *Many-To-Many relationship*. In this type of relationship, each record in the first table of the relationship can have many matches in the second table, and each record in the second table can have many matches in the first table.

Okay, so this one is a little fuzzy. An example should help. Say the publishing company publishes huge reference books that are written by teams of coauthors (it happens, it happens). The company has two tables in their database: one for their authors and one for their books. Each book is written by a group of authors, so the records in the book table have more than one match in the author table. At the same time, each author can be involved in writing more than one book. So the records in the author table have more than one match in the book table, too. Therefore, the relationship between the two tables is Many-To-Many. Is this starting to sound like a country western tune?

Back to Northwind to Test Your Relationship

A great place to become comfortable with table relationships is the Northwind database, which is no stranger to you. You already know that this database contains quite a few tables and so should also contain many relationships.

 To view the relationships in the Northwind database, open the database and then click the **Relationships** button on the Database toolbar. Then you're ready to get involved in some heavy duty relationships.

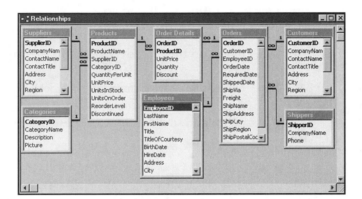

A well-related database.

Note that all the relationships defined in the database are One-To-Many relationships. It just makes sense that, in most cases, one of the tables will have records that have many possible matches in the table that they are related to.

Show Me Tells All

A great addition to the Northwind database is a menu item that says **Show Me** (it's right next to the Help menu when you open the Northwind database). This Show Me menu is a feature actually built into the database using macros. You can use the Show Me menu to get information on any and all of the objects in the Northwind database. It is a super resource as you work with the Northwind objects such as tables, forms, reports, and queries. Click the **Show Me** menu and a help box will appear with great information on all the objects that appear in the database. You will find that the Show Me information works a lot like the standard Help elements of Access.

Deleting Relationships

You may find it necessary to delete a relationship between two tables; for instance you may want to delete a field from a table that you have related to a field in another table (or you just might be feeling mean). Access will not allow you to delete the field from the table until you delete the relationship that this particular field is involved in (another example would be where you've inadvertently related two fields that should not be related). Open the Relationship window for the particular database; then select the relationship and delete away. For instance, you might have a number of related tables and decide that one of the relationships just has to go.

Check This Out...

The Key to Good Relationships
Remember, Access won't let you establish relationships between two tables using a field that is not the primary key for one of the tables.

Say you want to delete the relationship between the Orders table and the Employees table in the Northwind database. Maybe you've decided not to tie Employee information to your order system anymore. Click the line that shows the relationship; this selects the line. Then either click the **Edit** menu and select **Delete**, or press the **Delete** key on the keyboard.

Since you probably won't establish too many relationships that you then want to delete, Access wants to make sure that you want to deep-six the currently selected relationship.

Here is an example of a relationship.

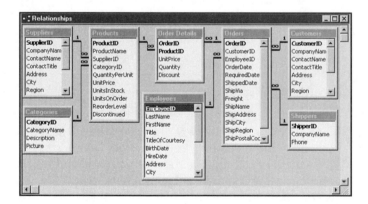

Access and the Office Assistant give you one last chance to save the relationship. If you are using the Office Assistant, it will prompt you with the question as to whether or not you truly wanted to delete the relationship (if you have the Assistant turned off, a dialog box appears related to the deletion). If you want to delete it, click **Yes** in the **Assistant Balloon**. One click and it's out of your hair forever. Of course, if this is all a big mistake, click **No**.

You may also want to remove unneeded tables from the Relationship window once you delete a relationship. Simply click any of the fields in the table and then press the **Delete** key on the keyboard. Access doesn't give you a second chance; as soon as you hit **Delete**, the table is gone from the window.

Don't worry too much, however; you aren't really deleting the table, just removing it from the Relationship window. You can put it back by clicking the **Show** table button on the toolbar. This provides you with a list of all the tables in the database. Add them to the Relationship window at your leisure.

When you finish in the Relationship window, click **Close** to return to the Database window. Access will prompt you to save any changes that you've made in the relationships if you've forgotten to save them.

The Importance of Good Relationships

Defining the relationships between the tables in your databases is super important if you ever want to do anything with the data that they contain. Defined relationships give you the ability to do queries and reports that pull data from more than one table. And while you may define your table relationships just to manipulate the data, a great side-effect is this whole concept of referential integrity. It will help you cut way down on data entry errors.

The Least You Need to Know

➤ Table relationships are possible because the tables involved share a common field. This shared field must be the primary key for one of the tables.

➤ To establish relationships between tables, click the **Relationship** button on the Table toolbar. This takes you to the Relationship window.

➤ Three different types of relationships exist. Most commonly you will have One-To-Many relationships between your tables—the individual records (one) in the table that has the common field as its primary key will potentially have a number of matches (many) in the related table.

➤ If you don't want two tables to be related, you can delete the relationship.

➤ Relating tables allows you to create database objects, such as queries and reports, using data from more than one table.

Part 3
So What's the Object?

Our modern society has become obsessed with the notion that everything we do these days have some significance—everything has to have a point, an object. We must constantly be growing and learning. The days of couch potatoism and junk TV have gone by the wayside and we must sit up in our chairs and watch PBS and learn something; everyone must be growing; and if you're not growing (metaphysically speaking) you must be nurturing someone who is growing.

Now, you've learned a lot about Access in this book (and have been growing into a real database maven); therefore when someone asks you "so what's the object?" You can answer, "which one?" Access actually offers you a number of different kinds of objects that help you view and manipulate your data. You've already worked with one of the most important Access objects—the table, the place where you keep all your data. In this next section, we'll explore some of the other objects available to you, such as forms and reports. Items that you can use to improve and streamline the database management process. "So what's the object?" Read on!

NEW '90s TREND: FAITH DEBUGGING.

Chapter 9

It's All in Your Form

In This Chapter

➤ Create forms for your database tables

➤ Use forms for data input

➤ Work in the Form Design view customizing forms

➤ Use the form's toolbox

➤ Create a new control for your form

I've always been bewildered by high-dive competitions; the competitors are, for the most part, judged on their form. Having a problem with vertiginous heights (I don't like high places), I've always felt they should all get a perfect 10 for just climbing to the top of that incredibly lofty ladder. Your databases can be a lot like a high dive; people who work online with your database—those entering, editing, and viewing the data—will in effect be judging your database by its forms.

Creating a Form

Working with forms is no big deal. Remember, they are just another one of the possible objects in your database bag of tricks. Forms are very useful for inputting, editing, viewing, and even printing data. You already had a quick look at forms back in Chapter 2, and you even created a form when you used the AutoForm feature for data entry in Chapter 6. So, as far as this chapter goes, you are already in good form—so to speak.

The forms that you design can make use of all the fields or just some of the fields that you find in the corresponding table. You can even design forms that use the fields from more than one table, allowing you to enter data in one form that inputs to two different tables.

The Wizard Will Know

As it has been (and will be) with many of the other features that you have already looked at, a wizard is available to help you create a form: the Form Wizard. To create a new form, or any other database object for that matter, you need to have a particular database open. In this case, use the Fromage Boutique database (you may have created this earlier) as an example.

Techno Talk

Wizards for Charts and Pivot Tables The Chart Wizard allows you to create various types of graphs to accompany the data in a particular table when displayed in the Form view. The chart (or graph) appears on a special form. The Pivot Table Wizard is a special cross-tab feature that allows you to compare data in a variety of different views.

With the Database window (for the Fromage Boutique database or any database) open in the Access workspace, click the **Forms** tab. This lets Access know that you want to work with either an existing form or create a new one. Click the **New** button.

The New Form dialog box appears. This dialog box allows you to choose what kind of form you want to create and how you want to create it. You can start from scratch in the Design view (just like you did when you created a new table) or use the Form Wizard (I vote for this choice). You can also use the AutoForm feature (remember, this uses all the fields in the table) to create three different kinds of forms: Columnar, Tabular, and Datasheet. There are also two other choices: Chart Wizard and Pivot Table Wizard, advanced features that you can ignore for the moment.

Select the form creation method and the table on which you want to base the form.

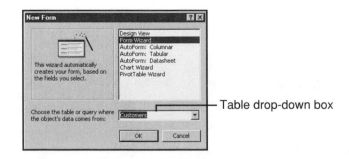

Table drop-down box

Click the **Form Wizard** to choose it in the New Form dialog box. Now, all you have to do is tell Access from what table you want to create the form. This means that the form will use the data and the fields that are currently in the selected table. Click the drop-down **Tables/Queries** box to choose the table. All the tables (and queries) in your database appear.

Keep this first form simple; base it on a simple table: Customers. Select **Customers** from the table list. Now all you have to do is click **OK**, and the wizard will walk you through the form creation process.

Pick Your Fields

The Form Wizard moves you to the next step in the form creation process; you pick which of the fields from the table you want use in your form. Use the series of command buttons to include or preclude fields from the new form. This screen also provides you with a Tables drop-down list if you select the wrong table in the previous step. See, the wizard is a nice person!

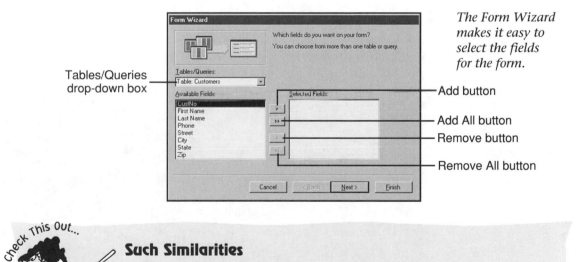

Tables/Queries drop-down box

Add button

Add All button

Remove button

Remove All button

The Form Wizard makes it easy to select the fields for the form.

Check This Out...

Such Similarities

This screen is very similar to the Table Wizard screen that you use to create a new table. Access supplies a list of possible fields and a series of buttons that allow you to select or remove fields from your new database object. Hopefully, you're getting the feeling that the Access wizards you use to create new objects will operate in pretty much the same general way.

If you want to include a particular field, for example, the CustNo field, you need to make sure to select the field in the Available Fields list and then click the **Add** button. Since you are going to use all the fields for your form, click **Add All**, rather than moving each field individually (this saves your clicking finger for playing games). Once you select the fields, click **Next** to move to the next step.

Don't Be a Lay-About, Choose a Layout

While the wizard does a lot of hand-holding during the form-creation process, it won't make the choices for you. You have to decide how you want this new form to look. You have four layout choices: Columnar, Tabular, Datasheet, or Justified.

A *Columnar* layout places each of the fields on their own line in a vertically oriented form; this type of form only shows one record at a time. A *Tabular* layout places the field names at the top of the form in separate columns and then lists the data records, each to a line, below the column headings. The *Datasheet* layout sets up the form to look like a table, using rows and columns. The *Justified* layout places the fields in equal rows across the form. These field rows line up or are justified on the right and the left.

To see a preview of a particular layout click its radio button; the preview appears in the left half of the Wizard screen. Once you've decided on a particular layout, make sure its radio button is activated; then, to select the type of form layout you want, click the appropriate option button.

The Form Wizard makes it easy for you to choose the layout of your new form.

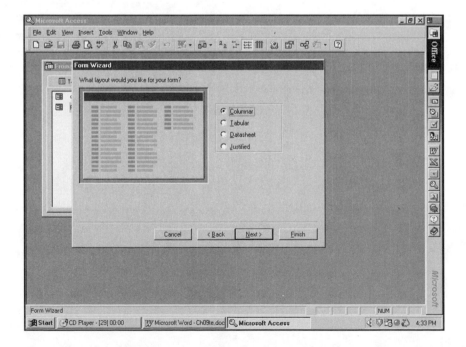

Check This Out...

Putting Your Layout on the Line

The type of layout you choose for your form will affect the arrangement of the fields on the screen; it's important to create a form that's easy on the eyes and makes data entry a snap. The Columnar layout is great for creating a form that is based on a table with only a few fields. This layout type also lets you view records separately. The Tabular layout works well when you have a lot of fields and what to be able to view a number of records at a time. The Datasheet layout can be used to hide certain fields from whoever is doing your data entry (things such as a salary field), but still let them do data entry in a datasheet-type environment. The Justified layout is similar to the Columnar layout, but places the fields in equal rows. Make sure you choose a layout that suits your data entry style!

The columnar layout (already selected) will work fine for the particular form that you are creating, so click **Next** to move ahead in the process.

You've Got to Have Style

Now Access tests your personal taste as you choose the style for the new form. The style is nothing more than the backdrop for your forms; for instance, you decide if you want your data to overlay a graphic of the world (International) or a night-time cityscape (Dusk).

Since this form is for your Cheese Shop (Fromage Boutique, remember?) database, use the Cloud style because it looks nice and fluffy like cottage cheese. Obviously, you can use a less arcane (or strange) process to decide on a style for your forms, but, hey, I'm writing this book. Click **Clouds**. Click **Next** to move to the next step.

It Was Fun While It Lasted

All good things must come to an end and form creation is no exception; you are looking at the last screen of the Form Wizard. This screen asks you to do two things: name the form and decide what to do next.

Every object that you create for a database needs a name, and Access is actually pretty good about coming up with names for you. In this case, you are basing this form on the Customers table in the Fromage Boutique database. Access figures that the form should have the same name as the associated table. You can, of course,

Check This Out...

Help You Can Count On You already know that the Office Assistant and the Access Help system offer you a lot of help as you work with the different database objects. The final screen of the Form Wizard has a check box named **Do You want help to display when working on the form?** If you do, select the check box.

change the name of the form by typing in a new name. In this example, however, you can leave the name as is: *Customers*.

You must also decide if you want to open the form that you created to enter or view data, or to enter the Form Design view and immediately alter the look or structure of the form. It makes sense to take a quick look at the form with the table's current data in it to see how much reworking it might need.

Make sure to select the **Open the Form to view or enter information** option button. Then click **Finish**. Congrats, you've designed a form!

Truly an Art Form

So you have a form, a very nice-looking form in fact, and you're probably wondering what to do next. Well, you can enter new data, edit old data, or just sit there and stare at the form. But hey, I know that you're too motivated to just sit there and stare (I'm giving you the benefit of the doubt).

Your new form appears! This one shows the first record in the Fromage Boutique database.

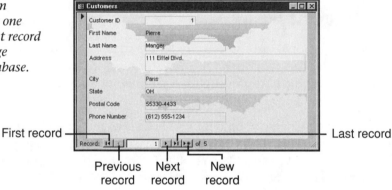

First record | Last record

Previous record Next record New record

Data Ho! If the table you based the form on already contains data, the form will display the first record. You can also easily move through all the records in the table.

Notice that the form has the same kind of navigation buttons that your tables have. You can move forward and backward through the records using these buttons. The New record button (an advance button followed by an asterisk) moves you to a blank record ready for data input.

Say that you're looking at the form and you don't like it. You want the fields to be ordered differently on the form. Believe it or not, you have complete control over the layout of the form.

Customizing Forms

Customizing forms is one of those things that can seem very simple on the surface but can become quite complex depending on what you want the form to actually do. Of course you're saying, "I want the form to be a data input platform." (That *is* what you're saying isn't it? You're so Access savvy!) And of course, this is one of the primary purposes of a form. But you can set up your forms to do all sort of things such as automatically fax a product order to a supplier or print an invoice for a customer.

Start with some of the basic form customization options, and then in the next chapter, you'll take a look at some of the more elegant things that you can do to a form.

SQL ▼	To enter the Design view for the form, click the **Form view** button on the Form toolbar.

Form Design Geography

It's always a good idea to get a feel for a new area like the one you're about to work with: the Form Design window. An understanding of the basic geography can save you a lot of headaches later. For instance, I don't know how many times I've stood in front of those maps at the mall and realized that knowing "you are here" is really only reaffirming the fact that I am lost.

You may want to work with the Form Design window maximized, so click its **Maximize** button.

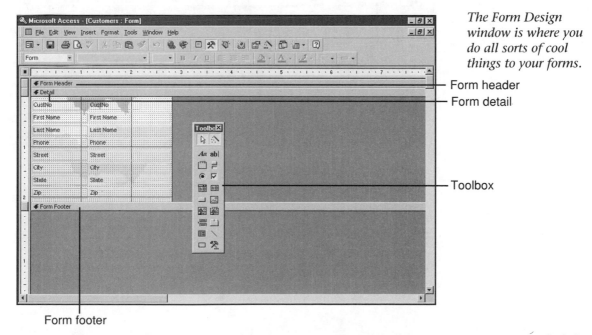

The Form Design window is where you do all sorts of cool things to your forms.

— Form header
— Form detail

— Toolbox

Form footer

Check This Out...

Important Form Design Tools When you work in the Form Design view, it makes sense to have the Ruler, Grid, and Toolbox showing. To see each of these items, click their respective menu choice on the **View** menu.

The Form Design window has three parts: header, detail, and footer. The *header* area is where you display the name of the form and any other information or items that you want repeated when you view the records in the Form view, such as any special command buttons that you create to open related forms or do special things such as print the form. The *detail* area contains all the fields and actually appears on the form when you are in Form view or print the form. The *footer* area is at the bottom of the form window and you can use it for items such as the date or other information that you want to appear on each of the records as they are viewed, including short directions on how to use the form.

You can enlarge or squish any of these three areas to accommodate a change in its own size or the size of another area. If you place the mouse pointer on any of the lines that divide the areas, the mouse pointer becomes a Sizing tool (go ahead and try it). Click-and-drag the **Sizing** tool to increase or decrease the size of one of the form's areas.

The Sizing tool makes it easier to change the size of any of your form's areas.

Form Header —⌐

Sizing tool —

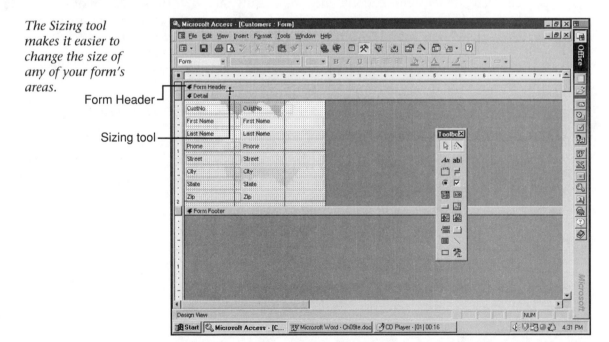

Headers and Footers From Top to Bottom

There are two different types of headers and footers related to forms. *Form Header and Footers* appear on your form when you are in the Form view; each record or form screen shows the header and footer information. *Page Header and Footers* appear on each printed page of a form.

Taking Control of the Form Controls

Pay special attention to the detail area of the Form Design window; this area of the Form window is where you decide how the data will be entered and represented in the form. For instance, you will usually want your data to appear as you type it. Text will be text and numbers will appear as numbers. However, you can, for instance, set up a numerical control that charts the data rather than displaying it numerically. We'll talk about some of this advanced control stuff later.

Two kinds of boxes appear: labels and controls. The *labels* are the field names that you create when you design the table the form is based on. The *controls* dictate how the data is input into the form. You will work with the different control possibilities in the next chapter, but I did want to introduce the concept to you now.

You can re-arrange the labels and controls on your form to make the data-entry process easier. You can also add or delete labels and controls. Remember, however, that when you delete a label and a control, you will no longer be entering data in a field that still exists in the table that you based the form on.

Your (Form's) Name up in Lights

The first thing you should do is give this form a title; yeah, I realize you named it when you created it using the wizard. But this title will be big and beautiful and appear in the header area of the form.

First, you have to make some space for your title in the Header area. Place the mouse pointer on the line that divides the header area from the Detail area. A Sizing tool appears. Hold down the mouse button and drag the Header border downward about a half inch (use the ruler to help you estimate).

Expanding the Header area of your form gives you room for a form title.

Header area ⎯

Sizing tool ⎯

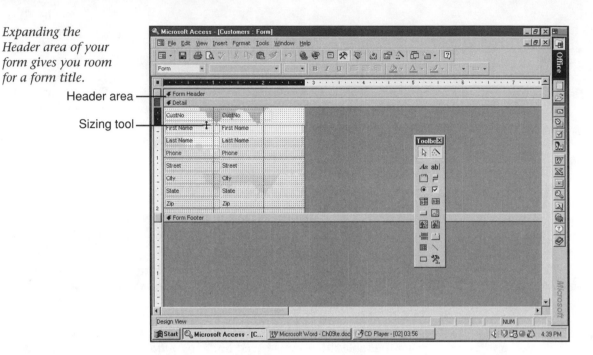

Now you need to add text to the Header area.

The Toolbox

In the Form Design view, you have a set of tools available to help you customize your forms. This set of tools appears on a Toolbox toolbar. You can drag the Toolbox around in the window until you find a spot that you like.

In this particular situation, you want to put new text in the Header area. Do this by clicking the **Label** button on the Toolbox. A new mouse pointer appears—a cross-shape above a capital **A**. This pointer is a Drawing tool.

Missing Toolbox? If you can't find the Toolbox, don't worry. Simply click the **View** menu and then click **Toolbox** to display it.

Place the mouse pointer where you want to create the new label (in this case in the Header area of your form). Hold down the mouse button, and drag the mouse pointer to draw a rectangle in the Header area. When you let go of the mouse, the rectangle becomes opaque and an insertion point appears in the upper-left corner.

Now all you have to do is type the text that you want to put in the box, in this case, type **Customer Information**. You're half way home to creating a great title for your form.

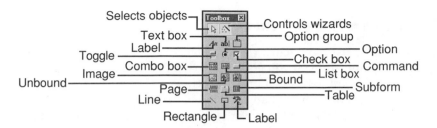

Selects objects — Toolbox
Text box — Controls wizards
Label — Option group
Toggle — Option
Combo box — Check box
Image — Command
Unbound — List box
Page — Bound
Line — Subform
Rectangle — Table
Label

The Toolbox gives you all the tools you need for Form design.

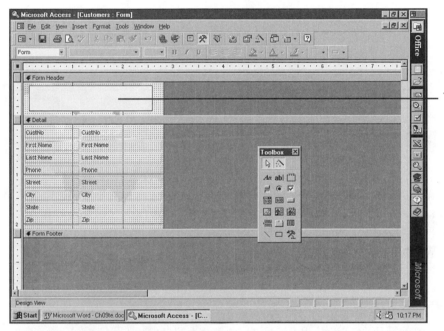

The label tool makes it easy to add a title or other text to your form.

— The new label

Appearance Is Everything

Things are looking good. You have your label in the Header area and you typed text into it. Now it makes sense to format the text so that it looks good. Move the mouse pointer to the edge of the title rectangle. When the mouse pointer becomes an arrow, click. The insertion point disappears and the text rectangle is selected.

With the text area selected, you can take advantage of all the great font attributes that are available on the Form Formatting toolbar. You can change the font style you are using, change the font size, or make the text bold, italic, or underlined.

119

What's That Button's Name?

If you forget what a particular button does, you can always point at it with the mouse and you will get a ScreenTip that displays the button's name. If you want additional info on the button, click **What's This** under the Help menu and then click the button; you'll be given a thumb-nail sketch of the feature or command that the button invokes.

The Form formatting toolbar makes you one click away from a number of features and commands related to forms.

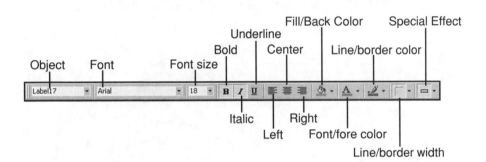

 Increase the size of the font, and also make the text bold and italic. First, make sure to select the label box you created. Then click the drop-down box for **Font size**; select the new size, **18**. Click the **Bold** and **Italic** buttons to add these attributes to your text.

Text Too Big?

If your text does not fit in the label rectangle you created, place the mouse on any of the square sizing handles and drag to increase the size of the rectangle until it accommodates the size of your text.

Give Yourself a Hand: Moving Controls

You can also reposition a label box on the screen. Lay the mouse pointer anywhere on the rectangle border (not on the sizing handles) and a hand appears. Don't worry, it's a friendly hand. Once you see the hand, click-and-drag to change the position of the rectangle. This capability to reposition a label box allows you to tweak the design of your form. You will find that any and all labels and controls can be moved using this method. This gives you complete control over the look of your form.

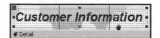

Repositioning the title text in the header area.

You Have Complete Control!

You can move and size every control and label in the detail area exactly the same way that you did for the title text. You can even offset the label from the control by using the alignment handles (large black handles at the top of the boxes) that appear when you select the label and control for a particular field.

 You've done a fair amount of work on this form and it would be a shame to lose it. Whenever you want to save the design changes that you make to a form, click **Save** on the toolbar.

It's Always the Details

Now that you have a great looking title for your form, you can move on to the Detail area. This form would probably be more appealing and easier to use if you re-orient the controls to a more horizontal positioning. To do this, you have to widen the form. Widening the form is no more difficult than sizing any of the label or control boxes you find in it. Lay the mouse pointer on the right edge of the form. The mouse pointer becomes a Sizing tool; then drag it to a new position. This is where the ruler comes in handy. Drag the form border to the 7" mark on the ruler.

You can widen your form by dragging the right border to a new position.

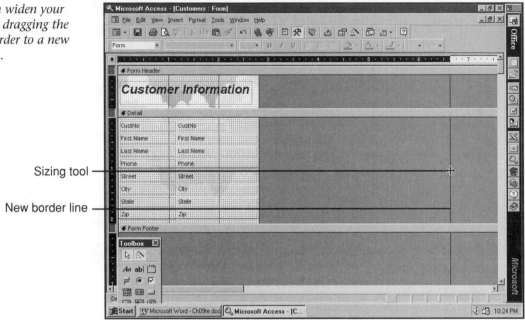

Sizing tool ──

New border line ──

Complete Control

The controls and their accompanying labels are basically what you used to call fields back when you were working on tables. When you drag a control to a new position, its label accompanies it (the opposite is also true). Notice, however that the labels and the controls reside in separate, but connected, boxes. You can size each of these boxes separately, and exactly the same way you sized the title label box in the header area—using the sizing handles that appear when you select the box.

Start re-arranging some of the controls. The CustNo label box and Control box (the CustNo Label box is on the left, the Control box on the right) are already in a good position—the upper-left corner of the detail area. It would be nice to drag the First Name label and Control box just below the CustNo control. Select the **First Name** label or Control box and then position the mouse pointer on the boxes' border. You see a hand pointer, which allows you to drag the control and its label to a new position (if you place the mouse pointer on a sizing handle, you get a Sizing tool). Drag the **First Name** control under the **CustNo** control.

This leaves room (since you enlarged the size of the form) to place the Last Name control just to the right of the First Name control. This leaves a big gap, so you might as well move the Phone control under the First Name control.

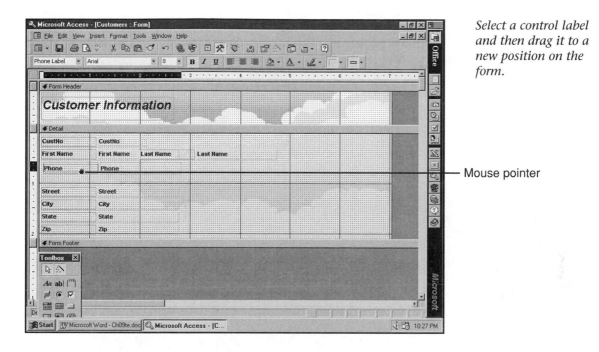

Select a control label and then drag it to a new position on the form.

Mouse pointer

This re-arranging of the controls should make data entry in the form a little easier. You expect someone's last name to follow their first name. It is also a good idea to arrange the Street and City, State, and ZIP on the same horizontal line. To do this, however, you will have to resize the Label and Control boxes associated with each field.

Sizing the Labels and Controls

Changing the size of the labels and controls is easy. Click the label or control to select its box and then use the mouse Sizing tool to increase or decrease the height or width of the selection.

In this form, you need to change the width of the address controls and their labels to make them all fit on one line. Move the Street control under the Phone Number control. Now comes the tricky part. Select the label for the Street control. Place the mouse pointer on the Sizing handle on the right side of the box. Drag the Sizing handle to the left to decrease the width of the label.

Notice that the Street Control box remains in its original position; it does not move to the left to take up the space that you opened up when you decrease the width of the Street label. Click the **Street** Control box to select it (it's the rectangle that's hooked to the Street label). Use the Sizing handle on the left side of the control to drag it toward the Street label. This closes up the space between the label and the control. Then all you have to do is use the sizing handle on the right size of the Control box to decrease its width slightly so it's about the same size as when you started.

123

*You can easily size
the label and the
controls in the form.*

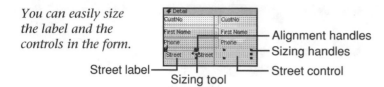

Alignment handles
Sizing handles
Street control
Street label
Sizing tool

Out of Control

Check This Out...

Control Size Is Important
Remember that the controls have to remain wide enough to display the data that you will eventually input into the fields using this form.

Now comes the real test. The plan here is to get all the address information on one line. This means that you have to size and move the labels and controls for the City, State, and ZIP fields.

Once you line up all the Address controls on one line, you will have a lot of open space on the form. You can close up some of this space by dragging the bottom border of the detail area until it is just below the Address line. The form looks great.

Techno Talk

Don't Lose Control With a Double-Click

If you inadvertently double-click one of the controls, you will open the control's Properties dialog box. This box allows you to set a number of parameters related to the control, such as the control source (where the data for the field is coming from) and additional field validation rules. To close this dialog box, click **Close**.

Your form is the best!

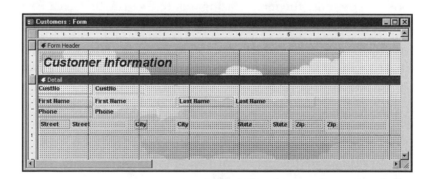

124

Wow! You did a great job creating this form. It is definitely ready for some heavy-duty data entry. In the next chapter, you'll raise the stakes of form construction and look at some elegant form design possibilities that will amaze coworkers, friends, and family.

The Least You Need to Know

➤ The easiest way to create a form is with the Form Wizard.

➤ If you don't like the way the form turned out using the Form Wizard, customize it in the Form Design view.

➤ In the Design view, your form has three areas: header, detail, and footer.

➤ The detail area is where you build and arrange the controls used for data entry on the form.

➤ Use the header and footers areas for information that you want to see on each record when you use the form to enter, edit, or view your data.

➤ You can move, size, and delete controls and labels in your forms.

Chapter 10

Reforming Your Forms

In This Chapter

➤ Add a text box to a Form Footer

➤ Work with the Expression Builder to place a date in a control

➤ Create list boxes and combo boxes for easy data entry

➤ Add a Command button to a form

➤ Add a subform to a form

➤ Use color, borders, and shading to make your forms look great

In the last chapter, you explored some of the design aspects of the database form. Now you are going to take one more giant step and look at some things that you can add to your forms that will get you a standing ovation at the office water cooler. Plus, you can put together a form that will make the data-entry process extremely easy. So, go for it!

Putting Your Foot(er) in Your Form

You can add new labels and controls to your forms when you are in Form Design view (but you already knew that from the last chapter). It's just a matter of using the right tool from the Toolbox. So you're not accused of neglecting the Footer area of your form, you had to place a new control in it.

Techno Talk

blah blah
blah blah
blah bl ah
b l b

Taking Control of Your Form Controls

The controls in your form are really made up of two parts: a label that denotes what kind of data will be found in the control (a label for the date control might be *date*) and the control itself, which holds the data. Some controls will be tied to specific fields in the table that the form is associated with (such as First Name and Phone). You can also place math formulas in your controls using the Expression Builder; expression types can range from formulas that add your data to an expression that places the current date in your control.

Use the same form that you used in the last chapter as an example. It was the Customers form from the Fromage Boutique database. Once you are in Form Design view, drag the footer border down so you have a little room to work. Now you can create the control.

Expand the Form Footer with a quick drag of the mouse.

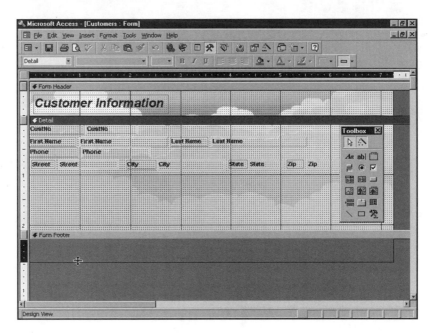

Click the **Text box** tool in the Toolbox. Drag a small rectangle on the left side of the footer area. A new control is created. Notice that Access created an empty label (it does have a label box number in it). Place the mouse pointer in the label box until the pointer turns to an I-beam. Double-click the current text in the label box to select it, and then type **Date**. You can widen the label box if necessary to accommodate the text entry.

Controls Unbound

Notice that the new control you added to the form is currently *unbound*, meaning that it is not associated with any particular data. The other controls in your form are *bound*. Controls such as First Name, Last Name, and Phone are all bound to their field namesakes in the Customers table. Whenever you use a wizard to create a form all the controls created will be bound to their respective fields.

Controls can also contain data that is not associated with a particular field in the table that the form is based upon. These controls are called *calculated controls*. You use the Expression Builder to create the expression (which can range from a complex math formula to a simple expression that returns the current date) that goes in the control.

You can take an unbound control and either associate it with a particular field in a table, making it a bound control, or place an expression in it, making it a calculated control. In your current situation you want a control in the Form Footer that gives you the current date; you're dealing with a situation where you need (yes, you guessed it) a calculated control.

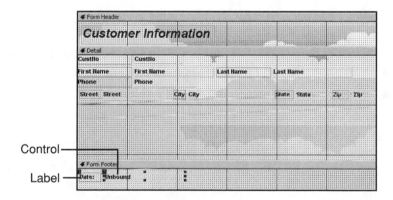

The new Label and Control box in the footer.

Double-click the edge of your new Control box. The Control Properties dialog box appears. This box allows you to choose the format and the source of the information that will appear in the control. Click the **Data** tab in the dialog box. You want to attach an expression to this control that provides the current date. Click the **Control Source** box.

The Right Click IS the Right-Click

To get to shortcut menus that give you quick access to the features and commands you want quickly, right-click any database object or control. For example, right-click a form control and then click **Properties** to set up the control for data input.

The Control Proper-
ties dialog box gives
you the ability to
attach an expression
to your form.

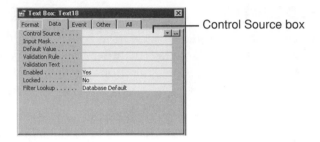

Control Source box

Notice that the Control Source box contains a drop-down arrow and a button marked with an ellipsis. The drop-down arrow (when you click it) displays a list of the fields contained in the table associated with this form. This form associates with the Customers table; that table's fields appear in the Control Source box.

Techno Talk

blah blah
blah bla
blah bl
b

Controls are Bound and Determined

If you add a new control to a form that is going to be used to enter data in the associated table, it must be a bound control. If there is not a field in the table that will accept the data entered in the form control, create a new field in the table. Access likes to keep this database stuff all nice and neat by binding the controls in your forms to the data fields in your tables.

The button marked with an ellipsis takes you to the Expression Builder feature. Click **Expression Builder** to take a look at this great feature.

Express Yourself

The Expression Builder allows you to build calculated controls. These can be as simple as a control that takes the First and Last Name field and places them side-by-side in the new control. Or you may want to build a control that returns the answer to a mathematical calculation. Calculated controls can, obviously, be quite complex, but in this case, you want to build a calculated control that displays the current date.

In the first column of the Expression Builder is a list of possible items that you can use to build an expression for your control. These items include such things as tables, queries, forms, and reports as well as other items such as Functions, Constants, Operators, and Common Expressions. You can see that building an expression for a control may be complicated. Keep it easy by using one of the Common Expressions (no, not a smiley face).

Click the **Common Expressions** folder. In the second column, you get a list of ready-made expressions—items that will put the page number or the current date in your control. I know it may be hard to remember what you were doing with the Expression Builder in the first place, but all you wanted to do was create a control that would return the current date in the Footer area of your form.

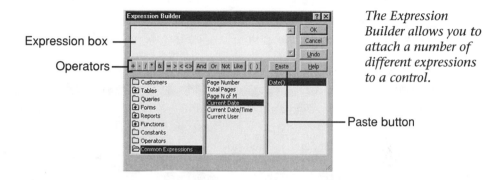

Expression box

Operators

The Expression Builder allows you to attach a number of different expressions to a control.

Paste button

Click **Current Date** in the second column of the Expression Builder. The actual element that will end up in the expression you are creating appears in the third column of the Expression Builder—*Date( )*. Notice that it is selected. Now you have to paste the expression element into the Expression box (at the top of the Expression Builder), so click the **Paste** button. Now that you have the expression in the Expression box, all you have to do is click **OK** (which you should do now).

You still need to close the Control Properties dialog box, so click its **Close** button. The date expression appears in your Control Source box. This means that you can return to the form.

Some Smooth Operators

Techno Talk

The operators that appear in the Expression Builder window are used to create the various expressions that you place in your calculated controls. You will notice that many of these operators are typical math symbols such as +, -, and *—characters that serve as the addition, subtraction, and multiplication symbols. You would typically employ these symbols to build expressions that did some mathematical calculation in a field or group of fields. For instance, you could build an expression that multiplies a field containing the number of items sold by the price, which will appear in another field. Other operators are also available such as And, Or, Not, and Like. These operators can be used to build conditional statements that return data that only meet certain criteria.

Is It a Date?

Dealing with the creation of a new control and the complexities of the Expression Builder may have tired you out, but there is still one more step to perform. You want to see if the expression you placed in the footer actually works. The easiest way to do this is to leave Design view and return to Form view. Your moment of truth is just a click away.

SQL ▾ Click the **Form View** button on the toolbar. Access displays the first record in the Customers table in your revised form. Look at the bottom of the form; there's the current date!

It is indeed a date!

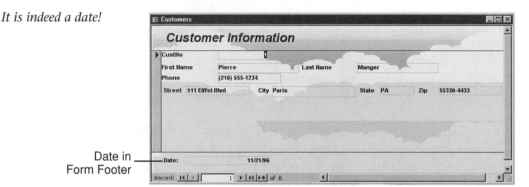

Date in
Form Footer

That was some slick work you did there. You will find that it can be very useful to include certain types of information in the footer of a form. Continue your exploration of form design, and look at some great ways to make data entry a piece of cake.

Adding a List Box or Combo Box to a Form

You're probably getting a feel for the fact that a well-designed form can make your data entry chores much easier. Each record can be viewed separately, different form layouts give you a choice of how the controls are arranged on the form, and new controls can be created that can place a date or the result of a math expression into your form. Well, hang on, because you're going to be introduced to two more types of form controls that really make data entry a breeze: the *List box* and the *Combo box*.

Both of these control types take advantage of the fact that certain tables in your database will be related. Put your thinking caps on for a second to find out the nuts and bolts of table relationships that make list boxes and combo boxes possible. When two tables are related by a common field, the field must be the key field for one of the tables. An example would be a Products table that is related to a Suppliers table by the common field, Supplier ID. This field will be the key field for the Suppliers table.

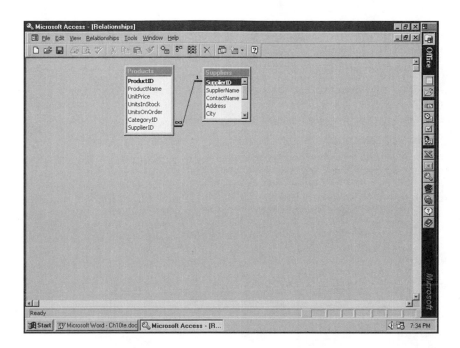

The SupplierID field is shared by the Products and Suppliers table, making it easy for you to create a form that uses a list or combo box for data entry.

Every time you add a new supplier to your Suppliers table, you will assign a Supplier ID to them (or let Access autonumber the suppliers via an autonumber field). You also need to have the Supplier ID information appear in your Products table. So why not set up a situation where you can view a list of the Supplier IDs from the Supplier table when you need to enter this information into the Product tables? Take it even one step further—wouldn't it be nice if you could use the mouse to select from a list of the Suppliers and their IDs when you have to enter them in the products table during the data entry associated with a new product?

Well, hold onto your hat, because that is the purpose of the List box and Combo box controls. These controls supply you with a list of the correct field data; all you have to do is click one of the choices and it appears in your form. You enter data into the form (which ends up in the associated table or tables) without any typing. It's all mouse work. You can create a form for a table like the Products table in the Fromage Boutique database by using the Form Wizard. Once you have the form, switch to Design view. This is where you create the List Box or Combo box control that will supply you with a list of Suppliers.

You're on My List (Box)

When adding a bound control to a form, (you should probably make space for it in the Detail area). Calculated controls, like date or page number, can go in the Header or Footer area. This means you may have to move controls that are currently in the Detail area, or increase the size of the Detail area. Remember that you want this new control bound to the SupplierID field in the Products table. Because you are creating the control from scratch you will have to designate which field in the Products table the control is associated with.

Fast Forms!

Remember, the easiest way to quickly design a form based on a particular table is to use the Form Wizard. Also, keep in mind that a form does not have to have a control in it for every field in the associated table; the number of controls in the form are totally up to you.

The Detail area is expanded to accommodate the new control.

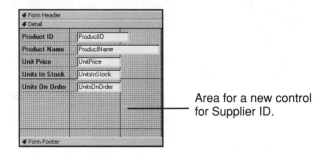

Area for a new control for Supplier ID.

I'll Take Box Number One, Monty

Adding the new box to the form is easy. It's just a matter of making a choice from the Form Toolbox. Access provides you with two different types of controls for list boxes: list box (surprise, surprise) and combo box.

The *list box* allows you to create a control that will pull its choices from a table, a query, or a list that you type in. A *combo box* is even cooler; it sets up a control that does all the things the list box control does, but it also lets you manually type in the data that you want, totally ignoring the offered list. You will find that a combo box is very useful if you have a situation where the data that appears in the drop-down list does not provide you with the correct data. For instance, you could have a new supplier that you haven't entered into the Supplier table yet. Since their name won't appear on the list, you can type it into the form control. Go ahead and set up this new control using the Combo box.

Creating the Combo Box

Creating the Combo box control and its accompanying label takes a tiny bit of artistic ability on your part. Well, not really! Simply drag the mouse to draw the combo box on the form.

One other important thing that you should know about is the Control Wizards button on the Toolbox. When this button is selected (depressed), you will get assistance from a wizard when you use tools on the Toolbox, such as the combo box and the list box. For instance, if you have the Wizard button selected, when you create your combo box, the Combo Box Wizard appears and walks you through the necessary steps. It makes sense to take advantage of this wizard whenever you can, so make sure to select the **Wizards** button (it will be a lighter gray than the other buttons).

Now create the box. Click **Combo Box** on the Toolbox. Place the mouse pointer in the detail area of the form (or where you plan on placing the new control). Then drag to create a rectangle below the other controls in your form that will represent the combo box. As soon as you do this (it takes a second or two), the Combo Box Wizard appears.

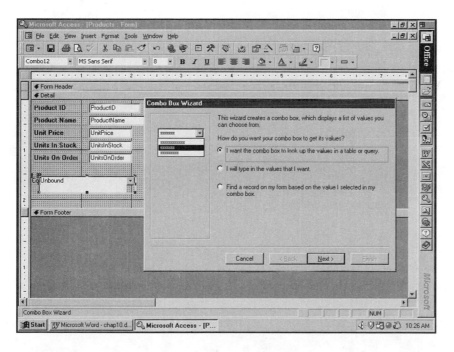

When you create this rectangle, the Combo Box Wizard knows you mean business.

The Combo Box Wizard helps you create your combo boxes. The Combo Box Wizard starts the creation process off by asking you to select one of three methods that the wizard can use to get its value: You can have the combo box look up the list values from a table or query. You can type in the values for the list. Or you can have the wizard find a record in the current form based on the value in the combo box.

The first choice, a combo box that lists values found in a table or query, is the best choice because when new data is added to the field that the combo box is bound to, your list of choices will reflect the new data—it is updated on the fly. For instance, if six new suppliers are added to the Supplier IDfield in the table, these new choices will immediately be available in the combo box. The second choice, typing in the values, will give you a usable list of possibilities, but you will have to manually update the list if the available choices change. You can completely ignore the third possibility, using the control to find records in the current form, because it will not give you a bound control (remember, a bound control is tied to a specific field in the table that the form relates to). This type of combo box is used to find records that contain data that matches the combo box list.

Make sure you select the **I Want the Combo Box to Look Up the Values in a Table or Query** option button. Click **Next** to go to the next step.

I'd Like the Table by the Window, Please

Now the wizard wants to know what table in the database you want to derive the list of values from. You want to be able to choose Suppliers from the list, so it makes sense to get the list of values from the Suppliers table.

The Combo Box Wizard wants to know what table to use for the combo list.

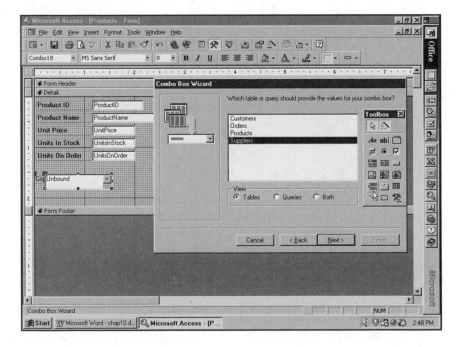

The wizard wants you to select the table that will supply the combo box values. Select the table that you want—in this case, **Suppliers**—and then click **Next**. Now the wizard displays the fields that are in the Suppliers table. This is where things get tricky.

Choosing the Field for the Combo Box List

Let's recap what you are trying to accomplish by creating this combo box. You want to create a control that provides you with a list of data. In this particular case you have a Products form that requires you to enter the Supplier's ID for each of the products. The combo box list will be derived from the Supplier's IDs that have already been entered in the Suppliers table.

On the surface, this all seems fine and dandy. However, there is a small, yet annoying, flaw in the plan. The combo box will give you a list of numbers—1, 2, 3, and so on. You will have to memorize the supplier name that is associated with each of the ID numbers; otherwise, you won't be able to enter the Supplier ID for a particular product into the form.

Don't despair—there is a way to set up the combo box so that it gives you a list of the supplier names, but actually enters the Supplier ID into the SupplierID field in the associated table. It might sound like magic, but it's not really all that hard to do.

The wizard wants you to choose which field in the table will supply the values for your form's combo box. Well, you want the list to display the suppliers' names. So, click **SupplierName;** then click the **Add** button. Now you want this combo list in your form to enter the SupplierID in your table, so click the **SupplierID** field and then click the **Add** button to add it to the Selected Fields box. Click **Next** and move to the next step.

Sizing Your Combo Box

Now you have to determine the width for your combo box. You can size it just like you would size a column in a table or any other control on a form. Just place your mouse on the right border of the box and drag to the right or left.

A more important aspect of this particular screen is the **Hide Key Column (Recommended)** check box. This box is selected by default and makes sure that only the SupplierName field information (or other fields that you chose) appears in your combo list. The SupplierID, which is the key field for the Supplier table, will be invisible.

The reason that this box is selected by default is that it sets you up with a combo box list that only shows the information that you want to appear in the form (in this case, the supplier name). Because the SupplierID is the unique identifier for the table, it must be associated with the list (any list box or combo box you create will have this same option) supplied by the combo box. Access figures that you won't want to view a two-column list in your combo box, so it hides this information by default.

137

*Your combo box lists
the SupplierID
values.*

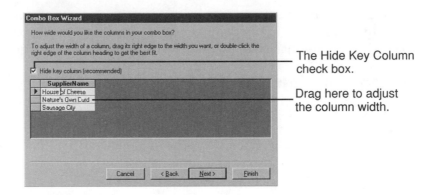

The Hide Key Column
check box.

Drag here to adjust
the column width.

You won't always have to adjust the width of your combo box columns; you can double-click the right edge of the box to get the best fit. When you finish, click **Next** to continue the process.

Telling Access Where to Put the Data

The next step in the process gives you the choice of having Access remember the values that you have in your combo box for later use or have it store the values in a particular field. You want the second choice.

Remember, the purpose of the combo box that you are creating is for data entry. The data that you select from the combo box list will be entered on the form. This means that the data will also be entered into the appropriate field in the associated table. It certainly makes sense to have Access store the data in the field.

Now, you may ask, when do I have Access remember the values in the combo box for later? You may have a situation where the value in the control will be used in a mathematical calculation. The result of the calculation is much more important than the value you choose from the combo list. Access will remember the value so that the calculation takes place and returns the result in the appropriate field. Selecting this radio button creates an unbound control. Access will not store the data in a field in a associated table; it will, however, list the data that appears in that field.

Click the **Store That Value in This Field** radio button. Click the **Field** drop-down list and select SupplierID. This is the step that you don't want to miss. It creates the combo box so that it shows you a list of supplier names (that's the field you chose in the first step of the wizard) that you can pick from. The supplier name will also appear in the form. However, if you check the associated table (Products), you will find that while the form shows the supplier name, the actual data that is being placed into the table is the Supplier ID. Pretty cool, huh?

138

Now you can cut to the chase and finish off the combo box. The wizard would like you to enter a name for the control. Type **Suppliers** and then click **Finish** to end the process. You may have to decrease the width of the Combo box control to see the combo box label in Form Design view.

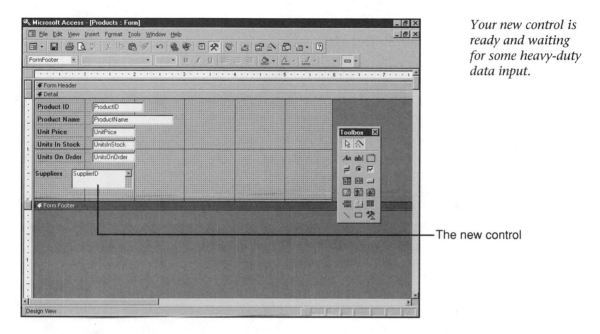

Your new control is ready and waiting for some heavy-duty data input.

The new control

Using Your New Combo Box

To see the combo box in action, you must return to Form view. Click **Form View** on the toolbar. Go ahead and try the combo box; click its drop-down arrow. The possible Supplier's names appear in the drop-down box. If you use the new form to enter data for a new product, all you have to do is enter the product's information and choose the supplier of the product from the Combo Box list. The great thing about all this is that the information entered in the form goes directly to your Products table. Now wasn't that a load of fun?

Techno Talk

Create Combo Boxes and List Boxes for Your Tables

You can also add combo boxes and list boxes to fields in tables. When you are in Table Design view, click the field you want to assign a combo or list box to. In the Field Properties window, select the **Lookup** tab. Designate the type of box in the **Display Control** and the value source in the **Row Source**.

Your new form in action.

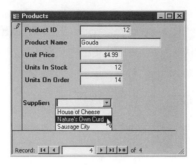

List boxes perform exactly the same way as the combo boxes do. You can either derive the values from a table, or create your own list. A list box, however, will not allow you to enter a value that's not on the list.

Adding Command Buttons to Forms

Now that you've added a couple of controls to some forms (in this and the last chapter), you're probably starting to feel in command. Well, take this form fun one step further and see how easy it is to add commands to your forms.

Commands are all around you in Access; you find them on the various toolbars as buttons and on the menu system as choices. Commands can start a quick and easy process like *print* or *save*, or embroil you in all sorts of choices like *build*, which invokes the Expression Builder.

You're in Command

Adding a Command button to a form is straightforward. Access already has tons of built-in commands that you can use to create buttons, or you can make a button that fires off a list of instructions that you've compiled as a macro or written in the Visual Basic language (you'll deal with macros later). Use your Products form that you stuck the combo box on as a guinea pig for command button creation. To create a Command button, you have to be in Form Design view.

Create the Command button using the Toolbox (just like your combo box). Make sure to select the Wizard button if you are going to need help creating the button. Command buttons go very well in the Header area of a form, so expand the Header area for this particular button.

Then click **Command** tool on the Toolbox and use the mouse to drag a button out on the form (in this example, in the Header area). As soon as you do this, the Command Button Wizard appears.

What's a Button to Do?

The Control Button Wizard lays it right on the line, asking you what you want to have happen when the button is pressed. It also gives you a box of command categories to choose from. Because you may have someone do your data entry with this form who doesn't know Access that well, it might be a good idea to put a button on the form that will close it.

To tell Access what you want the button to do, click a category of commands. For instance, click **Form Operations**. The wizard gives you a list of commands in the Actions box related to Forms. This button is supposed to close the form, so select **Close Form** in the Actions box.

The wizard gives you a preview of what the command button will look like for the selected action. Click **Next** to continue the process.

> **Buttons that Print** Placing a Print button on forms is also a good use of the Control Button feature. That way you are just one click away from a printed copy of the current record.

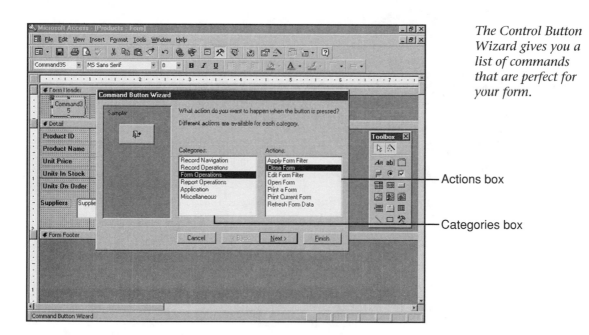

The Control Button Wizard gives you a list of commands that are perfect for your form.

Actions box

Categories box

Sew On Your Own Button

The wizard gives you one last chance to edit the look of the button that will appear on your form. You can use the Close button, a Stop button (my personal choice), or choose to mark the button with text of your choice rather than use a picture. So, select the picture (the Stop button) or type in the text you would like. Then click **Next** to continue.

All you have to do is name the button and decide whether or not you want the wizard to display help that will assist you in customizing of the button. So, say you name the button **Exit** and then reject the offer of help by clicking **Finish**.

The completed command button in Form Design view.

A Command Performance

Your finished button appears on your form. To actually test the button, return to Form view. When you finish entering data in the form, click the button. It closes the form (or performs whatever action you selected in the Command Button Wizard).

Adding a Subform to a Form

Because you're learning how to add things to forms, you might as well push the envelope a little bit and look at some of the other stuff you can stick on them. *Subforms* provide you with a way to view and edit data from two completely different tables. A subform is really just like any other form and is associated with a particular table. All you have to do is take a form that you've created (like your Products form) and make a place on it for the subform. The original form is now referred to as the *main form*. One thing you must keep in mind is that for this to work, the two tables must have a relationship. This means that they will share a common field.

In this example, the Products form is associated with the Products table, and the new form that will be created to serve as the subform—Orders—will be associated with the Orders table in your database. The two tables—Products and Orders—are related by the ProductID field.

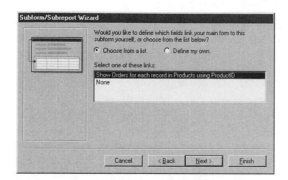

A form made up of a main form and a subform gives you access to two tables of data as you work.

You're the Sub(form) Commander

So, you have a Products form. It tells you the ID number of a particular product as well as its name, the unit price, the amount in stock, the amount on order, and the supplier—information that would be very useful for you to see as you add new customer orders to your database. Attaching an Orders subform to the Products main form allows you to enter your new orders and also keep on eye on how much of a particular item you have in stock as the orders are filled. By combining these two forms, you are able to keep an eye on two tables of data at once. You end up with one great form (consisting of a main form and subform) that can be used to enter or edit data in the two different tables.

Because the Products table and the Orders table are related by the Product ID (it's a One-To-Many relationship—Product-to-Orders), it will be a snap to set up a form (containing main and subform) that uses the fields from both tables.

You already know how to build a form: with the Forms tab selected in your Database window, click **New**. Select **Design view** or the **Form Wizard** and then designate the table that the form will be based on. In this particular case you will build your new form based on the Orders table. This supplies you with the subform.

You already have a form that can be used as the main form in this process—the Products form. Make sure you have the form open and that you are in Form Design view. Just as when you added controls and command buttons to this form, the first step is to make room on the form for whatever you plan to add.

Most likely, you will place a subform at the bottom of the current form below all the already-existing controls. Expand the detail area of the current form to make a space for the subform.

As you get ready to add the subform, keep in mind that this is another situation where you will want the Wizard button on the Toolbox selected. That way, when you select the new object to go onto the form, Access will invoke the appropriate wizard.

The expanded detail area is a perfect spot for you to place the subform.

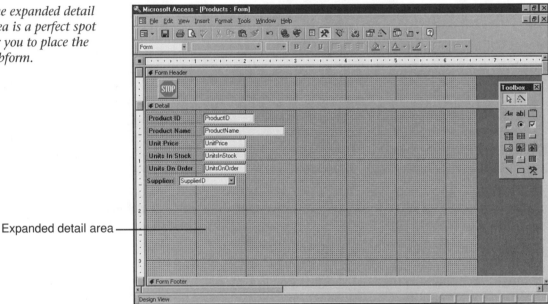

Expanded detail area —

Click the **Subform/Subreport** button on the Toolbox. A subform pointer replaces your mouse pointer, and all you have to do is drag a rectangle on the current form. As soon as you draw the subform rectangle, the Subform/Subreport Wizard jumps into the process.

Help, Mr. Wizard!

The Subform/Subreport Wizard walks you through the subform creation process. First, you must decide if you will build the subform from a table, meaning you will build a new form from scratch, (my choice) or use an already existing form. You would choose the latter if you had already created a form based on the Orders table using the Form Wizard.

Both of these procedures for creating the subform work equally well. The process will, obviously, move along a little faster, however, if you have already created the form you will use as the subform. For a better understanding of the overall process, let's build the subform from scratch. Click **Next** to move along.

Now the wizard wants you to select the fields that will go into the subform. This is easy. Select the table you want to get the fields from, and then add the fields that you want to use. In your example, select the **Orders** table and add all the fields. Once again, click **Next** to advance to the next step in the process.

The Missing Link

The wizard would now like to know how you want to link the subform to the main form meaning you need to select a field that the forms have in common. Your example has two possibilities: ProductID and SupplierID. Use **ProductID** because this is the field that defines the relationship between the two tables. It is the primary key for the Products table and is also contained in the Orders table. This is a necessity if two tables are to be related (the SupplierID is not the primary key for either of the tables, making it unusable as a field that relates two tables). The type of relationship that is common between the Products table and the Orders table. Each product can appear in the Orders table a number of times.

It is the relationship between the two tables (Products and Orders) that gives you the ability to combine the two forms based on these tables. The linking field provides the connection between the forms.

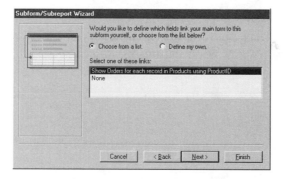

Choose the field that will link the forms together.

Once you select the linking field, you can move on to the next step by clicking **Next**. The last step in the subform creation process only requires that you name the subform (you can always go with the name that Access gives it) and decide whether or not you want help displayed as you work with the subform. Then click **Finish**.

Your Finished Subform

The best way to view the finished subform and get a feel for how it will work with the main form is to switch from Form Design view to Form view. Because the forms are linked by ProductID, when you move to a record in the main form (or input a new record) that contains a certain product, say cheddar cheese—ProductID 1. The subform displays the orders just for that particular product—ProductID 1.

The finished multi-form links the main form and subform together by one field, the ProductID.

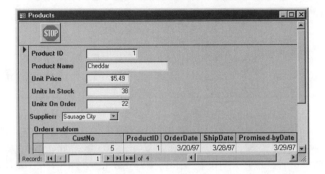

Dressing Up Your Forms with Color and Borders

Because you're on a roll with forms, take a look at a couple of ways to make them look better (think of it as a kind of form makeover). You can change the borders and colors of the controls and labels on your forms. All you have to do is be in Form Design view.

On the far right of the Form toolbar are a group of buttons that will assist you in changing the look of the form:

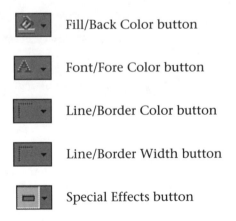

Fill/Back Color button

Font/Fore Color button

Line/Border Color button

Line/Border Width button

Special Effects button

To change the appearance of a label or control, select the item and then use the appropriate button to change a specific attribute. The only button that may seem a little mysterious is the Special Effects button. It can do things such as add a shadow effect to a control or make the control look raised, sunken, or etched.

The Least You Need to Know

As you can see from the last two chapters, there are many things you can and can't do with forms. Forms are definitely a formidable tool in your bag of database tricks. Here are the critical points to remember from this chapter:

➤ You can add controls to your forms that are bound to specific fields in your database tables, or you can link the control to an expression that will insert an item such as the current date.

➤ Expressions are the realm of the Expression Builder; use the Expression Builder to build expressions involving fields or expressions that return a specific result.

➤ You can create controls (list boxes and combo boxes) in your forms that take their values from a list based on a specific table's field or from a list that you create.

➤ Use can place command buttons on forms to close, print, or complete other actions.

➤ You can link subforms to a main form, allowing you to see the data from more than one table on one form.

➤ You can do almost all of the special things to a form using the Form Toolbox.

Chapter 11

Not a Stupid Question— Designing Simple Queries

In This Chapter

➤ Use the Query Wizard to create queries

➤ Create queries from scratch

➤ Deal with the Database Design window

➤ Set criteria in queries

➤ Perform math calculations in a query

Questions—sweet mysteries of life—answer a mind-boggling question and you might win the Nobel Prize; fail to answer a simple question on your driving test, and you might spend your mornings waiting at the bus stop. You can find questions everywhere, unfortunately answers aren't as easy to come by. Not so in Access, my plucky database maven. In this chapter, you will find out how easy it is to ask you Access database tables— *queries*—and always get the correct answers.

Understanding Queries

A query is a question that you pose to your database table or tables. You might want to know which of your salespeople has reached his sales goal for the year, or you might want to see a list of customers that live in a certain state. You can handle both of these situations with a query. In Access, you use different types of queries, depending upon the type of response you need. The most common type of query that you will run into as you work with databases is the *select query*. A select query finds and lists the records that satisfy the question that you ask.

You can also design queries that actually do something to a table—*action queries*. Action queries can be used to delete duplicate records in a table or move records to another table. Action queries always result in some kind of change to the table or tables involved in the query. You can even create queries that display their results in a cross-tab format that looks a lot like a spreadsheet. These tables are called *cross-tab queries* and provide you with a very unique way to look at the information that results from the query.

Access makes it easy for you to design queries. You can (just like tables and forms) create them from scratch or use a wizard. For your first foray into the wonderful world of queries, you'll start by creating a simple query that will list a subset of the customer records you have in a Customers table (you can use our Fromage Boutique Customers table as an example).

Creating a Select Query

Say that the Pennsylvania Legislature is debating a new bill that will place a surtax on cheese products. You decide that you better get a letter out to your Pennsylvania customers asking them to write their legislators condemning the proposed tax. Your Customers table contains customer records from two states: Pennsylvania and Ohio. So you need to come up with a simple query that will list just the Pennsylvania folks.

Techno Talk

Creating Database Objects from Query Results

Once you query a database table, you can use the query results to create a new table or a database report. Since Access makes it easy to create a report type that produces mailing labels, the logical outcome of this simple select query would be to eventually create mailing labels (maybe even form letters using Microsoft Word) for the Pennsylvania customers.

Before you start the query, make sure the Database window for the database that you're going to use in your query is open (in this case, the Fromage Boutique). Then it's just a matter of clicking the **Queries** tab and then clicking **New**. The New Query dialog box opens.

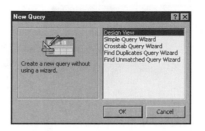

The New Query dialog box offers you several different ways to create your new query.

Keep It Simple

Access gives you several choices for creating your new query. You can create a new query from scratch, use a wizard to create a simple query, use a wizard to create a cross-tab query, use a wizard to find duplicate records, or use a wizard to find records in one table that have no related records in another table (these two tables would obviously have a relationship defined between them).

Once you use the different Query Wizards a couple of times, you may find that the fastest way to create a simple query is by creating it from scratch. However, the wizards do make the whole process extremely straightforward. Since this is your very first query, click the **Simple Query Wizard**. To move to the next step, click **OK**.

You Need Fields

You are probably getting the feeling that almost all this database stuff revolves around the data fields that you find in the records. Well, pass Go and collect $200 because the next step in the query creation process is to pick the fields that you want to use in the query.

First, select the table or query you want to use for this particular query in the **Table/Queries** drop-down box (in this case, choose the **Customers** table). Once you select the table, you can include all the fields available or just use some of them. Since you are designing this query to find a subset of your customers (the people in PA, remember?), including all the fields won't hurt. To include all the fields, click the **Add All** button; then advance to the next screen in the Query Wizard by clicking the **Next** button.

The first screen of the Simple Query Wizard is where you select the table and the fields that you want to include in your query.

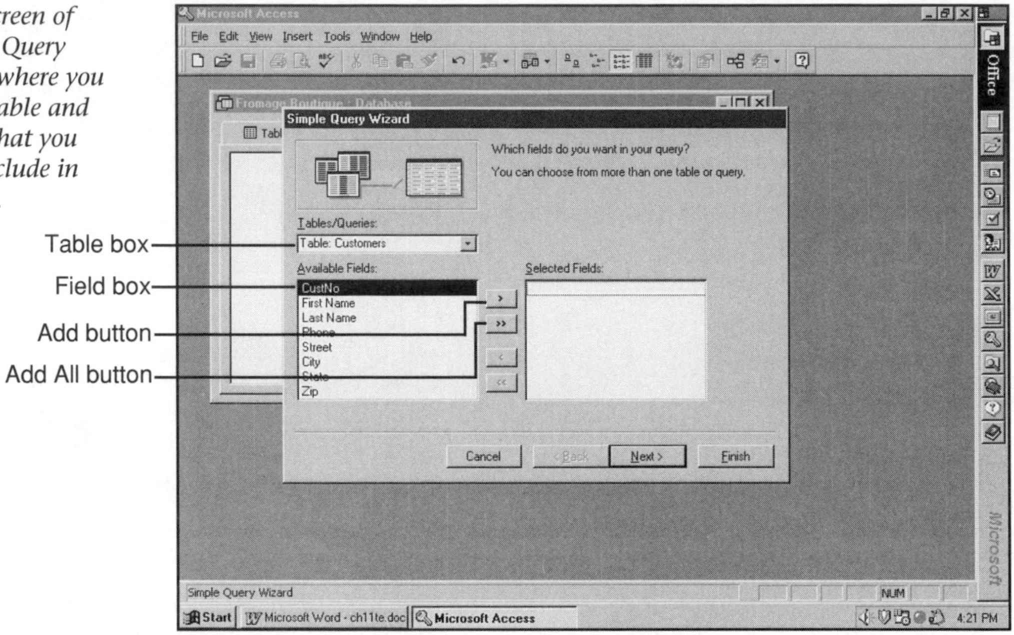

Table box

Field box

Add button

Add All button

Pulling Up to the Query Wizard Finish Line

The Simple Query Wizard really doesn't waste your time; you reach the last step in the process quickly. You are given two choices on the final screen of the Simple Query Wizard: You can open the query to see the results, or you can immediately modify the query in the Query Design view.

If you've been paying attention to the Simple Query Wizard screens, you may have noticed that you haven't done a whole heck of a lot to create this particular query. All you did was choose a table and some fields from the table. You haven't defined the question that the query will ask.

Obviously, you are going to have to modify this query's design to get the results that you want—a list of our customers in Pennsylvania. So, click the **Modify the Query Design** option button. Now all you have to do is name the query (or go with the name the wizard picks) and click **Finish**.

When you exit the Query Wizard, you are taken directly to the Query Design view, and your query—actually your query to be—is ready and waiting to be modified.

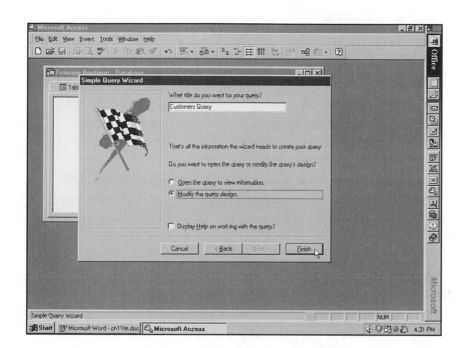

The final screen of the Simple Query Wizard asks you to name your query.

The Query Design Window

When you enter the Query Design view to either create a new query, or edit an existing query (which is what you're doing now), you will find that the Query Design window is divided into two panes. The top pane shows the table or tables that have been selected for the query. You can add tables to the query by clicking the Show Table button on the toolbar. To remove a table, click anywhere on the table and then press the **Delete**.

Queries by Design

Two quick ways to enter the Query Design view: click the **Query view** button on the Query toolbar to edit an existing query; then select the **New Query** button to design a new query from scratch.

153

The Query Design window lets you specify the tables and fields to be used in your query.

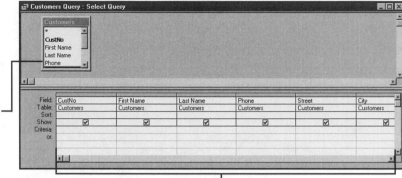

Tables selected for the query

Fields selected for the query

A Real Pane in the Bottom

The bottom pane of the Query Design window displays the query design grid, which lists the fields that you designated in the Query Wizard; these fields appear in a series of boxes (from left to right). Each field lists the name and the table that the field is from.

Access associates other criteria with the field that performs a particular action when you fire off a query such as: a sort parameter associated with the field, whether the field should be shown in the query or not, and any selection criteria associated with the query. If you remember, you only want to list the customers in Pennsylvania. Do this by putting a match criteria (the abbreviation *PA*) under the **State** field.

Cleaning Up the Window Pane If you do not want the Table row to appear in the lower pane of the Design window, you can use the **Table Names** command on the **View** menu to hide it.

You can change all of the query parameters associated with each field. The field selected, the table selected, sorting parameters selected—you control these three items using drop-down boxes.

For instance, if you want to sort the Customers records that appear in the query by the Last Name field, click in the **Sort** area under this particular field and either select an **Ascending** (my choice for an alphabetical listing of the customers) or a **Descending** sort. You will make your sort selection (Ascending, Descending, or not sorted) via a drop-down box that appears when you click in the field's sort area.

You should also keep in mind customers with the same last name. You may also want to set up your sort so that it sorts ascending by the First Name field as well. Click in the First Name field sort area and then select Ascending from the drop-down box.

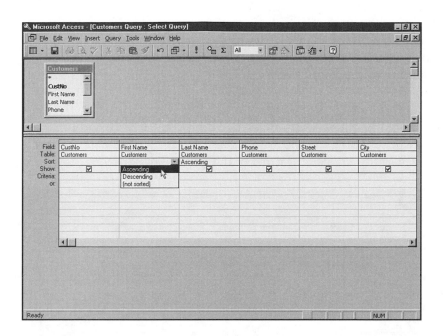

Clicking in the Sort row allows you to select the type of sort you want to accomplish when you run the query.

Index Your Tables

There is a way to speed up queries when you are dealing with large database tables: indexes. Access uses indexes to look up data, which means it can find an indexed field or sorted more quickly. The primary key field in your database table will already be indexed. However, you can also index other fields, especially those that you use frequently in queries where the field is related (joined to a field in another table).

To index fields and view the indexes already in a particular table, make sure you have the table open in the **Design** view; then click the field you want to index. In the Field Properties box for the record, click in the **Indexed** box; then select **Yes (Duplicates OK)** or **Yes (No Duplicates)**. **Duplicates OK** allows more than one record to have the same data in the index field (such as a last name field). **No Duplicates** assures you that no two records will have exactly the same data in the field.

For this sort to work correctly, the Last Name field must appear in the Query box before the First Name field. This is because the sort proceeds from left to right; the field you want to sort by first must be the first field designated in the Query box; the other fields involved in the sort then follow in the order that you want to sort them by.

It is very easy to change the order of the fields shown in the query box. Click in the **Field Name** row for a particular field. A drop-down arrow appears. Click the drop-down arrow and Access supplies you with a list of all the fields that you included in the query (yes, fields from all the tables that you select for the query will appear). Select the fields so that they are ordered appropriately for a sort that uses more than one field. In this particular situation you would click the **First Name** field name in the Field Row. To change the field name select Last Name from the list. Now all you have to do is change the second Last Name field to First Name by repeating the above action and selecting First Name from the Field list box. In effect you've flip-flopped the order of the fields to be sorted.

Clicking in the Field Name row allows you to control the order that the fields are sorted in.

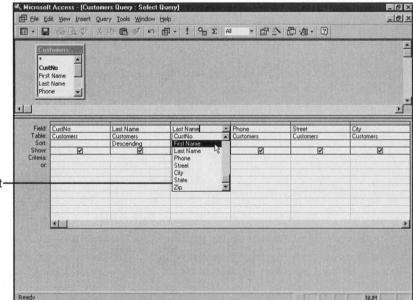

Field Name drop-down list—

Fields: To Show or Not to Show

You can also decide not to show some of the fields that are currently listed in the lower pane of the Query Design window. For example, you may not want the CustNo field and the Phone fields to show up in your final query (especially since you may want to use the query to generate mailing labels later).

A check box for each field appears in the **Show** row of the Query design grid (just below the **sort** row). Just select the Show check box below **CustNo** to hide that field in the query; Access removes the check mark and the field will not appear. Do the same thing to the Phone field, and it will also not show up in the query results.

What's My Criteria?

Queries get their power from the conditional statements that you place in the **Criteria** row of the Query Design grid. What is a conditional statement, you ask? It is a limiting parameter that makes the query produce a subset of your original table or tables. These statements can be as simple as **=PA**, where you are saying that you only want the records that have **PA** in their State field, or as simple as **>500**, where you only want the records where a particular numerical field has a number of more than 500 in it.

The Or box allows you to expand the conditional statement so that the query will either satisfy the condition you place in the Criteria box or the condition you place in the Or box. An example would be a query that displays fields for customers from more than one state (you would type PA or OH in the Criteria box).

In your sample query, you only want to see the records that have **PA** in the **State** field. To accomplish this, scroll to the State field in the lower pane of the Design window, and type **PA** in the Criteria box.

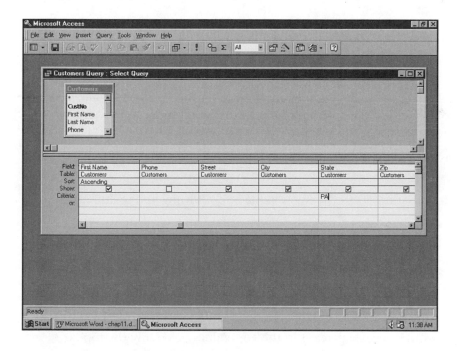

Entering the limiting condition in the State field's criteria box.

Every Query Has a Toolbar

One incredibly helpful bag of tricks that you should not neglect to discuss is the Query toolbar. There are buttons on this toolbar that let you run the current query, change the

157

query type, display a Totals row in the grid box that you can use to put formulas in the query; there is even a button that allows you to add more tables to the Query window.

The Query Toolbar provides you with quick access to a bunch of useful features.

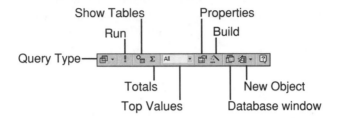

A Query with a View

A Query with a View

SQL ▾ You can also use the **Query** view button to switch back and forth between the results of your query and the Query Design window. This allows you to fine-tune your query on-the-fly.

The buttons that you use on the Query toolbar will obviously depend on a particular need as you build your queries. Below is a quick summary of what some of the more important buttons on this very useful toolbar do.

The Query Type button allows you to change the type of query that you are designing on-the-fly. You can choose from a number of query types including Select, Cross-Tab, and Make-Table.

This one is easy; click this button when you are ready to run your query.

The Show Tables button opens the Show Table box, allowing you to add tables to your query.

The Totals button adds a Totals row to the Query grid box. You can use this row to perform calculations such as totals, averages, or counts.

The Top Values box can be used to find the highest or lowest values resulting from the query. For instance you may want to see the top 20 percent of your sales using a query. You would set up a query that would sort sales in Descending order and then you would place 20 percent in the Top Values box. Only the top 20 percent of your sales figures will appear when you run the Query.

Running the Query

Once you establish the criteria for your query, you are ready to run it. The Customers query that you have been working on will (hopefully) select the records for the customers that live in Pennsylvania, and it should sort the records ascending by last name.

To run the query, click **Run** on the toolbar (it's the button with the exclamation point on it). Way to go! You set up (with Mr. Wizard's help) and ran a select query. Your sample query produced a sorted, subset of the original Customers table, the customers who live in Pennsylvania (PA).

The query results— a sorted subset of the original table.

Doing the Math—Formulas in Queries

Setting up the select query was really straightforward so cook some of that gray matter of yours and work with a query that incorporates a formula. Getting your queries to do math is easier than you think. Say that you have a Products table that tells you how many units of each product you have in stock and also tells you the unit cost of each item. You can run a query that will give you the total dollar amount that you have invested in each of the items that you have in your inventory.

Setting up a simple query from scratch that includes a math formula only takes a second. You select the **Queries** tab on the Database Explorer and then click **New**. In the New Query dialog box, select **Design view**.

When you click **OK** to start the query creation process, Access opens the Show Table dialog box, letting you know that this query isn't going to get very far if you don't choose a table.

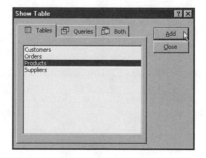

Select your table or tables for the query in the Show Table dialog box.

In this case, select the **Products** table and click **Add**. Once you add all the tables you plan to use in the query, click **Close**. As soon as you click Close, you are taken to the query grid box area, allowing you to refine or edit the query.

Selecting the Fields for the Query

The query grid box is familiar territory; this is where you place the fields that you want to use in the query. To add a field to the grid box, click in the appropriate field box and then on the drop-down arrow. All the fields in the table that you select will appear in the drop-down list. To select a field, click the field you want.

In your sample query, place the ProductName, UnitsInStock, and UnitPrice in the grid box. Remember, you can keep this query simple because all you want is the total invest-ment you have in each product in stock.

Expressing Yourself: Creating the Expression

If you think about what you want to accomplish here; it doesn't require brain surgery. You want to set up a formula that multiplies the units you have in stock with the unit price of the products that you have in inventory. You create this simple formula using the *Expression Builder*.

Make sure that you click in the field box just to the right of the two fields that you want to multiply (UnitsInStock and UnitPrice). This will put the answer in the last column of the query. This column, in effect, becomes your summary field in the query.

You can place a calculation in a query column to help summarize your data.

Expression Builder —

Fields in Query —

New Summary Field —

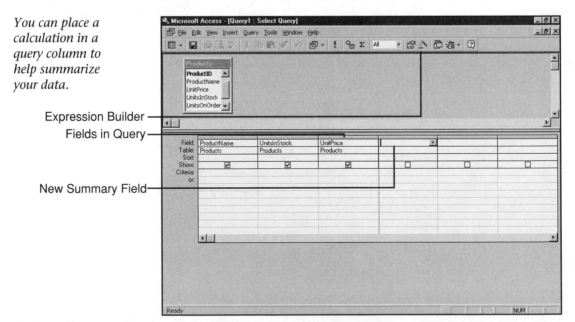

160

Once you place the insertion point in the field box that you will use for your total investment formula, click **Build** on the Query toolbar. And then you meet an old friend.

The Expression Builder

You can't say that you've never seen this thing before; you are now in the Expression Builder. You used the Expression Builder to put the date in one of your forms in Chapter 10.

The Expression Builder is divided into two areas: the upper part is the Expression box, where you will paste your formula, and the lower part is the Identifier area where you select the things that you'll construct the formula from.

Use the Expression Builder to create your formulas. In this case, you want to multiply two fields together. Since you find fields in a table, it makes sense to double-click the **Tables** folder in the Identifier area.

All the tables in your database are listed. You just need to double-click the table that you want to get the fields from. In this case, you would double-click the **Products table**. As soon as you select the table, the fields in the table are listed in the second box in the Identifier area. Now you are ready to actually build the expression.

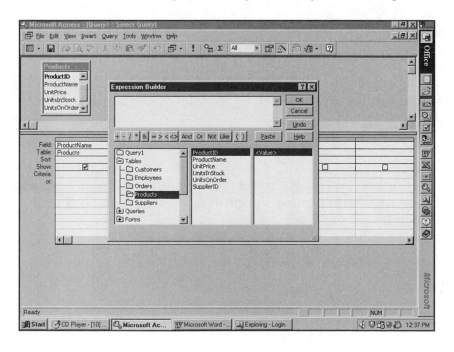

Working your way through the Expression Builder decision tree is just a matter of a few double-clicks.

161

Click the first field that you want to include in the formula, **UnitPrice**; then click **Paste**. Access pastes the field name into the Expression window.

Now you need to place a multiplication sign in the formula. The Expression Builder supplies a whole set of math symbols below the Expression window. Click **Multiply** (it has the asterisk on it) to place this symbol into the formula. Now all you have to do is paste the second field into the expression. Here you would click **UnitsInStock** and then **Paste**. That's it; formulas are that easy to build. Once you complete the expression, click **OK**.

The completed formula in the Expression window.

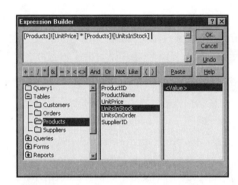

Express Yourself

You can use the Expression Builder to create formulas—expressions that return a time, date, or other value, and conditional statements. All the operators for conditional statements such as And, Or, Not, and Like are available with the other math symbols.

Run It!

Access pastes the expression into the grid box at the insertion point. The next step is to run the query and see if the expression actually works. The **Run** button on the toolbar will fire up your query.

The query appears in the Datasheet view. A new column appears at the end of the datasheet that contains the values that were created by your expression (a formula that multiplied two numeric fields).

The new column will have a heading that reads **EXPR1**. This stands for expression one. Since you probably don't want to leave this as the heading for the data column, you can return to the Query Design view and edit the name that appears in this particular field. For instance, you can select it (select **Expr1** in the design view, but leave the expression intact) and change it to Total, Current Investment, or something equally appropriate. Your new text will then appear as the column heading when you rerun the query or return to the Query Datasheet view.

Clearing the Query Grid If you ever need to clear the query grid, click the **Edit** menu, and then select **Clear Grid**.

Product Name	Unit Price	Units In Stock	Expr1
Cheddar	$5.49	38	$208.62
Brie	$6.69	23	$153.87
Swiss	$4.99	30	$149.70
Gouda	$4.99	12	$59.88

The finished query with the new expression column.

A Saved Query Is a Happy Query

When you create a query from scratch you will have to name it, if you want to save it. Click **Save** on the toolbar, and Access will prompt you for a name for the query.

Quick Fix Statistical Queries

Access queries also give you the capability to get quick statistical information on fields that contain numerical values. For example, this is a great way to get a total (Sum) of all the products you have in stock, or an average (Avg) of the number of support calls that you get at your little computer store. You can also use a query to find the maximum (Max), minimum (Min), or even standard deviation (Stdev) of a certain field or fields.

Say you want a quick statistical fix on the products you have in stock. You would start a new query (from scratch) and select the **Products** table in the Show Table dialog box. Once in the Query Design window, you would set up the numeric fields in the table (or tables) in the grid box.

To give yourself a nasty migraine and have the query compute a sum, max, and min for the number of products in stock. It's really simpler than it sounds.

Normally, you would set up the field in the grid box and then tell the query to sum it (or do some other calculation; you'll learn how to select the formula in a second). Since you want to calculate three different things using the same numerical field, place the field in the grid box three times. So, three columns in the Query box will be designated UnitsInStock.

The UnitsInStock field placed in the grid box three times.

Using the Totals Section in the Query Grid Box

Now you need to let the query know what the three calculations are that you plan on performing on the UnitsInStock field. The Query Design window has actually been hiding the place where these formulas go. Click the **Totals** button on the Query toolbar.

Check This Out...

Fast Math from the Totals Button

Access provides you with one math trick that you will use time and time again. The Totals button offers an easy way to place a totals formula or get a summary count of items. Use the **Totals** button to speed up the placement of calculations into your queries!

In the grid box, a new row appears—Total—below the Table row. Below each field that you have selected, there is a Total box; right now these boxes say **Group By**. Click in any of these Total boxes and a drop-down arrow appears. Click the drop-down arrow, and you will see a list of mathematical formulas and expressions.

In the first field box, select **Sum**. This gives you a field in the resulting query that gives you a grand total of all items in stock. In the second field box, select **Max**, which returns the maximum. In the third field box, select **Min**, which will return the minimum.

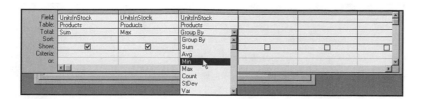

Selecting the formulas in the Total row.

Statistics from More Than One Table

While your example query made use of just one field, you can obviously place more than one numeric field (even fields from more than one table) in the grid area. Then select the formula for each field using the drop-down list in the Total row.

Once you set up your query and select your formulas, click **Run** on the toolbar to see the results.

And the Answer Is...

The query resulting from the kind of statistical query that you set up will be one row of numbers; the answers to your formulas. The column headings for the query datasheet consists of two parts: the first part references the formula that you used in the Total row, and the second part of the name references the numerical field that you ran the calculation on. So, the first column heading (with the answer appearing below it) would be **SumOfUnitsInStock**, meaning that Access calculated the total units that you have in stock.

Get the Most and Least Out of Your Queries

When you set up a query where you figure the max and min, you may also want to show which products relate to these totals; meaning what product is the max and what is the min. This is very easy to do. Include two columns in the grid box for **ProductName** and then select **max** and **min** in the group by boxes.

You can use queries like this to calculate statistical information for any field that holds numeric information. Everything from the sales totals on your latest book to the standard deviation on the frequency of a certain gene allele in an isolated salamander population (and you thought I only knew software stuff).

The query datasheet and its calculated results.

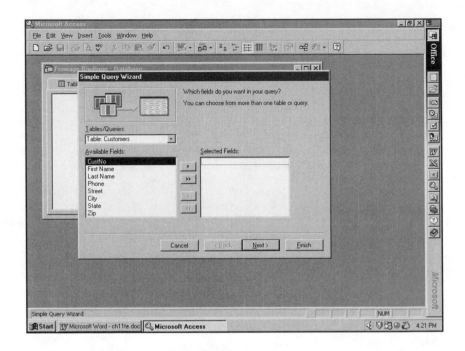

Wow! These queries are really something, aren't they? Take a second to get your bearings, take a deep breath now, and then move on to bigger and better things such as queries from more than one table, cross-tab queries, and queries that delete or move fields. See you in the next exciting chapter.

The Least You Need to Know

➤ Queries ask your tables questions; use queries to select certain records.

➤ Queries actually look a lot like a table and appear in the Datasheet view.

➤ The Query Wizard is a quick way to put together a simple query.

➤ The Query Design window is where you edit queries that you create with the Query Wizard or from scratch.

➤ The lower grid box area is where you designate the fields and the criteria (conditional statements) for your query.

➤ You can also use queries to perform mathematical calculations on your data, such as determining a sum, a maximum, or a minimum.

Chapter 12

Questions and More Questions— Designing Advanced Queries

In This Chapter

➤ Creating incredible multi-table queries

➤ Create a Crosstab query

➤ Place calculations in Crosstab queries

➤ Use queries that you create to create other queries

➤ Use Append and Delete queries

"The weather started getting rough, the tiny ship was tossed, if not for the courage of the fearless crew..." Oh, sorry, I was just relaxing in front of the idiot box (no relation to this fine series of books), and doing a little channel surfing. Since you're here, you must have weathered the last chapter, and I hope it convinced you that queries are much easier to understand than you first thought. Select queries are the easiest to create and probably the most used in database management.

In the last chapter you created several select queries (the first was a query that selected the customers from your Customer table who reside in Pennsylvania—a perfect example of a select query). In this chapter you will get the opportunity to explore other types of queries. First, however, you will learn how to create a select query from more than one table.

As you work with select queries from multiple tables and the other query types such as Crosstab, Delete and Append, all the query tips that you learned in Chapter 11 apply. Remember, if you ask the right question in the query, there probably isn't a database out there that won't give you the correct answer.

Creating a Query from More Than One Table

Let's take a look at how you create queries from more than one table. Come on, don't panic. You've already created forms from more than one table. Remember? So creating multi-table queries can't be all that bad. A great use for multi-table queries is to pull information together from a number of tables and then perform various query features such as sort, select, and summarize on the data.

You can create a multi-table query via the Query Wizard, or create it from scratch directly in the Query Design window. While this type of query isn't really the same as the select queries you did in last chapter you will still want to use select (which is the default query type) to set up this multi-table query. However, do keep in mind that the techniques used in building this query could also be used for other query types such as Crosstab, Append, and Delete—queries that you will explore later in this chapter.

The key to any type of multi-table query is that the tables selected for the query must be joined by relationships (yep, more of that mushy stuff). And, as you already know, relationships are based on common fields. The common field will be the Primary Key field for one of the tables and a regular field (meaning it's not the primary key).

Selecting the Tables for the Query

Let's say that you want to do a query that will include three tables: a Customers table, an Orders table, and a Products table. You would like this query to list—by product name—the orders that have been initiated by each of the customers.

This query won't create a datasheet subset of any of the tables involved as your Customer select query did in Chapter 11 (the customer subset was just customers living in Pennsylvania). It will combine information from the three tables so that you can see the customers, their personal information, and what products they've ordered on the same query datasheet.

For this whole query thing to work, relationships must exist between the tables. In our sample Fromage Boutique database, the Customers table and the Orders table are joined by the common CustNo field. They have a relationship. The Orders table and the Products table are joined by the common ProductID field, so they're okay too. I didn't say that all three of the tables had to be directly related to each other. There has to be a relational hierarchy between the tables you want to include in the query.

More Than One Way to Design a Query The tables can be selected for the query by adding them to the design window using the Show Table box, or by selecting fields from the tables in the Query Wizard.

To create this query, make sure that you have the **Queries** tab selected in your Database window. Click **New** in the Database window to create a new query. The New Query box opens. Make sure **Design view** is selected and then click **OK**.

The Query window will open. The Show Table box will also open. This is where you select the tables you want in the query. Double-click a particular table to add to the Query window. In this case, you would double-click the **Customers** table, the **Orders** table, and the **Products** table. Once you have selected all the tables that you wish to use in the Query, click **OK** in the Show Table box. The selected tables will appear in the top portion of the Query window. The relationships between the various tables will also be shown.

Create a Query From a Query

You can use queries in the place of tables when you set up a new query, allowing you to query a query (no, I'm not trying to be funny). Think about it; this would allow you to do some pretty refined questioning of a database (seriously!). For instance, you could create an Append query as you did in Chapter 11 to derive a table that holds a subset of your customers. You could then take this query table and query it for customers in a certain ZIP code range or sort the customers by name or location.

The selected tables and their relationships are shown in the top pane of the Query Design window.

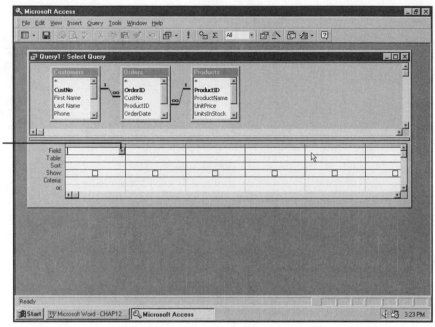

Click here to get a list of all the fields in the selected tables

Selecting the Fields for the Query

Selecting the fields for the query from three tables is no different than selecting them from one table. When you click in the **Field box** in the grid area of the window (lower half) a drop-down arrow appears. Click the arrow to select from a list of field names that includes all the fields in the selected tables.

It's Easy to Add Tables to the Query If you find that you need to add another table to a query, click **Show Table** on the toolbar and select from the dialog box. When you are finished, click the Show Table dialog box **Close** button.

Say that the purpose of this query is to put together a datasheet that can be used for calling your customers to let them know that their orders are in. So basically, you need to include fields in the query that give you the customers name and phone number, the date that you promised them the product, and the product's name. All the fields you need for this query will be available because you've included the appropriate tables in the query.

Selecting the fields for the query.

Field:	First Name	Last Name	Phone	Promised-byDate	ProductName	
Table:	Customers	Customers	Customers	Orders	Products	
Sort:						
Show:	☑	☑	☑	☑	☑	☐
Criteria:						
or:						

Results Are Everything

 Once you've selected the fields for the query, you can run it by clicking **Run** on the Query toolbar.

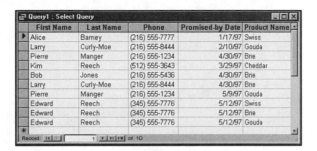

The query results list the customers and their product orders.

Notice that this query gives you the results that you want—customers and their orders—but it may not give you the results the way you want them. Each customer order appears in a separate row; this is kind of disconcerting when you have a customer that has placed more than one order. You could sort the query by last name, but you would still get separate entries for each order a customer has made. There is a better way to display this data by using the Crosstab query.

Here is a quick note on saving your queries. Whether you use the Query Wizard or design your queries from scratch, remember that you will need to name and save the query if you would like to be able to use it again.

A Good Crosstab Query Will Never Double-Cross You

Wow, try to say that really fast ten times! Crosstab queries display the information in a spreadsheet—like format that makes it easier for you to view and compare the data. Crosstab reports are perfect for summarizing numerical data from a particular field and then cross-referencing it to another field that has its data listed in the first column of the Crosstab report. For instance, if you wanted to see how many orders your customers have made by cheese, you could set up a Crosstab that would list all the customers in the first column and then give you a total (number or orders) that they have made for each cheese you carry in your inventory. The cheese types would be listed in the first row of the query. This configuration makes it easy for you to "cross-tabulate" a particular value as you visually scan the query.

Another excellent use for a Crosstab query is calculating the totals for the quarterly sales of a particular product. The Northwind database contains a Crosstab query that displays subtotals for each quarter by product.

*A Crosstab query
from the Northwind
database that
summarizes product
sales by quarter.*

Product Name	Customer	OrderYear	Qtr 1	Qtr 2	Qtr 3	Qtr 4
Alice Mutton	Antonio Moreno Taquer	1995			$702.00	
Alice Mutton	Berglunds snabbköp	1995	$312.00			
Alice Mutton	Bottom-Dollar Markets	1995	$1,170.00			
Alice Mutton	Ernst Handel	1995	$1,123.20			$296.40
Alice Mutton	Godos Cocina Típica	1995		$280.80		
Alice Mutton	Hungry Coyote Import !	1995	$62.40			
Alice Mutton	Piccolo und mehr	1995		$1,560.00		$936.00
Alice Mutton	Rattlesnake Canyon Gr	1995			$592.80	
Alice Mutton	Reggiani Caseifici	1995				$741.00
Alice Mutton	Save-a-lot Markets	1995			$3,900.00	$789.75
Alice Mutton	Seven Seas Imports	1995		$877.50		
Alice Mutton	White Clover Markets	1995				$780.00
Aniseed Syrup	Alfreds Futterkiste	1995				$60.00
Aniseed Syrup	Bottom-Dollar Markets	1995				$200.00
Aniseed Syrup	LINO-Delicateses	1995	$400.00	$144.00		
Aniseed Syrup	QUICK-Stop	1995		$600.00		
Aniseed Syrup	Vaffeljernet	1995			$140.00	
Boston Crab Meat	Antonio Moreno Taquer	1995		$165.60		
Boston Crab Meat	Berglunds snabbköp	1995			$920.00	
Boston Crab Meat	Bon app'	1995		$248.40		$524.40
Boston Crab Meat	Bottom-Dollar Markets	1995	$551.25			
Boston Crab Meat	B's Beverages	1995		$147.00		
Boston Crab Meat	HILARIÓN-Abastos	1995		$92.00	$1,104.00	
Boston Crab Meat	Lazy K Kountry Store	1995		$147.00		
Boston Crab Meat	Lehmanns Marktstand	1995		$515.20		

Creating a Crosstab Query

To create a Crosstab query, you use the Crosstab Query Wizard, which walks you through
the query creations steps, just like all the wizards in Access. Once you click **New** in the
Database Explorer (make sure you have the Query tab selected), you will select the
Crosstab Query Wizard in the New Query dialog box. As soon as you select your query
type, click **OK**. Now we'll see what this Crosstab stuff is all about.

Selecting the Fields for the Query

The very first screen of the Crosstab Query Wizard would like you to designate which
fields you want to use in the query. Before you can pick the fields, however, you have to
pick the table that holds the fields. There is one very odd thing about Crosstab queries;
you can't build them from more than one table. The Wizard tells you this; it says that if
you want to use fields from more than one table, you have to run a Select query first,
then use the Select query and its fields (which came from more than one table) to build
the Crosstab query.

Is this weird or what? Well not totally; you can design queries that use other queries as
the source for their fields. Queries look like tables, and most of the time they are just
subsets of tables with maybe a formula or two thrown in. So there is no reason for this
Crosstab thing not to work. And you already have a query (the Customer Orders query)
that holds the fields that you want to use in the Crosstab query.

For those of you that would like a quick query refresher, the easiest way to create the Customer Orders query that will be used to create the Crosstab query is via the Query Wizard. Make sure that you include the fields from the Customer and Orders table in the query. For more help creating a multi-table query check out Chapter 11.

Pick Your Table or Pick Your Query

It seems that the very first screen in the Crosstab Wizard is really crossroads with diverging paths. You must choose to base the query on a table or a query. In this case, choose query. Click the radio button to view **Queries**. Then you can choose the query that you want to use (Customer Orders). That's all there is to this step. Click **Next** to proceed.

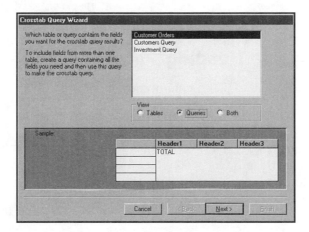

The first step in the Crosstab query creation process— select a table or a query.

Row, Row, Choose Your Row (Headings)

The next step in creating the Crosstab query requires that you make a choice; you have to tell the Wizard which of the fields in your original query should be used as row headings in the Crosstab query. To enter a field in the Selected Fields box, select the field and then click the **Add** button. You are limited to three row headings in the query.

Since the whole point of this Crosstab query is to be able to read the data from left to right and see which products have been ordered by which customer, it makes sense to use the customers' personal data as the row headings. In this case, use the Last Name, First Name, and Phone (number) fields as the row headings. Once you've selected the three fields that you want to use as row headings, you can click **Next** to move to the next step.

*The Crosstab
Wizard asks you
to select the row
headings for the
query.*

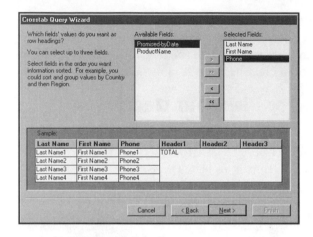

Choosing the Column Heading

Now the Wizard wants you to pick a column heading for the query. The field that you
pick will be used to create a column for each of the data values that are found in the
particular field in the original table or query.

The query that you are basing the Crosstab query on had a ProductName field that listed
the different names of the products you sell at the good old Fromage Boutique. It makes
sense to use the products name as the column headings, since you used the customer's
last name, first name, and phone number as the row headings.

Build Your Crosstab Queries from Summarizing Queries

Remember, Crosstab queries cannot be built from more than one table.
This is a real problem if you wish to use fields from multiple tables in
the Crosstab. So, it is necessary to build them from a pre-existing query
that pulls data together from a number of tables. Before you undertake
the creation of a Crosstab query make sure that you have built a simple query that
contains all the fields (from multiple tables if necessary) that you want to have in
the Crosstab.

Click the field name that you want to designate for the column heading, in this case
ProductName. Once you've selected the field for the column heading, click **Next**.

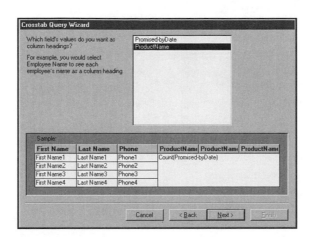

Selecting the field for the Crosstab column heading.

Calculations Anyone?

Now the Crosstab Query Wizard wants to know if you want to set up any calculations in the query. You can design the query so that certain calculations are carried out on the row and column intersections (just like a spreadsheet). In this situation, you have customers that have been promised a product on certain dates and so it might be nice to see how many total orders each of them has placed. What you can do is have the query count the promised by dates for each customer; this will give you the total number of orders that they have placed. The Crosstab query can also break down the number of orders that each customer has placed for each cheese type. So, the total number of orders for each customer will be found in the Promised-by date column and the orders by cheese will be summarized in the appropriate cheese column. Keep in mind that almost any field can be summarized mathematically. In the case of the Promised by date field and the various cheeses the number of times they appear in the original query is being totaled by the Crosstab query.

Notice that the Crosstab Wizard lists the fields (Promised-by-Date and ProductName) that you did not designate as row headings for the Crosstab query's column headings. When you designate the fields that will be in a Crosstab keep in mind that you will have to use them all; they must either serve as row headings, column headings, or be summarized mathematically. Click the **ProductName** field to select it. This will create a different column in the Crosstab for each of the cheese types. Now all you have to do is click **Next** to move to the next step in the process.

> **Check This Out...**
>
> **Crosstab Queries do Great Calculations**
> The whole idea of counting Promised-by dates to determine the number of orders that a customer has placed may seem a little odd. However, queries are capable of applying numeric functions to seemingly non-numeric fields such as a date ordered field. The functions available in the Crosstab query are Count, First, Last, Max, and Min.

The Crosstab Wizard asks you to select a field to serve as the column heading.

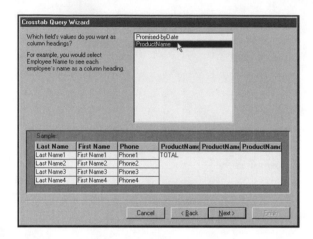

Calculating Totals Using the Promised-by Date Field

The Crosstab Query Wizard makes you use all the fields that you designated when you began the query creation process. So far, you've used the Last Name, First Name, and Phone fields as row headings. You used the ProductName field as the column headings (a different column will be created for each cheese type). You have not used the Promised-by Date field in the query.

No problem, the Wizard is aware of this and will make use of the field in the next step of the query creation process. Crosstab queries are great for summarizing information, especially in situations where you need a calculation done. The Wizard is asking what field information you want to use in calculations that will appear at the intersection of the rows and columns in the query. Since you want to see how many orders each customer has made (both total orders and orders of each specific cheese type), you will want to use an Access function that counts the number of times the Promised-by Date field appears for each customer (this counts each of the separate orders made by the customers).

This particular screen of the Crosstab Query Wizard provides you with several different formulas in the Function box that you can use to calculate results that you want to appear in the Crosstab query. In this particular case you will select the Count function. This will count the orders using the Promised-by Date field as previously discussed. Make sure that Count is selected in the Functions box. Then you're ready to move to the final step in the Crosstab query creation process.

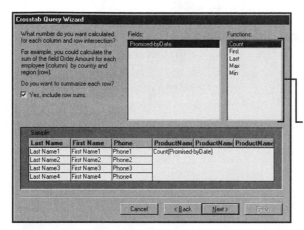

You can select a formula from the Functions box that will place calculated results in your Crosstab query.

Functions box

The End of the Line

Clicking **Next** one last time takes you to the last step in your query quest. Name the query (type the name in the name box) and then click **Finish** to view the results.

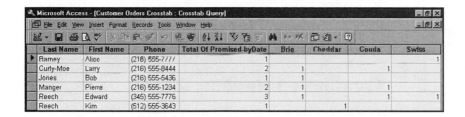

The completed Crosstab query.

This query looks marvelous. You have row headings (First Name, Last Name, and Phone Number), you have column headings (the product names), there is even a column that shows the total number of orders each customer has made (a result of the count formula).

You can now see how a Crosstab displays its data. If you follow a particular customer's name across the query toward the right, you can pinpoint which products the customer has ordered. The Crosstab query is definitely an improvement over the select query when it comes to viewing your data.

Using Append and Delete Queries

There are still two types of queries that we should take a look at before we close the book on this particular subject. But, wait! Don't close *this* book. Append queries allow you to copy records from one table and place them in (append them to) another table.

Quickly Copy Table Fields
You can copy the fields and all their parameters from an existing table to a new table. In the Table design view select all the fields of your existing table and copy them using the Edit/Copy menus. Create a new table and in the Design view, paste the fields into the table. It's very easy and very fast.

Setting Up Your Select Queries Fast The quickest way to set up a Select query that can then be easily turned into another type of query, such as an Append or Delete query, is via the Design view. With the Queries tab selected in the Database window click **New**. In the New Query box make sure the Design view is selected and then click **OK**. The Show Table box will appear; select the table or tables that you want to include in the query, then click **OK**. Then all you have to do is place the appropriate fields in the Field row of the query box. For more information on creating simple queries see Chapter 11.

For instance, you may have an Active Employee table. When an employee leaves the company, it makes sense to remove their record from the table. Using an Append query, you can move this data to a Former Employee table. Once you copy the data to the Former Employee table, then you can use a Delete query to totally remove their information from the Active Employee table. That way their data isn't cluttering up the active employee list, but you still know where to find this person's info if you need it.

I should reiterate the fact that running an Append query only copies the data from the original table to the new table. To remove the data from the original table you must also use a Delete query.

In your case, you have a Customers table that lists customers who live in three different states, Ohio, Pennsylvania, and Virginia. Let's say you've decided to make a separate table for the Pennsylvania customers because you are going to open up a new store in their state. This situation, then, calls for an Append query to copy the data to a new PA Customers table. Later in this chapter you will use a Delete query to remove the Pennsylvania customers completely from the original Customer table.

Creating an Append Query

To use an Append query you need a table that you can append the records to, and that table should have the same fields as the table from which you are removing the records. In our example, we need to create a table to hold the records of our PA customers—records we'll be taking from our current Customers table. The PA Customers table we create, therefore, will need to have the same fields as the current Customers table. Once you create the new table, make sure that you save it.

To create the Append query, set up a select query (from scratch or using the Wizard) for the table that from which you want to remove the records—in our example, the Customers table. All the fields that are contained in the table should be placed in the grid box in the Query Design window. In your example, you would choose the **Customers** table and use all the fields available. The new query, however, would be a Select query. This poses a problem (although an easily remedied one).

178

A Change Of Query Identity

You need to turn this select query into an append query. You can change the type of query that you are designing by clicking on the **Query Type** button on the Query toolbar. A drop-down list appears giving you several possibilities. Select **Append**.

As soon as you select Append, the Append dialog box appears and asks you to designate the table to which you want to append the records. You should type in the name of the empty table that you have created to accept the appended records. In this case you would type *PA Customers*, the new table for PA people. Then you should click **OK**. In normal circumstances you would probably already have a table that you are appending the records to. You would select that particular table rather than the sample PA Customers table that we created for this particular discussion of append queries.

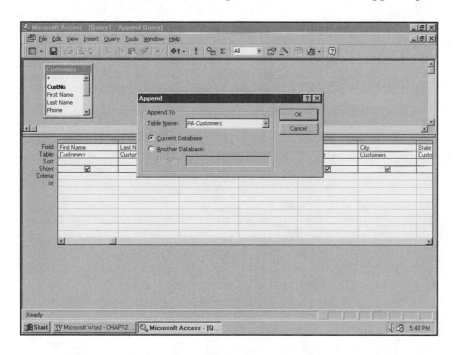

Selecting the Table that will receive the records from the Append query.

You will notice that a new row appears in the Query Design grid box after you have selected the table that will receive the records from the Append query. This row determines the fields in the new table to which you will append the field information. Since we are appending to a table that has exactly the same fields in it as the current table, the Append to: row will list the same field names as those listed in the query's Field row.

179

Setting Up the Append Criteria

Now all you have to do is set up a criteria that lets the query know which records it should append to the new table. We want the PA customers appended to the PA Customers table, so you would set up the criteria **PA** in the criteria box below the State Field (just like you did in the select query you created in the last chapter).

Enter the append criteria in the appropriate field column.

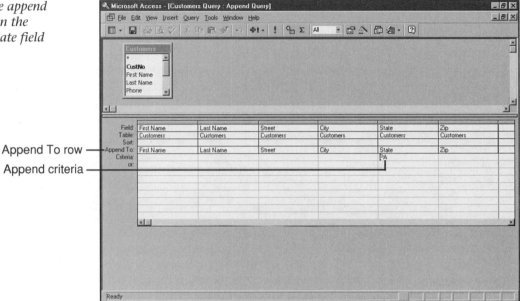

Append To row — Append To row

Append criteria — Append criteria

 Once the criteria is set, just click **Run** on the toolbar. Access knows that you are doing something fairly drastic here, so as soon as you attempt to run the Append query it tells you how many rows (records) will be appended by this query.

If you're confident that the query was designed correctly (and you should be), click **Yes** to allow the query to append the records to the new table. Remember, if the query doesn't work right, you can always go back and edit it's design. And if you end up with the wrong records appended to your PA Customers table, you can delete those records and start over. Access is very forgiving so don't hesitate to experiment and learn as you work with the various database objects such as queries.

A Query Well Run

It would be a good idea to see if your Append query actually performed as advertised. You can minimize the query and switch to the Table tab in the Database window and then open the table that the records were appended to. In the example that we've been working with a table (PA Customers) holding records for people from PA should be the result of the query.

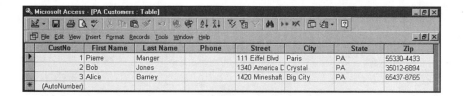

The Append query copies the appropriate records to the table that you designate.

Make-Table Query Makes New Tables Fast

Another way to quickly create a new table using records from a current table is the Make-Table Query. It works exactly the same way as the Append Query, however, it will create a new table from the records selected by the query. This means it takes care of the field creation for the new table.

Creating a Delete Query

You will find that if you open the original table (the table that you appended the records from), the records you appended are still there. Since you went through all the trouble to append them to a new table, you probably don't want them in the old table anymore. This is where a Delete query comes in. You use it to delete the records in the old table that you appended to the new table. The great thing about setting up the Delete query is that you can use the Append query that you designed; the only change that you make is to let Access know that the query is now a Delete query.

So in our present case, you still have the Append query in the Access window (we minimized it, remember?). So once you restore it (click its restore button) you can change it into a Delete query.

To switch a Append query to a Delete query, click **Query Type** on the Query toolbar and select **Delete**. A new row appears in the query grid box—Delete. This row can be designated as Where or From. When you are setting up a Delete query for a single table leave Delete box as Where. When you have multiple tables you can designate that certain fields from one of the related tables be deleted.

Deleting the Records

The last step in setting up the Delete query is to set up the criteria for the deletion. Since we already had the Append table set up to append the records with PA as the state, this condition is still present in the query.

Once you designated your criteria for the Delete query, you can click **Run** on the toolbar. Access let's you know how many records you are about to delete and it also lets you know that the deletion is final. You can't use the Undo feature to get your records back. To make the query a done deal, you would click **Yes**.

*The Delete Query—
there's no turning
back from this one.*

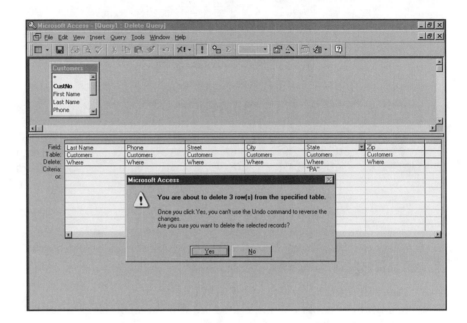

Here a Query, There a Query...

As you can probably tell by now, there are a lot of things that you can do with queries in Access. You can select records, append records, delete records, place data in a Crosstab query, do mathematical calculations; queries really do seem to be capable of doing it all.

The Least You Need to Know

➤ The tables that you use in multi-table queries must be joined by a common field—in other words they need to have a relationship.

➤ You can not only create queries from tables but from other queries.

➤ Crosstab queries allow you to view your data in a spreadsheet format where calculations can be carried out on the row and column information.

➤ Append queries are used to copy records from one table to another.

➤ Delete queries allow you to remove unwanted records from your tables.

Chapter 13

From Soup to Nuts—Creating Delicious Reports

In This Chapter

➤ Create informative single table reports

➤ Use the Report Wizard to create great reports

➤ Group fields in different report levels

➤ Edit your report designs

➤ Create multi-table reports that give you great summary information

I always loathed the first week of grammar school each Fall; you could bet that the teacher, who was probably reconsidering her profession after a Summer respite from this gaggle of screaming kids, would ask you to get up in the front of the class and give a report about what you did on your summer vacation. I would spend hours at home writing clever little (I thought they were clever) stories about what I did during my summer. I was building a database of facts to use during my report. However, typically, as soon as I took my place in the front of the room and cleared my throat to begin my great oration, I would drop all my index cards into an unsortable mess.

Reporting Your Database Information

Well, fear not, those days of unorganized reports are over. Access can take the information in your tables and spin reports that will present your data in a format that is well-designed and easy-to-understand. You will never have to write on another index card in your life!

You've already done a bang-up job dealing with tables, forms, and queries—all database objects that are primarily used online. Reports differ from these other database objects in that reports are designed to be printed. Of all your database manipulations, your reports are the most likely to be seen by your coworkers (and gasp, the boss) on the printed page.

You can create reports from single tables or from multiple tables (remember all that table relationship stuff we talked about?). You also have the same data and design control in reports as you did when you were working with forms.

Creating a Report From One Table

If you've tried to print out one of your tables, you've found you end up with several sheets of paper that spread the fields over the pages, and make it difficult to tell what data goes with what record. Let's say you just want to print out a readable list of your customers from a Customers table. What you need is a single table report.

Using the Report Wizard

As you have found with nearly all the other database objects that we've explored, the easiest way to create a new report is using a wizard. We'll fall back on our Fromage Boutique database, as we create a single table report from the Customers table via the Report Wizard.

Once you open a particular database, the next step is to click the **Report** tab of the Database window. You've already clicked the Explorer's **New** button to create other objects, so the next step should be second nature; click **New**.

There is more than one way to design a new report.

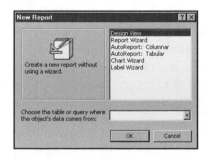

The New Report dialog box appears, offering you a couple of different ways to construct your new table. You can design the report from scratch, use the AutoReport command to build a quick report (columnar or tabular) using all the fields in a specific table, or you can use the Report Wizard to walk you through the steps.

Select the **Report Wizard** and then click **OK**. The next screen is very familiar; it's not unlike the Wizard screens that you've used to build forms and queries. You are asked to choose a table and specify which fields you would like in the report. The Customers table would be chosen in the Tables/Queries box, and since you want a report that gives all the information on customers available in the table, you'll want to include all the fields. The easiest way to include all the fields is to click **Add All** (it's the one with the right-pointing double chevron on it). After you've chosen the fields, you advance to the next screen by clicking **Next**.

Fast Reports with AutoReport

You can also use the **New Object** button on the Table toolbar to build an AutoReport for the currently selected table. It's the same feature that you used to build an AutoForm for data entry.

Are You With A Group?

The next screen wants to know if you would like to add any grouping levels to your report. You can set up the information in a defined hierarchy. Customer numbers, for instance, can be displayed as a major heading for each of the records.

You can arrange the information in any order you like. In this case, it would make sense to put the customer number at the top of each record in the report, and follow it with the last name, and then the first name. The rest of the information for each customer will be displayed in a columnar fashion under the levels.

To set up the grouping levels, which really are just headings and subheadings in the report, select a field and then click **Add**. Once you've chosen your levels (CustNo, Last Name, FirstName), you advance to the next screen.

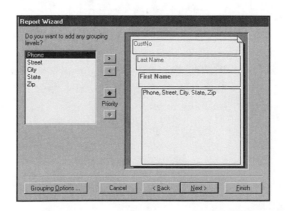

Field names and the field information can be grouped at different levels in a report.

185

Get Those Records in Order If you set up a report that doesn't group the information at different levels you can have the records appear in the report according to the sort parameters that you set.

What Sort of Sort Would You Like?

The Report Wizard now asks you if you would like to sort the records in the report by a field. You can actually sort the records by up to four fields. You don't need to sort your records in this situation because you have made the customer number (CustNo in our table) a first-level group. The records will be listed in the report in order by CustNo making sorting unnecessary. Click **Next** to move to the next step.

Your report can be designed to sort the data presented by one field or a number of fields; reports using group levels don't need to be sorted.

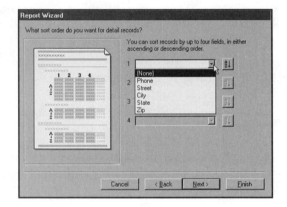

Pick a Report Layout

This whole report creation process has been pretty easy so far, but now you're going to have to put on your designer bérèt and decide on a layout and page orientation for the report. Several layouts are available. You can print the report stepped, blocked, as an outline (two different layouts) or in left-aligned columns (equally spaced on both the right and the left). All you have to do is click the **Radio** button for your specific choice. In this case, choose **Align Left 1**, which gives a balanced look to the printed page.

You can also choose the paper orientation for the report. *Portrait* is a regular sheet of paper in its 8.5" × 11" orientation. For *Landscape* you turn it 90 degrees and you have a page 11" × 8.5" If you only have a few fields in your table use the Portrait orientation. If you have a lot of fields use Landscape. You'll leave the page orientation as portrait and move on to the next step. So, click **Next**.

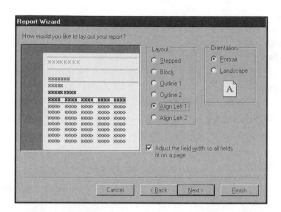

You select the layout and the page orientation for the report.

Even Reports Have Style(s)

Now you have to select a style for the Report: Bold, Casual, Compact, Corporate, Formal, or Soft Gray (who comes up with these things?). Since you are probably learning Access to help you ascend the corporate ladder of success (don't get stuck on one of its rungs) let's choose **Corporate**. Once you choose your style, you can move on to the next step by clicking **Next**.

An End in Sight

Wow! You are already at the last step in the report creation process. The Report Wizard gives you an opportunity to name your report or go with the name that it has selected for it. Since you used the Customers table as the data source for the report, the Wizard assumes you want to name the report Customers. Hey, makes sense to me!

You also must decide whether you want to preview the report or fiddle with the report's design. It probably wouldn't hurt to take a look at the report and then decide if you need to alter it in the Report Design view (yes, it's a lot like the Form Design view). Click the **Finish** button to take this report home!

Previewing the Report

I love previews; I mean, how many times have you left your local movie theater after sitting in the dark for two hours and lamented the fact that the previews you saw of coming attractions were a heck of lot more exciting than the film you just sat through.

Since reports are meant to be printed, Access takes you to the Print Preview window to show you the report that you created. Print Preview shows you your form exactly as it will print and gives you the chance to return to the design screen to make changes.

Use Print Preview on All Your Objects

You can also use Print Preview to take a look at any forms or tables that you may want to print. Seeing the different database objects as they will appear on the printed page can help you decide whether you really want to print them or not; it can save you a lot of paper.

Print Preview has its own set of command buttons along the top of the window. You can click **Print** to send your report to the printer or you zoom in and out on the page. You can also click **Close** to exit the Print Preview mode.

If you move your mouse around when you are in the Print Preview mode, you will notice that the mouse pointer has become a zoom controller (it looks like a magnifying glass). When you are zoomed out on your report (you can see the whole page) the zoom controller contains a plus (+) sign. This means that if you click the mouse button, you'll zoom in. When you are zoomed in, the zoom controller contains a minus (-) sign. Click it and you zoom out.

Print Preview gives you the ability to zoom in and out as well as print your report.

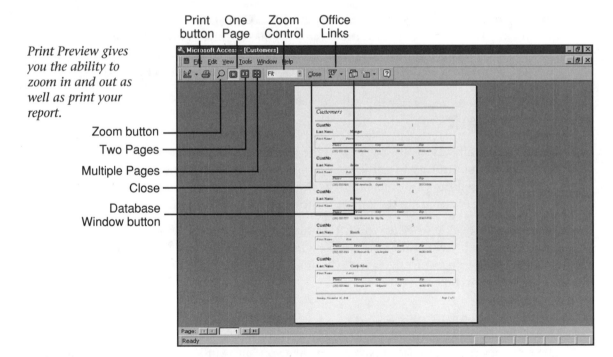

Print button · One Page · Zoom Control · Office Links

Zoom button

Two Pages

Multiple Pages

Close

Database Window button

Techno Talk

Export Access Data to Word and Excel!

You can also export your Access reports to other members of Microsoft's Office Suite of applications. You can send your report to a Microsoft Word document or analyze the data in the report using Microsoft Excel's spreadsheet capabilities. Use the OfficeLinks button to quickly take advantage of this powerful feature.

Once, you are finished previewing your report, you can send it to the printer or close the Print Preview window.

The Report Design View

When you close the Print Preview window, you are taken to the Report Design view. The design view offers you a Toolbox that contains the same tools that were available when you were working on forms. In the Design view you can delete or add field controls and labels to the report.

You can also size and move the controls and labels. For instance, you may find that a report based on a table with a lot of fields has squished the field data and the field labels on the report (see, you should have chosen landscape page orientation). You can click a field or label and use the sizing boxes to change the width or height of a particular item.

Techno Talk

Get Those Widths Right When you initially set up the grouping levels in the report via the Report Wizard you can change the average width of the field controls in the report by clicking **Grouping Options**.

Redesigning the Report

You will probably find that if you used the Report Wizard wisely, you won't have to do a whole lot of redesigning on your report. You already know that manipulating the controls and their labels is all mouse work. You may, from time to time, want to give a report a personal touch.

When you use the Report Wizard to generate the report, it automatically puts two controls in the report's footer area, the date and page numbering. Since we didn't have a lot of records in our Fromage Boutique Customers table, the entire report only filled one page. When you only have a one page report, it seems kind of senseless to have a page number on the page. To remove the page numbering all you have to do is remove the appropriate control.

Since the page numbering control is in the footer area, you may have to scroll down to select it. Once the control is selected all you have to do is press the **Delcte** key on the keyboard to remove it. Whenever you make any changes to your Report design make sure you click **Save** on the toolbar to save them.

Picture This...

You can also add text and other items to your report design for purely cosmetic reasons. Since this is a report for the customers of a cheese shop, it might be nice to include a picture logo in the report design.

Check This Out...

Make Your Reports Beautiful

All the font attributes (bold, italics, under-line) and border and color buttons on the Report toolbar can be used to enhance the look of your reports.

Adding a picture to a report is really a snap (or is that snapshot?). You may have to expand one of the Report areas to place a graphic. For instance, you may want to expand the report header in your report for a company logo. Once you have a place picked out click the **Image** button on the Toolbox. Then you use the mouse pointer to drag a rectangle onto the report (pick your spot) to hold the image.

As soon as you create this control that will hold your image, the Insert Picture dialog box appears. This dialog box is like any other File Open or Insert dialog box; you pick the location of the item that you want to use (in this case a picture) and then you specify which item you're talking about.

The images that come with the Microsoft Office 97, and the Access 97 software, will commonly be found in a Clipart subdirectory that resides inside the Office directory that is created when you install the software. Two directories reside in the Clipart subdirectory. One directory is named Popular and will contain images that have been installed to your computer's hard drive. Other images are also available in a directory named ClipArt On Office CD. This provides you with several subdirectories of additional ClipArt.

Once you open the appropriate directory, you can also preview the images listed; all you have to do is click the image. Let's take a look at the various images available on the Office CD. There should be a picture that will be perfect for our customers report. Let's look in the Office directory and see if there isn't a picture of some cheese that we can use for our Fromage Boutique Customers report.

Access and Office offer a number of great graphics that are easy to insert into your report.

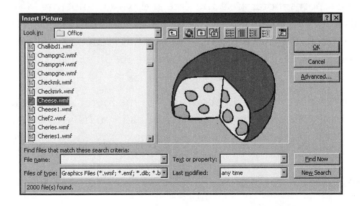

Scroll down through the images in the Office directory. Notice that the images are listed alphabetically. If you scroll down far enough you will find cheese.wmf; a great picture of a great (or is it grate?) piece of cheese. Once you have the image selected, you just click **OK**. The Picture will be inserted into the control box that you placed on the report.

Many of the images provided with Access 97 and Office 97 are quite large. Meaning, you will have to adjust the size of the Image control that you placed in your report to accommodate the graphic. Click **Image Control** and then use the sizing handles on the control to enlarge it.

In the case of our cheese image, it fits nicely into a fairly small Image control. You can move the image by clicking on the control and then dragging it to a new position. Images provide a great way to dress-up your reports!

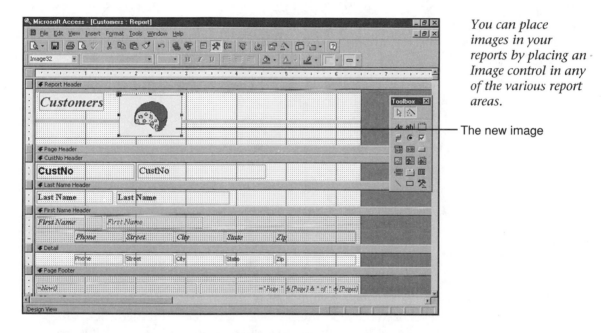

You can place images in your reports by placing an Image control in any of the various report areas.

The new image

With the help of the Report Wizard, creating reports can be really quite simple, and bare-bone reports can be created quickly using the AutoReport feature. Let's expand our look at reports, and figure out how to create a report that is based on more than one table.

Reports Created From More Than One Table

You can use the Report Wizard (or design the report from scratch) to generate a report that uses more than one of your database tables. When you designed your single table report, the wizard asks you to specify the table and the fields that it was to use. When you build a multi-table report, it's just a matter of selecting fields from more than one table.

I know this sounds really easy, but there is one catch. The tables that you take the fields from must have a relationship. If they don't, the Wizard will not let you mix the fields in the report. It tells you that the tables that you are taking the fields from are not related and it bounces you to the Relationship window.

Check This Out...

Queries Into Reports You can also base reports on queries. This allows you to manipulate the data in a table or tables via a query, and then generate the report from the query results.

All is not lost, however. You just establish the appropriate relationship between the tables and then start the Report Wizard again. This time it will accept your field choices.

For instance, let's say you have two tables in your database related to your products: a Products table (listing the items you sell) and a Categories table (defining the major groups that your products fall into). You want to print a report that lists the products by category.

It's easy to check or to define relationships between your tables. Make sure the Database window is open for the particular database and then click **Relationships** on the toolbar.

A One-to-Many relationship exists between the Categories table and the Products table.

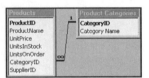

Since a relationship exists between these tables, you would start the Report Wizard. When you reach the screen where you pick the fields for the report, you would select the fields you need from both tables. This is done by selecting one of your tables—Categories—in the Table drop-down box. The fields found in the Categories table will be displayed in the Field box. To add the fields to the report select the field or fields and then click **Add**. Once you've selected the fields you will use from the Categories table, select the **Products** table in the Table drop-down box. Select the fields that you will use in the Field box, and add them to the report.

Techno Talk

Use a Main Report and Subreport to Summarize Data from Multiple Tables

You can create reports that show data from more than one table by creating a main report and a sub-report. This is done in a similar fashion to the method that you used to create a main form and a subform. You create a report from one table and then, in the Report Design view, add a control for a subreport. You can then set the parameters for the control, such as the table that should be used for the subreport and how the information should be formatted.

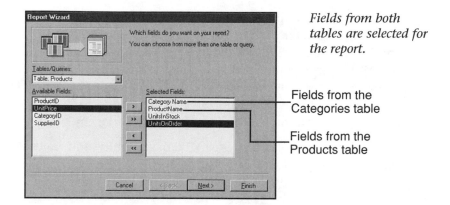

Fields from both tables are selected for the report.

Fields from the Categories table

Fields from the Products table

Boy, Is This Report Wizard Smart

Once you've determined the fields that you want to include in the report, you can advance to the next screen in the Report Wizard. If you've chosen fields from more than one table, the wizard will ask you how you want to view the data in the report.

For instance, we used fields from a Categories table and a Products table. So the wizard wants to know if you want the report to show the data by Category or by Products. We want this particular report to list the field information by Categories—which obviously means that you would tell the wizard to list it by category.

Once you determine how the data should be listed, the wizard also gives you the option of grouping the information as you did in the single table report. Since the report will list things by the main heading—Categories—you may want to select the field for the item name (ProductName in this particular case) and make it one of the major heading groups.

Even though you are asking the wizard to create a report from more than one table, it still affords you all the options that were available for the single table report such as sorting the data by a particular field, and the full range of report layouts and styles.

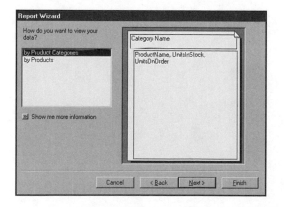

You select how you want the combined data from the two tables to be listed in the report.

Since you are grouping the data by headings, you won't need to sort the data, so you can skip the wizard screen by clicking **Next**. The next two screens are where you select the report layout and then the report style. Make a selection in each and then click **Next** to continue. Once you complete the steps in the report creation process (including naming the report), the new multi-table report will be displayed in the Access Print Preview window.You can zoom in and out on your report or send it to the printer. If you decide not to print you can exit the Print Preview window by clicking **Close**.

Reports provide you with a great deal of flexibility, and really are the best way to assemble your data for printing. In the next chapter, we'll take our survey of Access reports a little further, and look at how you can easily create mailing labels, set up a report that does calculations, and place a chart in a report.

The finished multi-table report.

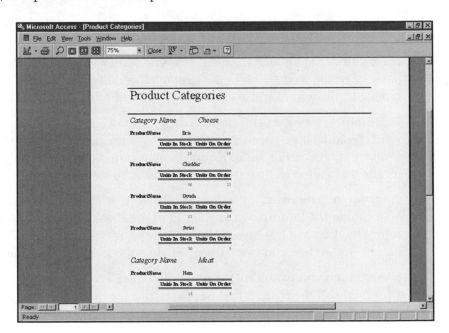

The Least You Need to Know

➤ The easiest way to create a report is via the Report Wizard.

➤ You can edit your report designs in the Report Design view. This let's you fix anything that the wizard didn't take care of.

➤ You can group fields on your reports so that you get a series of headings and sub-headings making it easy to make sense of the information shown on the report.

➤ Multi-table reports can also be created using the Report Wizard. This type of report makes it very easy to summarize data from two or more related tables.

➤ The Print Preview window allows you to scrutinize your reports before you print them.

No Need for a Calculator—Doing Math in Reports

After the last chapter you're probably feeling pretty good about your ability to take a bunch of seemingly unrelated data and use Access to spin a pretty good report. Reports are meant to summarize information; it is their raison d'être—their reason for being (use the idiom *raison d'être* to impress friends and family. For example: *The apparent raison d'être of my cat is to walk on my keyboard when I'm trying to type.*

Placing a Total in a Report

If you buy the supposition that reports exist to summarize, then it makes sense to have your reports summarize numeric information. Meaning it would be great to design a report that can return a total on a bunch of numbers. Let's say that you run a design and architectural firm called *Daring Designers*. And let's also say that you are creating a database to help you track company expenses. So, you would probably have at least an Employee table, an Expense table, and a Department table in your database. The tables would also be related by shared fields.

The easiest way to create this database would be to create a blank database and then use the Table Wizard to create the various tables in the database taking advantage of the ready-made fields that the wizard provides. The Employee table should contain the fields Employee ID, First Name, Last Name, Extension, and Department. The Expense table should contain the fields Expense ID, Employee ID, Amount Spent, Date Submitted, and Expense Description. The Department table should contain the fields DepartmentName, Department ID, and Office Location. Obviously, if you were building a database for your own business, the tables in the database and the fields in the tables would be set up to meet your own particular needs. For more help building your tables and working with fields see Chapters 5 and 6.

Practice Makes Perfect

The Northwind database that ships with the Access 97 software is also an excellent resource. It provides you with ample tables and data to practice building the various database objects. You can also use the Northwind database tables as examples of well-designed tables as you build your own databases.

The tables and relationships in your Daring Designers Database.

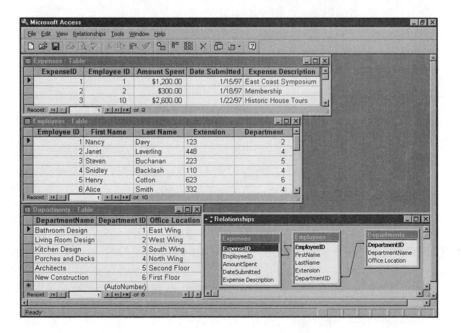

Once you have a proper database set up with the right tables, you can generate the reports. Your first step would be to build a report (either via the Report Wizard or from scratch) referencing the fields that will supply your data—such as Employee Name, Expense Amount, Expense ID, and perhaps the department that the employee belongs to.

Report It With the Wizard

The easiest way to build this report would be via the Report Wizard. Your data would probably exist in at least two tables: an Employee table and an Expense table. Remember, you can mix fields from different tables to design a report.

Expenses

Expense Description	Department Name	First Name	Last Name	Amount Spent	Date Submitted
East Coast Symposium	Living Room Design	Nancy	Davey	$1,200.00	1/15/97
Membership	Porches and Decks	Janet	Leverling	$300.00	1/18/97
Historic House Tours	Architects	Steven	Buchanan	$2,600.00	1/22/97
Miscellaneous	Porches and Decks	Sridley	Backlash	$1,800.00	1/23/97
Concrete Supplies	New Construction	Henry	Cotton	$920.00	1/24/97
National Conference	Porches and Decks	Alice	Smith	$1,560.00	2/3/97
CAD Software	Architects	Ebb	Palooka	$2,200.00	2/5/97
Appliances	Kitchen Design	Cleo	Katrina	$5,500.00	2/7/97
West Coast Conference	Bathroom Design	Steven	Buchanan	$1,400.00	2/8/97

A sample of a tabular expense report grouping information by expense.

Reports From More Than One Table

When building a report that uses more than one table or query as a source of information, you must decide how you want the data to be presented. For instance, if you are building a report using information from two tables: an employee table and an expense table, you can either set up the report to list the expenses by expense number (using the expense table to provide the report's view of the data) or list the expenses by employee (using the employee table to provide the report's view of the data).

Once the report is built, you will want to make sure that you switch to the Design view, so that you can add a totals formula to the report. How and where you add that formula is our next exciting topic.

Don't Put Your Footer in Your Mouth

You already know from our earlier discussion of reports that they contain page header and footer areas—places where you can put data or other information that you want to repeat on either the top or bottom of each page of the report.

Techno Talk

blah blah blah blah blah blah

Footer Facts Information that you place in the report footer will only appear at the end of the report (the last page). Likewise any information placed in the report header will appear at the beginning of the report. Information that you would like to repeat on each page of the report should appear in the page header or footer.

Your reports can also contain report headers and footers— areas that you can use for report names (the header area), or for summary information such as a totals formula (the footer area). Obviously the report header would appear at the very beginning of the report, and the report footer at the very end.

Since we want to place a formula in the report footer, the first thing you will need to do is expand the footer area. It's just a matter of placing the mouse on the footer area's bottom border and then dragging the sizing tool to give you the space that you need. That seems pretty painless doesn't it? Well, unfortunately, making a spot to put the formula is a lot easier than putting the formula in the spot. Now you have to face the tough stuff and place a new formula control in the footer area.

Adding the Totals Control

To place a totals formula in the footer area, you must add a new control to the report. In the case of the report that we discussed earlier, the employee expense report, it would make sense to place the total control under the control that listed the amount for each of the expenses.

To add the new control you click the **Text Box** tool on the Toolbox and then drag out a new control box in the footer area. You can then click the **label box** for the new control and assign it a name. In this case, you may want to label the control **Total Expenses**.

Check This Out...

At the Controls

You can select any of the controls in your report and drag them to new positions. Don't forget that you can also size all the label and control boxes in the report. Keep in mind, though, that reports can appear on multiple pages. Arrange your controls accordingly.

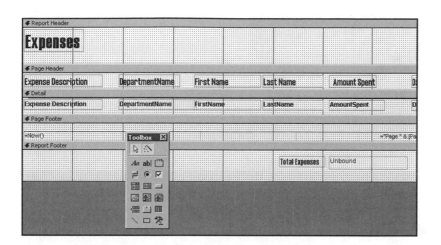

The new control in the footer area will total the expenses.

As soon as you're satisfied with the control's label and position in the footer area, you can set up the control to total the expenses. Click the control to select it, and then click the **Properties** button on the Report toolbar. The Properties box for the currently selected control will appear. Now comes the tricky part.

Control Properties are No Problem

When you want to change the properties of a control in your report, make sure you have the control selected before you click the **Properties** button. You can also place the mouse on the control and click the right mouse button. Then select properties from the short cut menu that appears.

The Source of All Data

So we aren't after the source of all data (but it made the heading sound more mystical); we just need to tell Access the source of the data for the new control that you built. The source will be a particular field and an expression such as a math formula (you put a date expression in a report in the last chapter). If you want a total to appear in this control you will have to designate the field that holds the data and then build an expression to total the information.

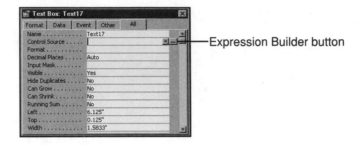

Getting ready to place an expression in the data control source box.

Expression Builder button

Click in the Control Source box. A button for the Expression Builder will appear. Click the **Expression Builder** button and get ready to build a formula.

Your Total Comes To...

Once in the Expression Builder, it's just a matter of choosing the right formula for the situation and having the formula act on the appropriate field information. The Builder gives you easy access to both the formulas and the fields.

In this particular case, we want to total a group of numbers (expenses), so we'll use the sum formula. Double-click the **Functions** folder to list the type of formulas available. A subfolder for Built In functions appears; double-click it and a huge list of possibilities appears. All the functions available in Access will be listed in the third column in alphabetical order.

Choose From Categories of Math Functions

The Expression Builder allows you to select sub sets functions by categories (the second column of functions in the Builder). Once you select a category of functions, the specific formulas appear in the third column of the Builder.

The Sum of It

We're going to use the sum formula, so scroll down through the third column of choices and select **Sum**. After you select a particular formula, you need to add it to the Expression window. You do this by clicking **Paste**.

The formula now appears in the Expression window followed by a pair of parentheses with **<<expr>>** inside them. What the Expression Builder is trying to tell you is that you have to place the field name inside the parentheses if you want the expression to total the data.

202

You enter the field name by first selecting **<<expr>>** with a click of the mouse. Then you double-click the **Tables** folder (or the **Query** folder if you are using queries to build the report) to select the table that holds the particular field. Double-click the appropriate table (in my example, *Expenses*).

The fields in the table will be listed in the second column of the Builder. All you have to do is select the correct field (in this case *AmountSpent*), and then click **Paste** to place the field name in the Expression window. Once you have your expression complete, click **OK**.

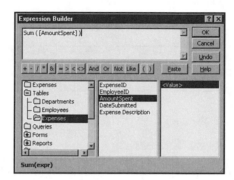

The completed formula in the Expression window.

Formatting the Total

Now that you've built a superb formula for your report, it makes sense to have the result of the formula appear in the report in an appropriate format. Since you are totaling expenses, you probably want the control's contents to be formatted as currency.

To format the control, click the **Format** tab of the Control's Properties box (you are returned to the Properties box when you exit the Expression Builder). Then click the drop-down arrow in the **Format** box. A bunch of different numerical formats are listed. In this particular case you would choose **Currency**.

Once you've completed your work in the Properties box, you can close it by clicking **Close** (the **X** in the upper-right corner). Now comes the fun part; you get to view the changes that you've made to the report—in this case the addition of a grand total at the end of your report.

Click **Report view** on the toolbar (it's the first button on the toolbar). You may have to scroll down and to the right to see the new total. It appears at the end of the report because it's in the report footer, remember? Now, wasn't that easy?

Check This Out...

Save It Or Lose It Make sure to save any changes that you make to the design of your report. This includes adding and formatting controls.

The completed report showing the total of all expenses.

Expenses

Expense Description	DepartmentName	First Name	Last Name	Amount Spent
East Coast Symposium	Living Room Design	Nancy	Davy	$1,200.00
Membership	Porches and Decks	Janet	Leverling	$300.00
Historic House Tours	Architects	Steven	Buchanan	$2,600.00
Miscellaneous	Porches and Decks	Snidley	Backlash	$1,800.00
Concrete Supplies	New Construction	Henry	Cotton	$920.00
National Conference	Porches and Decks	Alice	Smith	$1,560.00
CAD Software	Architects	Bob	Palooka	$2,200.00
Appliances	Kitchen Design	Cleo	Katrina	$5,500.00
West Coast Conference	Bathroom Design	Steven	Buchanan	$1,400.00
			Total Expenses	**$17,480.00**

Techno Talk

Count Those Entries

You could also place controls in the report that give you a count of the number of entries, or the average of a group of numbers. All the functions that you need to summarize data via controls are found in the Expression Builder. You can also place subtotal controls (and other mathematical expressions) in the detail area of the report to figure subtotals (or other results) for various groupings of data.

Adding a Group Subtotal to a Report

Now that you have a feel for calculations in reports, we can go one step further and take a look at grouping information in a report so that a subtotal is performed. For instance you may have different categories of items that you stock in your store and you would like your report not only to show you total number of items in stock (in the Report footer), but also subtotals for the units in stock in each category.

So let's say that you run a cheese shop (sound familiar?) and have already run a report using the Report Wizard that gives specific data on the items in stock and groups them into four categories: cheese, meat, gourmet crackers, and implements (you know, those important cheese eating aids). It should be no great shakes to edit this report so that you get a subtotal of the units in stock for each of the product categories.

The Design view of a report that displays data on items in categories.

Not All Groupers Are Fish

To make this whole subtotal of units in stock by category work, we have to find a way to let Access know that we want the information grouped—meaning it will have to know that it should add the items in stock for each category even though the category contains items that are not the same. For instance, a subtotal of the cheese category gives you the number of all the cheeses whether they are Cheddar or Gouda, or Bada for that matter. Ouch! Bada pun.

So to group this information together, you have to add a new section to the report. The information in your report may already be grouped by a particular field; for example, in our example report CategoryID is used to group the data (note the CategoryID header in the figure above). So, all you have to do is add another group section to the report for CategoryID, or group footer section. Then you can place your subtotal formula in the new section. Now you're probably thinking that you knew that this stuff was going to get complicated eventually, but actually adding a new section to the report is pretty easy.

Adding a New Report Section

Grab your mouse and let's create a new group footer section for the report. Click **Sorting and Grouping** on the toolbar. This opens the Sorting and Grouping dialog box. This dialog box is used to both sort and group information in the report (like you couldn't figure that out). We want to add another section to the report for the CategoryID field. First, you either select a current field or add a new field to the Field/Expression column. In this case you would click the **CategoryID** field.

Adding Fields for Sorting and Grouping?

To add a new field to the Sorting and Grouping box, click in the first empty row in the Field/Expression column. A drop-down arrow appears in the box, allowing you to choose a field. You should also be careful not to delete the fields currently listed in the Sorting and Grouping box. They were placed there when you originally set up your report and chose how the information should be grouped.

A Group Properties box appears for the currently selected field (in the bottom half of the Sorting and Grouping box) showing whether or not a Group Header or Group Footer currently exists for the field. In your example, the CategoryID field does have a Group Header. It's very easy to add a Group Footer.

Choosing the Group Field

The field that you use to set up a new group header or footer should be a field that either was used (in the original report), or can be used to group the data in your report. In the case of our cheese report all the products were listed by category (first all the cheeses were listed, then all the beverages were listed, etc.). This makes the CategoryID field the logical choice for the new footer section. Another thing that you should keep in mind when you set up new sections in a report is where you want the new grouped information to appear. The Group Header would appear above the group information. The Group Footer would appear below.

Setting the Group Properties

In the Group Properties area of the Sorting and Grouping dialog box click in the **Group Footer** box. Then click the drop-down arrow and choose **Yes**. Once you've chosen to add a new Group Footer or Header, you can close the dialog box. The new Group Footer (or Header) area will appear in your report.

Giving the group footer a Yes vote in the Sorting and Grouping dialog box.

Adding an Expression to the Group Footer Area

Now that you have a place in your report for the subtotal formula (the CategoryID footer in our case), you might as well add your expression. You've already been through this drill once.

You place a new control in the new footer area, and then click **Properties** on the toolbar. Once you select the **Data** tab of the Properties dialog box for the new control, you click in the **Control Source** box and then use the **Expression Builder** to build your formula.

The subtotal formula that you place in the Group footer will be exactly the same as the formula that you would place in the report footer to get a grand total—the sum function and the name of the field you want to total.

In your example, you wanted to subtotal the number of items in stock in each category, so the formula that you would create in the Expression Builder would be:

> *Sum ([Products]![UnitsInStock])*

Group Subtotal versus Grand Total Remember that by definition the Group footer will only provide information relating to the group of data that you designated, in this case the categories of items. This is why you can use the sum function to get a subtotal rather than a grand total.

The New footer area and the subtotal expression for the report.

Viewing the Edited Report

Once you've finished the editing of the report in the Design view, all you have to do is click the Report view to see your changes—even the addition of a group subtotal. See how simple it is to add new sections to existing reports?

A portion of a finished report that has a group footer with a subtotal.

Products by Category

Category Name		Cheese	
ProductName		Brie	

Product ID	Units In Stock		Unit Price
2	23		$6.69

ProductName		Cheddar	

Product ID	Units In Stock		Unit Price
1	38		$5.49

ProductName		Gouda	

Product ID	Units In Stock		Unit Price
12	12		$4.99

ProductName		Swiss	

Product ID	Units In Stock		Unit Price
3	30		$4.99

Total Items in Stock	103

Check This Out...

The Old Switcharoo

As you refine your reports, you can easily switch back and forth between the Report view and Design view by clicking the **View** button on the Toolbar.

The techniques that you used in this chapter to add formulas and new areas to your reports can be used whether you build your reports via the Report Wizard, or from scratch. Don't be afraid to experiment. Remember, the changes that you make to a report aren't final until you save them.

The Least You Need to Know

➤ You can place mathematical expressions in your reports by simply creating a new control and then placing a formula in the control by using the Expression Builder.

➤ The report Footer area provides a good place to put a grand total for a tabular report that you want to summarize numeric fields.

➤ Every control on our report will have a Properties dialog box associated with it. You use this box to determine the format, the control source, and other attributes of the control.

➤ You can add sections to your reports via the Sorting and Grouping dialog box. This box is also where you select the fields that you wish to use to group information in the report.

Chapter 15

Pride of Ownership— Enhancing Your Reports

Now before you start whining about how sick you are of reports, just let me say that this is definitely going to be the final word on the subject. I mean, I could go on for another five or six chapters on reports—I love reports. Oh, well, I guess I'm sick of them, too; so this is definitely going to be your last look at this highly versatile and useful database object.

Adding a Subreport to a Report

As you already know, reports are great at summarizing the information in your tables and queries. You can take this concept one step further and set up reports that contain two parts—the main report which may list the data in great detail and a subreport that can serve to summarize the information given in the main report.

For instance, you may have a report that breaks down the expenses amassed by each of your employees. It may also be useful to see the information broken down by department, which would require a second report. The fact that you take the more general report on department expenses and attach it to the report on expenses for employees allows you to present the data in two very different ways in the very same report.

A Report Within a Report

This whole idea of a report within a report is very easy to execute. First, you build the reports that you want to combine—perhaps one specific report and one general report. You can use the Report Wizard or build these reports from scratch in Report Design view.

Reports and Forms

Reports are very similar to forms. When you want to create a report from scratch, you add the controls to the Report Design view using the various tools on the Toolbar. You can add headers and footers to your reports and also divide reports into sections.

So, once again let's say that you run Daring Designers. And the Daring Designers database has an Employee table, an Expense table, and a Department table. Information on creating the tables found in this database can be found in Chapter 14; you can also get similar results using the comparable tables found in the Northwind database as you explore the techniques described in this chapter. You would use the fields from these tables to design your two reports. So, in keeping with the example, you would have a report that summarizes expenses by employees and a report that summarizes expenses by department.

The easiest way to create these two reports would be via the Report Wizard. The first report summarizing the expenses by employee would use fields from the Employee and Expense tables. The report summarizing expenses by department would use fields from the Expense table and the Department table.

After you have the two reports completed, open the more general of the two reports in Design view. The more general report will be longer, perhaps consisting of multiple pages when it is printed. The longer report will serve as the main report, and you will attach the more specific report (in this case, expenses by department) as a subreport.

Expenses by Employee

LastName	Backlash
First Name	Shirley
DepartmentName	Porches and Decks

Date Submitted	Amount Spent	Expense Description
2/8/97	$1,560.00	National Conference

LastName	Buchanan
First Name	Steven
DepartmentName	Architects

Date Submitted	Amount Spent	Expense Description
1/23/97	$1,800.00	Miscellaneous

First Name	Robert
DepartmentName	Bathroom Design

Date Submitted	Amount Spent	Expense Description
2/7/97	$5,500.00	Appliances

LastName	Cotton
First Name	Harry
DepartmentName	New Construction

Date Submitted	Amount Spent	Expense Description
1/24/97	$920.00	Concrete Supplies

LastName	Davy

A look at the two reports that will become the report and subreport.

Expense by Departments

DepartmentName	Office Location	Date Submitted	Amount Spent
Bathroom Design	East Wing		
		2/7/97	$5,500.00
Living Room Design	West Wing		
		1/15/97	$1,200.00
Kitchen Design	South Wing		
		1/22/97	$2,600.00
Porches and Decks	North Wing		
		1/18/97	$300.00
		2/3/97	$1,580.00
		2/5/97	$2,200.00
Architects	Second Floor		
		1/23/97	$1,800.00
		2/8/97	$1,400.00
New Construction	First Floor		
		1/24/97	$920.00

Techno Talk
blah blah blah blah blah

Changing the Design of the Report Wizard

When you design a report via the Report Wizard or from scratch, you can easily change the overall format of the report. When you are in Report Design view, click the **Format** menu, then click **Autoformat**. You can then select from a number of formats.

Adding the Subreport Control

You've added controls to forms and reports, so creating a spot for the subreport should be no big deal. You do have to decide, though, which section of the main report you want to use for the subreport.

You can place the subreport in any of the non-repeating sections of the main report, such as the report header and footer, but it probably makes sense to place a subreport that summarizes the information at the very beginning of the main report. That way, when you print out the report, the less detailed report will appear on the first page, with the more detailed breakdown of the data following. Most people won't even leaf through the entire report. They just want to see the overall picture that the subreport provides.

So, a good place to put the subreport is in the Report Header of the main report. Expand the Header area to accommodate a new control that will hold the subreport. If the report label for the current report resides in the Header section, you may want to drag it to the very bottom of the section. Also, if you used the Report Wizard to create the report, there may also be lines that you will want to select and rearrange in the Header section.

Be Careful Where You Put Your Subreports

Don't place the sub-reports in the page header or footer sections. These areas are used for information that you want to repeat on every page of the printed report. Report headers and footers make better places for subreports.

Summarize at the End

There is also certainly a case for placing your summary information (in a subreport) at the end of a larger, more detailed main report. That way, people leafing through all those pages can view a good wrap-up of the data in the ending subreport.

To add the control for a subreport, click **Subform/Subreport** on the Toolbox. Drag out a rectangle that will accommodate the controls and labels in the subreport. As soon as you place the subreport control in the main report, the Subreport Wizard is activated.

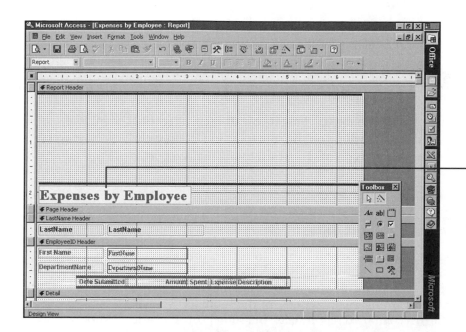

An expanded Report Header section with the report title moved to the bottom of the section.

The report title

You can add an existing report or create a new report to add to the current report.

Selecting the Subreport

The wizard gives you the option of using an existing report or building a new report for the subreport. If you created a report for this purpose, you would obviously choose the existing one and then click **Finish** to return to Report Design view. If you selected to build a new report using the Subreport Wizard, complete the steps in the report building process. You will find that your new report has been placed in the main report.

Obviously, the fact that you can use an existing report or create a new report to use as the subreport places you in a chicken-or-the-egg situation. If you have a report that you created via the Report Wizard that is appropriate for the subreport, select it when the Subreport Wizard gives you this option. Otherwise, you must complete all the steps necessary to build a new report that will serve as the subreport.

You can view the subreport by double-clicking its control (click right in the middle). A second window will open, showing you the subreport in Design view. You can modify the design of the subreport at this point. To return to the main report, close the subreport window.

Too Many Report Titles

When you add a subreport to a main report, the new control that you create will have a label that displays the name of the subreport. The subreport will probably also have this name in the header of the report. So, rather than having two titles for the subreport showing in the printed version of this combined report, click the subreport label and then press **Delete** to get rid of it.

Viewing the New Report

You can click **Report View** to see the subreport and main report as they now appear in Print Preview mode. And you can always return to Design view via the View menu if you want to make any modifications to the report design.

Adding Page Breaks to a Report

You may find that when you add a subreport to the beginning of a main report, it forces the main report to move down the first page of the printed combined report. It may make sense to push the main report to a second page and allow the subreport to occupy the opening page of the report. Adding page breaks to your reports is really quite easy. It's accomplished by using the Page Break tool on the Toolbox.

To add a page break to a report, make sure that you are in Design view. Click the **Page Break** tool in the Toolbox. Place the mouse pointer where you would like to place the page break and click the left mouse button. A page break symbol will appear on the left side of the section, showing you exactly where the page break will fall.

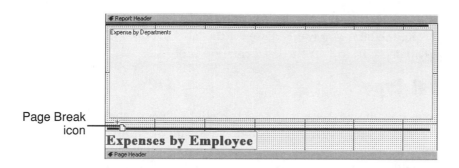

Place a page break between a subreport and the main report.

Page Break icon

After you've placed your page break, you can view the report in Print Preview mode to take a look at the changes you've made. After you have completed the design changes to your combined report, make sure to save the changes.

Creating Mailing Labels

You've created single table reports, multi-table reports, even multireport reports (subreport and main report); now it's time to tackle a report type—mailing label. It may seem on the surface to be a piece of cake compared with the tables you've already created, but it's historically been one of the worst nightmares of the database aficionado.

In fact, the hoops that you used to have to jump through to create mailing labels using your database are probably the main reason that businesses have kept at least one typewriter at their offices; it was easier to type the labels on the typewriter than to create them via the database.

Well, those days of cranky databases are over, and Access provides you a very straightforward path for creating of mailing labels. Yes, you guessed it; there is a Label Wizard that walks you through the process.

To create mailing labels—which really means to create a report—you have to have a table or a query to base the report on. Obviously, because you're doing labels to go on envelopes or packages, the records in the table or query must contain all the mailing information you need for each individual.

Using the Label Wizard

Once you have the appropriate table or query, you're ready to create the labels. Open the database from which you want to create the labels. Make sure the Report tab is selected in the Database window. Click **New**. When the New Report dialog box appears, select the **Label Wizard**, then select the table you want to use for the label data in the Table drop-down box. Then you can click **OK** to start the label creation process.

Selecting the Label Type

The Label Wizard makes it really easy for you to select the right type of label for your report; you don't have to deal with any of that "banging a square peg into a round hole" stuff; you select the label type by *Avery number* (Avery is a label brand name). The Avery number for your labels will be on the box or package that the labels came in. Now aren't you sorry that you threw that box away?

A Label is Only a Label

Avery is one of the largest label-producing companies, and their label sizes (along with 3M and others) have become the business standard. More than likely, the labels that you use for your printer are Avery labels or clones of Avery labels (don't take this as an endorsement of Avery labels—just supplying you with the facts).

For instance, let's say that you want labels for a letter that you are sending out to your customers; a commonly used Avery number for envelope labels is 5160—a label $1 \times 2 \frac{5}{8}$ inches. You would select the 5160 label number in the Avery Number box. Once you've selected your label number, all you have to do is select how the labels are fed into the printer—Sheet Feed or Continous. As far as laser printers and inkjet printers go, you will use sheet-fed labels, so you would select **Sheet Feed**.

Set the label parameters in the Label Wizard.

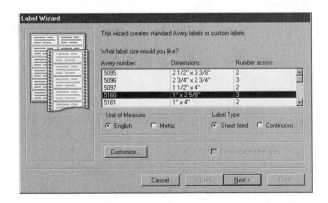

Custom Labels are Just a Click Away

You can also click **Customize** and edit the settings for any of the label types. This allows you to use odd-shaped labels or labels that do not have an Avery size equivalent.

Once you've set your label parameters, click **Next** to move to the next step.

Printing Labels

For the few users who still own one, a few words should be said about creating mailing labels on a dot-matrix printer. You may have to edit the user-defined page size before you can create label reports. To edit the paper size and set the default printer, you must enter the Microsoft Windows Control Panel via the **Taskbar Start** button. In the Control Panel, click the icon for your dot-matrix printer. Click the **File** menu, then click **On Properties**. In the Printer's Properties dialog box, click the **Paper** tab. Under **Paper Size**, click the **Custom** icon. In the User Defined dialog box, type the width and length of the label that you will use. Once you have set the label parameters, click **OK** to exit the dialog box. Avery, 3M, and other label makers still provide tractor-feed labels that can be used to print the labels that you create in Access on your dot-matrix printer.

Dressing Up Your Text

"It's better to look good than to feel good," or so Billy Crystal use to say in one of his many odd incarnations on *Saturday Night Live* (yeah, I know that was a long time ago). And, unfortunately in today's business world, appearance may be everything; so it's important that even your mailing labels look good. The next step in the label creation process is to select the look and color of your font.

Drop-down boxes are provided that let you choose the font type, font weight, font size, and font color. You can also click check boxes that will make the characters italic or underline.

Keep Your Labels Readable Simple fonts without serifs (like Arial, for example) are really your best bet for mailing labels. You probably should avoid italics as well. The post office can really get cranky when you bring in a huge pile of letters and their scanners can't discern the address on the label. They really don't like sorting things by hand.

Once you've selected the various font attributes, you can click **Next** to continue the process.

Have It Your Way

Now you have to choose what you would like on your label (not your cheeseburger). More than likely, you will want a name and address on a label that you will use for mailing. This Label Wizard screen lists all the fields available in the table or query that you chose to build the labels from.

To add a field to the label, select the field and click **Add**. You can press the spacebar when you need to put a space between fields, such as a first name and a last name field. To drop down a line on the label, press the **Enter** key.

Once you've selected the fields for the label, take a look at the sample label and make sure that you have all the fields that you need. If things looks good, you can advance to the next step.

Select the fields for the label.

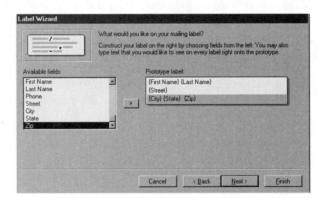

Order In the Sort

Now the Label Wizard wants like to know if you would like to sort the labels by a particular field(s). Sorting the records allows you to print the labels in a particular order. For instance, if you want to get the cheaper bulk rate on your mailing, you may want to sort the labels by ZIP code. Other possibilities are also available such as sorting the labels by last name and then first name (in case you have more than one customer with the same last name).

Mailing Labels

You may want to contact your local post office and find out exactly how you should format and sort your mailing labels. Different bulk mailing rates require you to do different things with your mail. For instance, a comma after the city used to be widely accepted. Now the post office wants your labels with spaces only, no commas.

Once you've selected the field(s) you want to sort the labels by, click **Next** to continue.

The End of the Road

The last step in the label creation process will look quite familiar. It is the final screen that you get when you create any type of report using a wizard. You are required to either name the report (yes, remember labels are a form of report) or use the name that the wizard has assigned to the report. You also have the choice of viewing the report—in this case, mailing labels—as it will print, or you can go directly to Design view to modify the report.

If you chose your mailing label size correctly, you will probably find that the field information will fit just fine on the label; you may want to go directly to the Print Preview view. More than likely, your labels look marvelous. But you may have one little problem...

But the Post Office Wants All Caps

The newest edict out of that fine government institution, the post office, is that mailing addresses should appear in uppercase characters. So, your mailing labels probably are not uppercase. I mean, you didn't think to set up your tables in all caps, so now you're stuck.

Well, not really. You can modify the report so that the labels will print in uppercase characters. To do this, you will simply add an input mask to each of the controls in the mailing label report.

Make sure that you're in Design view. Then click the first control in the mailing label report. Now you need to access the Properties box for all the selected controls, so click the **Properties** button on the Toolbar. Click the **Format** tab of the Properties box and then place the insertion point in the Input Mask box.

There isn't a built-in input mask that will change your control's characters to uppercase, so you will have to build one from scratch. It's actually quite easy. The > sign is used to tell Access to put things in uppercase. So type a > (greater than sign) in the Input Mask box. Then you have to specify the number of characters that should be put in uppercase. The ? serves as a wildcard character for one text character. You want to type in enough question marks (after the greater-than sign) to accommodate the longest control entry (it might be a person's name or street address).

In Case of Uppercase
You can also set up Input Masks for uppercase data entry in your tables or forms.

You will have to set up this uppercase input mask for each of the controls in the mailing label report. So, select each one and then follow the procedure outlined earlier. Once you've set up the input mask for uppercase characters for all the controls, you can preview your new improved report. See—mailing labels can be fun!

Designing an input mask for uppercase characters.

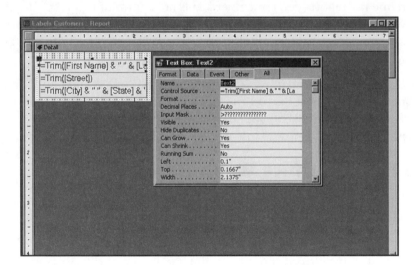

All Out of Breath

Wow! This report saga has gone on and on and on. It just shows how important reports are to your databases. You can design great tables, set up super relationships, and create incredible queries, but if you can't print a simple report, no one will be able to appreciate all your hard work. And don't forget, reports can be a lot of fun.

The Least You Need to Know

➤ You can place a subreport on a main report, allowing you to show two different takes on the data. The subreport can be a summary of the data, and the main report can supply all the details.

➤ Depending on how elaborate your report is, you can place strategic page breaks between the different elements of the report. This allows you to control how the information will print out.

➤ The Label Wizard walks you through the mailing label creation process. All you need up front is a table that will provide the data to the wizard and the Avery label number off the box of labels that you are going to use.

➤ Input masks can be used to change the way the data in your report controls will print.

Printing Database Objects

Have you ever been in a meeting where the participants are poring over a laser printed copy of a report? Suddenly one of your coworkers points out that there is an obvious error on one of the pages. At the very least it's a typo, at the most it's the result of a formula that doesn't even come close to the correct answer. If it's your report, you look for an open window to jump out of, and if it's not, you sit thanking your lucky stars and hoping that this never happens to you.

It Might Look Good, But Is It Right?

In the realm of printouts, databases have come a very long way from the prehistoric software packages of yesteryear (which is only about three years ago). Think about it; Access allows you to design extremely professional looking reports and forms; even the tables and queries look good. Back in the "old days" you were lucky if you could get your output into rows and columns.

Couple the desktop publishing capabilities of Access with the inexpensive laser printers and color inkjet printers available today and it's pretty easy to make your printed materials look like a million bucks. However, no matter how good your work looks, it's not worth
a tinker's cuss (which is roughly equivalent to a wooden nickel) if the information isn't accurate.

This means that you have to be extremely careful when you enter your data and extremely thoughtful and methodical when you design your mathematical expressions, reports, or queries. So knowing that exactitude is as important to you as it is to me, I'll get off my soapbox and you'll tackle the real subject matter of this chapter—printing your database objects.

A Word About Reports and Your Other Database Objects

You've already spent some time discussing the printing of reports (don't tell me you skipped those interesting and pithy chapters on the subject). As I said on more than one occasion, reports are the ideal format for printing your database information, and Access provides you with a set of very flexible report design features because of this fact.

You will find, however, upon occasion, that you just want to print a table, or a form, or maybe even a macro—nothing fancy; you just want a hard copy. For instance, you may want to send a printout of a table to a coworker for proofreading, or you may want to show off an incredible form that you designed for data entry. Access provides you with a couple of different ways to put these objects onto the printed page.

Check This Out...

Design View's Hard Copy
You can also print forms and reports in their Design views. Open the form or report in the Design view and then click **Print**.

Quickly Printing a Database Object

The fastest way to print a database object is to select the object in the Database Explorer window. Once the object, such as a table, is selected, click **Print**. Your database object will be sent to the printer.

Printing an object this way dumps the information to the printer that is currently selected in your Windows setup. If you want to have more control over the print job, such as which printer you will print to or what paper size you would like to use for the print job you must follow another route to printing—the Print command on the File menu.

Unsolicited Headers and Footers

As you already know headers and footers are areas where you place information that you want to appear on either the top or bottom of every page of a printout respectively. When you print tables, forms, and queries, the printouts will automatically be assigned headers and footers. The header information will consist of the table or form name and the current date. The footer information will consist of the appropriate page numbers.

Using The Print Dialog Box

When you click the **File** menu and then click the **Print** command, the Print dialog box appears.

Preview Your Print Jobs

You can preview the printout of any of your database objects by clicking on the **Print Preview** button on the Database or object specific toolbar. Use the mouse pointer to zoom in and out on your object in the Print Preview window.

The Print dialog box allows you to select certain print parameters, such as the printer you would like to use for the current print job. It also gives you control over the print range and the printer's properties.

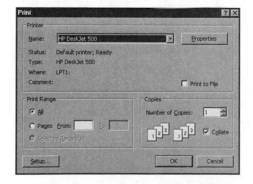

The Print dialog box allows you to select your printer and print range.

Selecting a Printer

Depending on your home or office situation, you may have your computer connected to more than one printer (especially if you are on a network). The Print dialog box has a drop-down box that will list all the printers that you have access to. To select a printer other than the current printer, click the drop-down arrow and choose your printer from the list. Once you choose the correct printer, click **OK** to send the print job to the printer.

Corralling Those Pages on the Range

The Print dialog box also allows you to select the range to be printed. This range can consist of a page, a group of specific pages in a sequence, or all the pages in the database object. To print a single page, click **Pages** and type the page number in the From: box. This set of steps is also used to specify a page range with the only additional step being typing the page range in the To: box.

You can also print a set of specific records by selecting the records in the table prior to invoking the print command. This is a great way to get a hard copy of important or new records that you would like to look over or verify.

Getting the Deed to Your Print Properties

The Print dialog box also gives you control over the Print Properties associated with the current printer. These properties range from the paper size that you want to use, to the print quality of the output from the printer.

When you click the **Properties** button in the Print dialog box, the Properties box for the currently selected printer appears. This dialog box contains three tabs: Paper, Graphics, and Device Options.

Paper, Paper—Read All About It

You are obviously going to use different paper sizes when you set up your print jobs. For instance, you may have a report that you want to place on one 8.5"×14" legal sheet of paper rather than spreading it over two 8.5"×11" sheets. Or you may have your printout set up to place names and addresses right on envelopes rather than printing out sheet-fed labels.

The Paper tab of the Properties dialog box allows you to select the different paper sizes and types (such as regular sheet versus envelopes). This tab also gives you the option of printing in portrait or landscape and allows you to set the paper source.

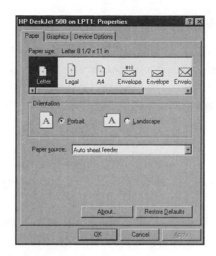

The Paper tab of the Properties box gives you control over paper size and page orientation.

You Don't Have to Be Graphic

Your graphics have to look good. The Graphics tab of the Properties dialog box is where you set the options for how the graphic elements in your database objects will print.

When You Go Too Far—Restore Defaults

If you really mess up the settings for how your graphics print, click **Restore Defaults** in the Graphics tab to put everything back the way it was before you started going wild on the graphic print parameters.

This tab gives you control over the resolution (the intensity of the image produced by the dots per inch printed) of the graphic, the dithering of the graphic (this is how the colors or shades of gray are blended), and the intensity (degree of lightness and darkness) of the graphic.

Global Choices

All the settings in the Print Properties dialog box are global settings. When you change these, you affect all the potential print jobs that you will print from all your various software packages so be careful.

You Always Have Options

The third tab on the Print Properties dialog box is for Device Options. This tab gives you control over the print quality of your print jobs and can be used to increase the speed at which the printer operates. Increasing the speed of your printer from the normal setting to a faster setting (in most cases there is only one other setting, fast) may affect the quality of your print job negatively. So you may not have as many options as you think when print jobs are concerned.

Once you set the various parameters and possibilities in the Print Properties dialog box, you can click **OK** to close the dialog box and return to the Print dialog box.

Getting a Break on Page Breaks

You can print each record, group, or section of a report or a form on a separate page by using the form or report property sheet. To access the Property Sheet, double-click the section selector when you are in the form or report Design view. In the Property Sheet you can select several different ForceNewPage properties for the section such as placing a page break before the section or after the section.

Once you've selected your printer and the print range and set the print properties, you're ready to print. To send the job to the printer, click **OK** in the Print dialog box.

Breaking the Code—Printing Your Macro Design Information

One thing that you should probably discuss before you bring our discussion of printing database objects to a close is the printing out of your macros. You can actually print a kind of mini-report that details the actions that you have placed in a particular macro. Open the macro in the Design view or select the macro in the Database window. Click the **Print** or **Print Preview** button.

Access will start the Database Documentor—a feature that gives you detailed information on the design of your various database objects. The Print Macro Definition dialog box will appear, giving you a set of check boxes that allow you the option of precluding certain information. There is a check box for the macro's properties, its actions and arguments, and its permissions.

Once you've designated the information you want to include in the macro documentation report, click **OK**. The results of the documentation will either go to the printer or to the print preview screen.

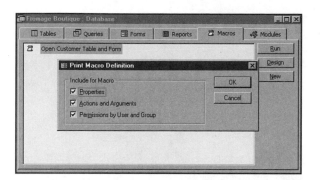

The Print Macro Definition dialog box lets you decide what information should be included in the documentation report.

Database Documentor is Always Ready and Willing

You can use the Database Documentor to detail the design of any of your database objects. The Documentor is particularly useful for documenting the macros and visual basic applications (modules) that you create. To document a database object click the **Tools** menu, point to Analyze, and then click **Documentor**.

Are You Setting Me Up?

If your database object is small, such as a table holding just a few records, or a short summary report that definitely fits on one page, you probably aren't that concerned about how the printout will be affected by such things as margins or page orientation. However, when you print a large object such as a long report or a multipage form, you may want to change the margins and select the page orientation.

To Access the Page Setup dialog box, click the **File** menu, then click **Page Setup**. The Page Setup dialog box allows you to set margins, page, and column parameters for your forms and reports.

The Margins tab of the Page Setup dialog box allows you to set the margins for your printout and also to determine whether or not you want the column headings in your datasheet to print out (the Print Data Only check box).

The Page tab allows you to select the paper size, paper orientation, and the printer that should be used for this particular print job. The source of the paper, such as a special feeder for labels or special paper (envelopes), can also be selected in this tab.

The Column tab gives you control over the grid settings in a multi-column report or form. You can select the row spacing as well as the column size in the final print out.

The Page Setup dialog box allows you to set the parameters for printing great-looking reports and forms.

Is It Just Resting Or Is It Dead?

So you've covered all our bases and you'll never have a problem printing out any of your database objects, right? Wrong! A time will come when you click in all the right places and still don't get a printout. When this happens there's a chance that something weird is going on with the printer or your connection to the printer; yes, it becomes a hardware problem. So when your printer seems to be doing something more than just resting, consult this short trouble-shooting list to get your print jobs back online.

➤ Make sure the printer is on and online (I know you already checked this).

➤ Make sure there is paper in the printer or that the paper that is there isn't jammed.

➤ Make sure that you are looking for your printout at the right printer (which printer did you print to?).

➤ Check your printer cable; is it still connected to the printer?

➤ Scream for your network administrator and make up a story about how that particular printout is for the big, big boss.

➤ Go to lunch and then see if anyone fixes the printer problem while you're gone.

Spelling It Out

Since accuracy was one of the themes of the opening paragraphs in this chapter, it makes sense to take a moment and discuss the Spelling feature that is available in Access. Most of the errors that are introduced into a database are done during data entry (other errors would be things like incorrectly designed reports or queries—especially where formulas are involved). So it makes sense to try and catch these errors in the beginning.

The Spelling feature, obviously, won't be able to check the numerical information that you input, or help you enter proper names, but it may help you avoid embarrassing typos and misspellings. Let's take a look at how you would spell check one of your Access database tables.

Using the Spelling Feature

To spell check the information in a table, query, or form make sure you have the appropriate item open. Click **Spelling** on the currently available toolbar or you can Click the **Tools** menu and then click **Spelling**.

The Spelling dialog box will appear. Words flagged as misspelled will appear in the dialog box. A list of suggestions will also appear that you can choose a correct spelling from. An **Add** button allows you to add words to the dictionary. If Access flags a proper name or a word not in the dictionary that is correctly spelled, you can either add the word to the dictionary, or click **Ignore** to ignore the word and continue with the spell check.

There is also a button in the Spell checker window that allows you to bypass the current field. This is great if you want to ignore entire fields in a table and still continue the spell check process.

Using the Spelling feature in Access.

Typos Are Nasty

While a spelling feature is not as crucial to a database as it is to a word processor, you will find that it can help cut down on your data entry problems by catching various misspelled words.

Be Politically Correct with AutoCorrect

Well not really, but Access has another great feature that will help you cut down on typos called AutoCorrect. AutoCorrect will replace common errors as you type. You can even add commons errors that you make and their correct spellings, so that AutoCorrect will fix them as well. To set up AutoCorrect to work as you enter information into your tables and forms, click the **Tools** menu and then select **AutoCorrect**. Select the **Replace Text As You Type** box and you are good to go!

Closing the Curtain

As we bring our little tale of printing and proofing to a close, I want to take one last opportunity to bug you about your database data. Don't print it out if it isn't right. Databases are supposed to be a collection of facts—enough said.

The Least You Need to Know

➤ You can print out any of your database objects, just open or select the object and then let it fly with the print command via the Print button on the toolbar or the Print command on the File menu.

➤ All of your print parameters, both global and object specific, can be set via the Print dialog box. To access this box, click the **File** menu, then click the **Print** command.

➤ The Print Preview command can save you a lot of paper. It makes sense to preview your print jobs before you send them to the printer and kill another tree.

➤ The page margins and other page attributes for a print job are controlled by the Page Setup dialog box.

➤ Not all your print problems will be software problems. Check out your hardware when you can't seem to get that database object to print.

Part 4
Expanding Your Database Brain Power

You are probably feeling really good about all the database knowledge that you've crammed in your head via this witty, yet kindly text. Your fingers dance over the keyboard as you work with your database objects; you're really using your head to design databases of epic proportions and ultimate simplicity.

Suddenly, as you work with Access, you slam up against a mental brick wall; you happen upon a feature that you have no knowledge. Well fear not, this book hasn't gasped out its last breath yet and we are going to take a look at some of the more advanced features and concepts that you may have to deal with as you build your dulabases. Want to know how to import data from other software packages, password protect your files so no one can access them (except you), and how to customize the Access application window to your own liking. Turn the page and expand your database brain power!

CHEAP TROUBLESHOOTING SEMINARS.

Chapter 17

OLE—Taking the Bull out of Object Linking and Embedding

"Woolly bully, woolly bully, woolly bully..." Oh, hi, I'm just getting in the mood for the this exciting chapter—OLE (and wondering whatever happened to Sam the Sham and the Pharaohs). Ever seen those video clips on the news of the annual running of the bulls in Pamplona, Spain? It is utter chaos, people screaming and running everywhere—the same kind of chaotic mess that breaks out when you're sitting around the office and someone mentions the mystical acronym *OLE*.

What is OLE?

OLE stands for *Object Linking and Embedding*. It is actually two different ways to take items created in any of a number of applications, and place them into your current application, in our case Microsoft Access. The application where these items or *objects* are created is called the *source* application. The application that you place the object in (whether linking or embedding) is called the *destination* application, and in our case, this is (yes, you guessed it) Microsoft Access.

Database Objects versus Linked or Embedded Objects

You are already quite familiar with database objects, things like tables, forms, queries, and reports. These types of objects allow you to manipulate and store your data. A linked or embedded object is a little different; it can be a graphic, a video clip, a sound, a spreadsheet, or a chart—you name it. You can link or embed any item that originates from an application that follows the Microsoft Windows OLE rules.

The Object of Your Objects

The word *object* is probably one of the most overused in the computer lexicon. Object can be used to describe certain kinds of programming; it is used to describe database objects (but you already knew that); it is also used to describe items linked or embedded into applications. Make sure that whenever you see the word object used as a computer term, you determine the particular context in which it is being used.

Linked or embedded objects can be placed in your database objects. You can place an OLE field in a table and store linked or embedded photos of your employees in that particular field. Or you can place an embedded or linked graph in a report to help your clients understand a complex set of statistics. When you place objects in your database via OLE, you should be aware of the different natures of linking and embedding. So the big question is whether you should link or embed, because there is a difference.

To Link or Embed—That Is the Question

When you link an object to your database you are creating a connection between the source application file and Access. The object does not reside in the Access database file but is represented there by a linking code. When you need to update the file, it is done in the original source application and the results of the update are seen in the Access database. For instance, you can link a Microsoft Excel Chart to an Access Report. When you activate the Chart with a double-click, its source application is started—Microsoft Excel and the file.

The great thing about links is that you could have the same object linked to several different destinations. When you update the file in its source application, the file is updated in all the places that it is linked to. Another cool thing about linking is that the object is not stuffed into the destination file (it resides outside of it as a separate file, remember?) So, a linked object does not greatly increase the size of the destination file. It doesn't bloat up, making it easier to handle.

Embedding gives you the same results as linking but is kind of the flip side of the coin. An embedded object does become part of the destination file and so increases its size. It is basically a transplanted copy of the original file. Since the embedded file resides in the destination file, updating the original file in the original application does not update the embedded copy.

One really wild thing about embedded objects is that they are dynamic—meaning they can be manipulated and updated right in the destination application. When you activate an embedded object, the server application will open up in a window inside of the destination application. In many cases, the menu system of the server application will temporarily replace that of the destination application. So you are in essence running the server application from inside the destination application.

A good example of this would be an Excel chart embedded in an Access report. Double-click the embedded chart, and the Access menus and toolbars are temporarily replaced by the Excel menus and toolbars. You edit the object, and when you click outside the object window, the menus and toolbars of your destination application are returned to you.

You may be asking, "When do I link and when do I embed?" And the answer to this question really depends on the object that you want to link or embed in your Access database. Objects, like spreadsheets built in Excel or reports written in Word, are dynamic, meaning the information in them is updated constantly. They are best linked to Access. This allows you to update the object in the application you created it in and still have the current results linked to your database objects like a report or form.

Objects such as scanned photos, or video clips of your vacation that are static and are not updated over time, can be embedded into your Access database. This makes the object part of the database file. Now that you have some of the OLE theory down, let's take a look at how easy it is to link and embed. You'll start with an OLE field in a table.

> *Techno Talk*
>
> **OLE Ready** All the applications in Microsoft Office 97 are totally OLE compliant. This means that you can link and embed objects between Access, Word, Excel, PowerPoint, and Office utilities like Microsoft Chart 97.

Working in the ~~Oil~~ OLE Field

You've already worked with tables, so you know how to design the fields that hold your data. Linked and embedded objects (OLE objects) are basically the same as any other data type . You really treat them no differently than a person's address or their social security number; you build a field and place the data or object into it.

Let's say that you want to build a table that will hold information on a set of vacation photos. And to make it even more interesting, your photos have been scanned into your computer as Windows bitmap images.

Sidebar Title?

Graphics can come in a number of different file formats. You can tell the particular format by the file's extension: Windows Bitmap (.bmp), AutoCAD Format 2-D (.dxf), Computer Graphics Metafile (.cgm), CorelDRAW (.cdr), Encapsulated PostScript (.eps), HP Graphics Language (hpgl) file, Kodak Photo CD (.pcd) file, PC Paintbrush (.pcx) file, and Tagged Image File Format (.tif) file, to name a few.

To create an OLE object field in a table, open the table in the Design view. Click in an empty field row and then name the field. So, for example, if you were designing the field for bitmap pictures of your vacation photos, you may want to call the field *Scan of Photo*.

Selecting the Data Type for the Field

Now comes the hard part; you will actually exercise your free will and make a choice. After you type the field name, either press the **Tab** key or click in the **Data type** box for the new field. Click the drop-down arrow and select **OLE Object** from the list.

That's all there is to it; you made a field that will hold OLE objects. Now you need to figure out how to get the objects into the field.

Setting the Data type for the OLE field.

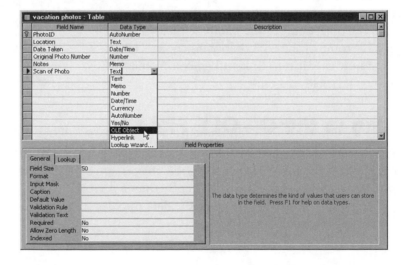

Insert Object Here

You've got your OLE field, now you need to come up with some OLE objects. To insert OLE objects into a table, you need to be in the datasheet view, which should make total sense because that's the table view that you use when you enter data. Make sure that you save the table design before you switch to the datasheet view. Click in the field when you want to place the object (remember it needs to be an OLE field). Now you can insert the object. Click the **Insert** menu, then click **Object**.

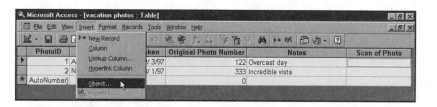

Getting ready to insert an OLE object into a Table.

As soon as you invoke the Insert Object command, the Insert Object dialog box appears. A wide range of object types are available in the object list. You will probably find an object type for just about every software you have installed on your computer. Select the object type you want to use. Once you select the object type, you need to decide whether you will create a new object or use an existing one.

To Paste or Not to Paste

You can link or embed objects from any application that supports Windows OLE. For applications that do not support OLE, you can still copy items and then paste them into Access. These pasted items will not have the dynamic character of OLE objects (meaning you can't update them without pasting a revised file into the field).

New or Vintage Object

The great thing about OLE is that you can use an object that already exists, such as a picture or a graph, or you can create one on the fly. For instance, let's say you want to embed a picture (a bitmap) into your table.

If you select the **Create New** radio button and then click **OK**, you will be whisked into Windows Paint (or the application that creates the OLE type you've selected), and given the opportunity to create a brand-spanking new object.

There is also a check box in the dialog box that (if selected) will display the OLE object as an icon (an icon that related to the server or source application), rather than a full-blown representation of itself. If you select the **Create from File** radio button, you will have the opportunity to select a currently existing file to be placed in the field.

So, let's say that you want to create the object from an existing file; click the **Create from File** radio button. The dialog box changes. A Browse button appears that allows you to look for, and specify, the file that you want to use as the object. You are also given access to a check box that determines whether the object should be linked or embedded.

When you click the **Browse** button, a dialog box appears that gives you the ability to look through the directories on your computer and select the file you want to embed or link. Once you select the file, click **OK**. When you are practicing linking and embedding graphics in your Access tables, you can use any of the images that are included with your Office and Access 97 software. However, if you have a scanner, you may want to create your own images to place into the database.

Selecting the file to embed or link into the Access table.

You will be returned to the Insert Object dialog box; the name of the file that you selected will appear in the File Name box. The application that the file was created in will also appear above the file name if it can be readily identified via the file extension.

Ready to embed the object.

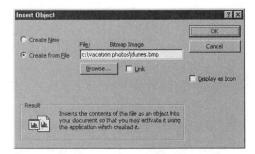

240

Click **OK** to embed (or link) the object. You will not see the actual object in the table field; a file type name will appear designating it. For instance a bitmap image will say *Bitmap Image*. An Excel spreadsheet would be tagged as *Microsoft Excel Worksheet*.

For instance, in our vacation pictures database, the images are bitmap images (.bmp files). So, it says Bitmap Image in the field. The application associated with bitmap files in Windows is Microsoft Paint (or some other graphics package; file associations will depend on the software that you've installed on your computer).

PhotoID	Location	Date Taken	Original Photo	Notes	Scan of Photo
1	Australia	2/3/97	122	Overcast day	Bitmap Image
2	New Zealand	3/1/97	333	Incredible vista	Bitmap Image
(AutoNumber)			0		

vacation photos : Table

Record: 2 of 2

Embedded bitmaps in a sample vacation photos database.

To actually view the object, double-click the field. This will start the source or server application (in this case Microsoft Paint). You can even edit the objects once you have entered the application. Any changes that you make will be saved with the embedded or linked object. In the case of the embedded object, the changes are stored in the object itself, which now resides in the Access table. When you are working with a linked object, the changes are stored in the original source file.

Check This Out...

When Linking and Embedding...

Remember that when you are working with embedded and linked objects that the embedded object becomes part of the target application (making the database file larger); the linked object remains outside the application and is only represented in the database table, form, or report.

Techno Talk

blah blah blah bla bl bl

Update Your Links

You can edit and update the OLE objects that you link into your tables and other database objects. Click the **Edit** menu and then click **OLE/DDE** links. A list of the current links will be displayed in a dialog box. This dialog box can be used to update links if files have been moved or to replace current links with new links.

Have Your Object and See It Too

A great way to view the objects that you embed or link into a table is to design a form for the table. In the form view, you will be able to actually see the embedded objects. Make sure that when you create the form it has a control that is bound to the OLE object field in the table. You may have to edit the size of the control box in the form to accommodate the size of the object. You can do this easily by sizing the control in the Design view and then switching to the Form view to see the results.

Creating Forms with OLE fields

Just a reminder—you can create your form using the Form Wizard, from scratch in the design view, or by clicking **New Object** on the toolbar and selecting **Autoform**. If you select the OLE field as one of the fields for the form in the Form Wizard you will automatically be given the appropriate control. This also holds true for the Autoform, which uses all the fields in the table to create the form. If you want to build the control from scratch, you should use the **Object Frame** button in the Toolbox.

Paste Special is Very Special

Another way to link an object to a field, a form, or report control is to open the source application and copy the object to the Windows clipboard. Open the destination table, form, or report in Access, and then click the **Edit** menu and select **Paste Special**. In the Paste Special dialog box, select the object and then click **OK** to paste it.

So, in our example, each form created for the table would display a graphic of a particular vacation photograph. As you can see (if you're viewing your objects), linking and embedding objects into tables and forms is really quite easy.

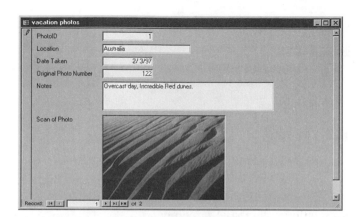

Viewing an OLE object in a form.

Creating and Embedding a Chart in Access

Another OLE object that you will probably get a lot of mileage out of is the chart—a graphical representation of your data. You already know from our discussion of objects that you could build a chart in any number of applications, such as Excel, and then embed or link it into an Access database form or report. However, you don't even have to leave Access to create extremely professional looking charts and graphs because of the mini application Microsoft Graph 97.

Build Your Charts with Graph 97

Graph 97 ships with Microsoft Office and each of the Office components—Access, Excel, PowerPoint, and Word—if you purchase them separately. You must make sure that when you install Access or Office that you also install Graph 97.

Microsoft Graph 97 is available to you as you create and edit your forms and reports. Placing a graph into a report, for instance, is no more difficult than placing any other type of control. The interesting thing about Graph 97 is that it only creates embedded objects. It does not have the capability to save its own products, which could then be lined to your Access object.

243

Placing a Chart in a Report

Let's say you want to place a chart in a report. The first step would be to create a report that details the data; the whole point of adding the chart to the report, then, is to graphically summarize the data. Most people relate better to graphs than they do to columns and columns of numbers.

Oops! Where's the Data?

One thing that you should be aware of before you start clicking on the menus and trying to build a chart, is that you will have to tell the Graph 97 program where to find the data. More than likely, if you've built your databases correctly, the data will be held in a group of related tables (It's a relational database, remember?).

For instance, let's say that you have a database that tracks employee travel expenses. You have a table for the employees, one for the expenses, and a table for the various departments—such as marketing or sales. You want to build a chart that would show what percent of the total expenses each department has spent (a pie chart would do nicely). However, no one table holds all the data that you need for this chart. So you need to build a simple query (since the relationships between the tables make it easy) that will list just the department names and their total expenses. Then you can build the chart from the query.

Creating the Chart

Let's stick a chart in a report. Open a previously-created report in the Design view. You will probably have to increase the size of the one of the report sections, such as the report header, so that you have a place to put the chart.

Use Your Imagination

When you are working with a report in the Design view, try to imagine how things will look on the printed page and place your controls and objects accordingly. If you have trouble imagining things, just cheat and switch to the Print Preview mode to take a quick look at how you page design is shaping up.

Fuel Your Charts with Queries

Queries are very good building blocks for charts. They have the capability to summarize or select certain information in your tables and then perform math on any values in the resulting query. Use queries to your advantage.

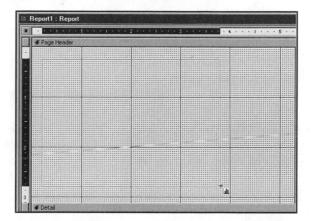

Placing the new chart in the report.

Click the **Insert** menu, and then click **Chart**. The mouse pointer becomes a charting tool. Use it to drag out a space (a rectangle works well) in one of the report sections for the chart. As soon as you create the space for the chart and release the mouse button, the Chart Wizard appears.

Make a Chart Button You can also place a button on the Report toolbar for creating a chart. See Chapter 22 for some friendly help on customizing toolbars.

The Chart Wizard

The first step in the chart creation process via the Chart Wizard is to choose the table or query that you want to base the chart on. Since you were really smart and did a query of your data (even if you didn't, you're still smart for buying this book), you can build the chart simply and easily by selecting that particular query and advancing to the next step in the chart creation process.

The next step is pretty typical of all these Wizards that you've been using to create things like queries and reports. You need to choose the fields that will be used to create the chart. For a simple chart, you typically need two fields to get the job done. These include the name of the particular items you are talking about (such as department names), and then the amount, or number, associated with each item (such as total expenses).

Having More Than One Axes to Grind

Most charts that you create from your database data will be simple x, y charts. Meaning that they will possess two axes. Two axes charts include line graphs, simple bar charts, and pie charts. The information on the x axis is usually textual such as the name of an employee or a kind of newt. The y axis will contain the related numerical information such as sales in dollars or number of newts counted.

In our example, you have been talking about building a chart that shows the expenses for each department in our company. To build a chart from this data, you would need to designate the department name and then the total expense relative to each department (this was another reason to build the query; the query can total (sum) amounts for you). Once you've selected the fields for your chart, you can move to the next step.

Selecting the fields to be used in the chart.

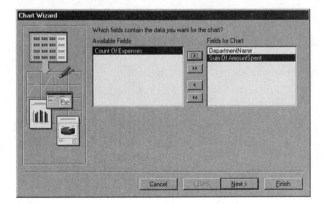

Choosing Your Chart

Isn't it great to possess free will and be able to make choices—like which stimulating television show you're going to watch this evening? Well, the Chart Wizard gives you a choice of chart types. There are bar charts, line charts, and pie charts—just to name a few.

Which Chart Is Best for You?

Bar charts work best for showing change over time. Pie charts are good at showing you how the parts relate to the whole. Line charts are good for tracking amounts over a time period.

Since you want to create a graph that will let us see how the expenses made by different departments relate to the total expenses, a pie chart would be the best choice. Once you've selected the chart type (you just click it), you can advance to the next step.

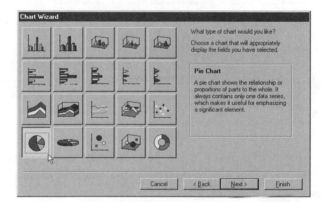

Selecting the Chart type—just click the picture!

Interior Decorating—Getting That Chart Layout Just Right

Now the Chart Wizard gives you a chance to manipulate how the information will be shown on the chart. You are give the opportunity to drag buttons that represent each of the fields in the chart to a specific place. You should be careful, however, because you could drag a field to a position that messes up the chart.

Just remember that most charts need just two types of information: values (the y axis) and text labels that relate back to the values (x axis). So you want to make sure that the field that contains the appropriate information appears at the right chart position.

For your pie chart, the values (the expense button) would be placed on the pie chart. The informational field (the name of the department button), would be placed outside the chart to serve as the series for the pie chart.

Placing the field buttons on the chart.

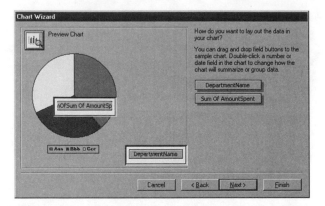

Setting Up the Chart Fields

If you do feel that you need to move the field buttons around on the graph, you can preview the changes that you have made by clicking the **Preview Chart** in the Wizard window.

Once you've placed your field buttons (again, in most cases you probably won't have to move them) in relation to the chart and the chart axes, click **Next** to move to the next step.

The Charts, They Are a Changing

The next step in the chart creation process gives you the option of setting up your chart so that it changes from record to record, reflection the potential change in data. This is great if you plan on placing the chart in a form; it makes sense for the chart to reflect the data for the record you currently have displayed. If you set up your form or report correctly (it is most likely based on the same table or query that the chart is) the fields in the chart that you are embedding in the form or report will use the same fields, making the matching pretty easy (because they will still have the same field name).

The Checkered Flag

The last step in the chart creation process has been the same for everything that you have made via the wizards; you've got to give them a name. So name your chart and then click **Finish** to end the process.

You new chart will appear in your report or form in the design view. To get a really good look how the form or report looks with the new chart, change to the Print Preview view.

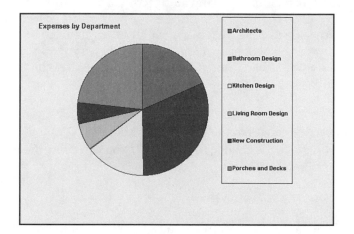

The report showing a new pie chart!

In your example, you made a pie chart that helped visually clarify a report that summarized expenses by departments. You can use charts in forms and reports for a great effect. In fact, you can include a number of charts in a multi-part report.

Editing a Chart In Graph 97

Even though you have been expending our brain cells on creating a chart for a report or form, I didn't want us to forget the core subject matter of this chapter—linking and embedding. You can edit the charts that you place in your reports or form and it's just matter of a double-click.

Make sure that you are in the design. Then double-click your chart. Wait a second, and Microsoft Graph 97 will appear. Inside the Graph 97 window is your chart, and a datasheet for the chart. The datasheet is the result of the data choices that you made when you were walked through the chart creation process by the Chart Wizard.

Microsoft Graph 97 has its own toolbar and menu, giving you access to a wide variety of commands relating to charting your data. You can use Microsoft Graph 97 to change the graph type that you are using, add vertical or horizontal gridlines behind the graph, or change the colors that are used in the graph.

Editing the Chart Colors

Since you are probably using a printer that only prints in black, you may want to change the colors used in your charts. Select a portion of a chart, such as a pie wedge or a bar and then double-click the item. A formatting dialog box will appear that allows you to select a gray pattern for the pie wedge or bar. Change each of the parts of the chart to a gray pattern and then print the chart.

When you complete your changes to the chart, close Microsoft Graph 97. Your chart is updated as soon as you make the change in Graph 97. You can print the results as soon as you return to the Print Preview window in Access.

You as Matador

As you can see, there are a lot of things that you can use OLE for in your databases. You can link or embed various objects in your tables and you can place objects in your report or forms. The OLE capabilities of Access allow you to create very complex and rich database objects, and while you may not get rich from your databases, your data will certainly be visually compelling—no bull!

The Least You Need to Know

➤ OLE objects are items, such as graphics, graphs, even video clips, that created in other applications. Access adheres to all the OLE rules, so you can link or embed just about anything into one of your database objects.

➤ Linking and Embedding are pretty much flip sides of the same coin—an embedded object resides inside of your database file making it bigger, and a linked object remains outside of your database file. Whether you embed or link, you can create the file from scratch via the server or source application or you can use a previously existing file.

➤ A great way to portray your data is visually via a chart. The Chart Wizard will walk you through the steps of chart creation. The actual behind the scenes creation of the chart, however is accomplished via Microsoft Graph 97 a mini-application. It can be used to create charts that you can embed in your database forms and reports.

➤ Your charts can be quickly edited by double-clicking on the embedded chart. This starts the server application, Microsoft Graph 97, which supplies you with all the tools you need to make your charts look great.

Chapter 18

Imports and Exports— Moving and Sharing Data

In This Chapter

➤ Import an Excel spreadsheet into Access

➤ Analyze the data using the Analyzer Wizard

➤ Normalize a flat file database by splitting the data into multiple tables

➤ Share Access data with other applications such as Microsoft Word

You probably have a pretty good feel for the internal workings of Microsoft Access by now, and you understand how to use the various database objects to manipulate your data. Unfortunately, not all the data that you end up working with will start out in nice neat tables; you may have to deal with the dreaded data from the outside; information that you desperately want to get into Access, but that currently resides in a file that originated in another software package.

You Always Externalize Everything

It's really not that uncommon to find that a large amount of data has been squirrelled away in a format that is not conducive to database management. You may even have a list of important contacts or other information stuck somewhere in a text document or a spreadsheet. Fortunately, for you and millions like you, Access can rescue your data. No longer will it be trapped in the land of the flat file.

Importing External Data

Importing data into Access is not really as difficult as you might think. The first thing you need to do is to make sure you know where the external file resides on your computer. Then it's just a matter of clicking the right menu selection.

Let's say you have a spreadsheet file that contains a list of transactions you made at your business, a cheese shop (surprise!). The spreadsheet details a number of orders that you made for customers. Since a spreadsheet is not a proper database, however, there is a lot of duplication of information. Each time a customer makes an order you have to retype all their personal data such as address and phone number.

A spreadsheet used to track orders.

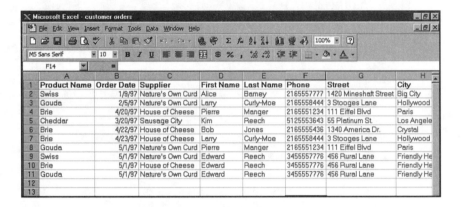

Notice that the spreadsheet mixes information like customer name and address with data regarding products and suppliers. This is the curse of the flat file database. When you work in Access, however, you don't have to retype customer information each time you place a new order because orders, customers, and products all reside in different tables. So it makes sense to take the spreadsheet data and import it into an Access table or tables.

Repetition—The Name is Flat File

The fact that you have to repeatedly enter the same data over and over in a spreadsheet used to track orders is a perfect example of a flat file database. It does not supply you with the option of creating separate tables for categories of information and then relating them for queries and reports as Access does.

Getting External

To import external data, open a new database or open an already existing database. Click the **File** menu, then click **Get External Data**. You are given two choices at this point, import the spreadsheet data, or link to the spreadsheet.

Waiting Forever?

If your system seems to be busy for a very long period of time as it tries to import the spreadsheet, you can halt the process by pressing the **Control** key and the **Break** key simultaneously. Once you break out of the import you can attempt again. However, close any applications that you may not be using to free up Windows' resources.

When you import the data, it will be placed in an Access table that has no link or connection to the original spreadsheet file. When you make changes in the spreadsheet, they won't affect the data in the table. If you link to the spreadsheet, however, you are dealing with the flip side of the coin. A link between the spreadsheet and the table means that if you update the information in the spreadsheet it will be updated in the table as well (by virtue of the link).

Think About Your Link
Remember that a link means that there is a source application (in the spreadsheet's case Excel) and a destination application (Access).

More than likely, you are not going to use the spreadsheet again, especially if you are going to all the trouble to import the data into Access; so in our example, you will forgo the link and choose the **import** command. As soon as you choose import or link, an Import dialog box appears and asks you to identify the file that you want to import.

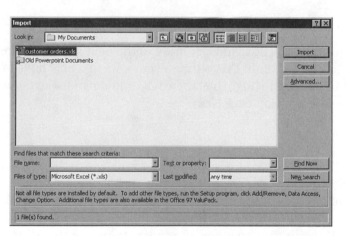

Selecting the spreadsheet file to import.

After you select your file, click **Import**. Access starts the Import Spreadsheet Wizard; it will help you with the conversion of the spreadsheet to an Access table.

Running Your Own Import Business

The Import Spreadsheet Wizard will walk you through the import process; the first step is to let the Wizard know which of the sheets in the Excel workbook that you are importing is the sheet you want to create a table from. Just click the particular sheet and then click **Next**.

The next step in the process requires that you tell the Wizard if the first row in your spreadsheet contains column headings that can be used for field names when the data is placed in a table. The answer is probably yes because most spreadsheets will use headings to identify the data types in each column. So you would click the **First Row Contains Column Headings** check box.

Letting Access know if the first row of the spreadsheet contains column headings.

Once you clicked in the check box, you can move to the next step in the import process. The next screen asks one question: Do you want your data in a new table or an existing table? If you want to use an existing table, there is a drop-down list to choose the table. Once you've made your decision click **Next**.

Fielding the Import

The Import Wizard's next screen allows you to determine which fields you want to include in the import. Each of the column headings in the original spreadsheet will be considered fields unless you specify otherwise. You can also change the field names for the fields and let the Wizard know whether a particular field should be indexed. Finally, you can also use this screen to change the data types for each of the fields.

Changing the field parameters is quite easy; a copy of the original spreadsheet is present on this screen, just click a particular column heading and then specify each of the parameters for the particular field. Once you've determined which fields you want advance to the next step in the process.

Turning the Key

You already know from your work with tables that each table needs to have a primary key that uniquely identifies each of the records. The next screen in the Import Wizard asks you to select a field to serve as the primary key or let it create a new field for this purpose. You can also choose to have no primary key, but I definitely advise against it.

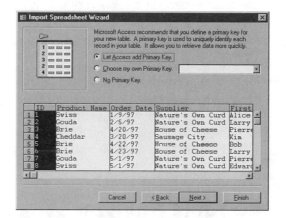

The Import Wizard will help you set up a primary key for your new table.

Let's say you decide to let Access create the primary key. It will create a new field called ID and assign a number to each of the records. Then you can click **Next** to move to the next step.

That's All Folks!

The last step in the import process is to name the new table that you will be creating from the spreadsheet data. Since our example deals with customer information let's be hyper-creative and call the table *customers* (or whatever you like).

The final screen of the Import Wizard also gives you two choices in the form of check boxes. You can check a box that will start the Table Analyzer and help you decide whether the new table should be broken into several smaller tables. You can also check a box that will display help on working with the new table when you exit the Import Wizard.

If your spreadsheet contained redundant data like the sample spreadsheet that you've talked about, you probably will want to run the Table Analyzer immediately and get the data in proper shape. Otherwise, the new table will be just as unwieldy in Access as it was in your spreadsheet software package.

Freud Would Have Been Proud— Analyzing Your Table

Whether you immediately invoke the Table Analyzer as you finish the import process or analyze your table at a later time, you will find that most spreadsheets that you import into Access will need some work before they can serve as proper database tables. The process of splitting a table's data (necessary because of the duplication of field information) into related tables is called *normalization*.

So What's Really Normal?

Since I'm not the best person to decide what is and isn't normal, I'm glad that the Table Analyzer exists. You can use the Analyzer to walk through the steps necessary to normalize a table. What is really great about this whole process is that you can break a document, like a spreadsheet into smaller related tables. Then you can use the related tables to generate forms, queries, and reports; just like you would do if you had created the database from scratch.

Working with the Table Analyzer Wizard

Using the Table Analyzer Wizard is very straight forward. Click the **Tools** menu, then point to **Analyze**, then click **Table** to begin the process.

Understanding the Problem

The first dialog box that appears in the Table Analyzer Wizard takes a look at the potential problems caused by a poorly designed table or imported spreadsheet. Examples are available that show you why duplication of data in a database table is not a good thing. Once you've taken a look at the examples provided in this dialog box, you can click **Next**.

Understanding the Solution

The next dialog box in the Wizard explains what the normalization process is and how it will potentially solve the problems in your table. Again, examples are offered to help you understand the process that will take place. Once you're satisfied that your table needs to be normalized, click **Next** (you probably feel that your coworkers should be normalized too, but the Wizard can't do everything).

Select Your Table

Now that you've decided to go ahead and actually try this normalization thing, the Wizard would like you to identify the table that will be processed. It asks you to identify the table that contains fields where values are repeated. Just click the appropriate table (in our example it would be the imported spreadsheet) and then click **Next**.

Brand New Tables

New tables will be created during the normalization process, but the original table will also still exist after you analyze it. You can delete it if you no longer need it after normalization.

Who Makes the Decisions Around Here?

The next stop in the table normalization process is to decide how to split the fields in the table; new tables will be created by the process and you have to decide which fields go where. You can split the fields yourself, or you can let the Wizard help you out.

If you do let the Wizard decide, you will have a chance to adjust the field locations. So, it probably makes sense, at least the first couple of times you do this normalization thing, to let the Wizard take the lead. Once you have decided whether or not you'll let the Wizard place the fields in the new tables, you can proceed to the next step in the normalization process. Just click **Next**.

Group(ing) Therapy

The Wizard will take a look at the fields in the original table and do its best to group them into new tables. You will find, however, that the Wizard is not infallible and probably will not be able to pull all the fields out of the original table and place them in appropriate new tables.

For instance, let's say that you had a spreadsheet (which you imported into Access) that tracked orders for your cheese shop. The spreadsheet included a field for the product ordered and a field for the supplier of the product. The other fields in the original spreadsheet relate to the customer, such as name, address, and so on.

The Wizard probably won't have any problem creating a customer table from these fields, or identifying the fact that a second table for suppliers should also be created. However, the Wizard may not break fields related to product out of the customer table and create a third table for products.

A Real Drag

The grouping of fields is probably going to require some input from you and will depend on the complexity of the original table. You will find that creating the new tables is a real drag—a quick drag of the mouse pulls a field out of a current table. Dragging a field into the group box creates a new table and also creates the appropriate relationship with the table that you drag the field from. You can then rearrange the fields in the tables anyway you like. Just drag a field from one table to another.

Tables created by normalization of a spreadsheet.

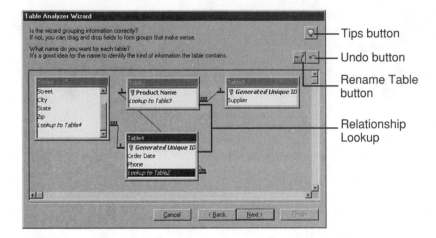

You can also drag the relationship Lookups that the Wizard has created, so that the tables have the appropriate kinds of relationships. You may even want to drag inappropriate relationships and create new tables that have yet to be totally defined by the normalization.

For instance, you would want a relationship between a newly created Supplier table and a newly created Product table, but neither of these tables would have a direct relationship with a Customers table (customers are usually related to orders). So, you would probably want to drag the relationship Lookup out to create a new table and eventually turn it into your Orders table.

To get a usable database out of a spreadsheet or other flat-file database, you will probably need to put your database thinking cap on and do quite a bit of field rearranging and table creating. The tables that the Wizard creates are really only the starting point for turning a flat-file database like the spreadsheet into a relational database that will really get the job done. Now, you know why I harangued you so much in Chapter 8 about the importance of table relationships.

Name That Table

When the new tables are created by the Analyzer Wizard, they are given temporary names like Table1, Table2, and so on. You will probably want to give the tables more meaningful names, and the Grouping dialog box provides you with an easy way to do this. Select the table that you want to rename. Click the **Rename Table** button. Type in the new name and then click **OK**.

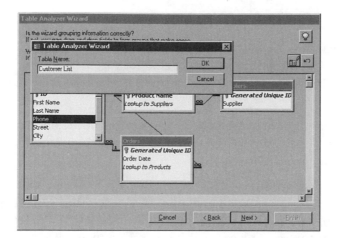

Naming one of the newly created tables.

The Analyzer Wizard Grouping dialog box also supplies you with an Undo button. You can use it to undo your last action. So if you name a table and change your mind or if you move a field and want to put it back, just click **Undo**.

Once you've created the tables that you need and arranged the fields the way you want them click **Next**.

> **Hot Tips on Table Creation** A Tips button in the Grouping dialog box gives you a list of things to keep in mind as you work through the table normalization process.
>
> *Check This Out...*

Locating Your Keys

When you deal with database tables, there is no way to get away from the concept of the primary key. Every table needs one; it supplies the unique identifier for each record in the table. The Analyzer Wizard knows this; the next step in the normalization process is to make sure that each of the new tables created has a primary key.

You can specify a field in a table as the primary key by selecting it and then clicking the **Set Unique Key** button. If a table does not contain a field that would be appropriate for the primary key, you can create a new field in the table by clicking the Add **Generated Unique Key button**. This Table Analyzer dialog box also equips you with an **Undo** button and a **Tips** button.

In our example, the Customer List table has an ID field but it has not been designated the key field. To make it the key, click the field and then click **Set Unique Key**. Once you've made sure that each of the tables has a primary key, you can click **Next**.

One Last Check (Actually Two)

As soon as you click **Next**, the Table Analyzer will take one last look at your new tables and try to determine if the fields that you've grouped together really make sense as a unit (meaning a table). If it finds a table that may contain unrelated fields, a message pops up letting you know.

You decide whether or not to continue with the splitting of the fields. If you want to continue, click **Yes**. If you want to backtrack and take another crack at arranging the fields in the new tables, click **No**.

The Analyzer also checks the new tables for any typos in field data that may have been duplicated (such as a customer who has a number of orders, but you misspelled their name in one order). If you don't have any repeat field data with different spellings, the only indication that this takes place is a short on-screen message when the final splitting of the fields is analyzed. If you do have misspellings or other typos, Access will walk you through the data and give you the chance to choose from a drop-down list of correction or to leave the data as is.

Pass Go and Collect a New Query

You've breezed through the Table Analyzer and are sitting pretty at the finish line. The last choice that you need to make in the table normalization process is whether or not you want to create a query from the new tables that duplicates the grouping of information that was found in the original table. This is an excellent idea and allows you to have all your original information in the query, giving you the option of deleting the original table (which you really don't need anymore).

After you decide about the query (I vote yes, let the Wizard build the query) click **Finish** to end the normalization process. If you said yes to the query, Access will build and display it on screen.

The query will be given the name of your original table and the original table's name will be changed to include _old to identify it. You can now delete the original table. The new tables created from the normalization process can now be filled with appropriate fields and data and then used to create forms, queries, or reports.

Exporting Data from Access to Other Applications

Now that you have a feel for how easy it is to pull data into Access, we should take a look at the flip side of the coin and see what it takes to put Access data in other applications. Two obvious uses of Access data would be spreadsheets and word processing documents.

For instance, you may find that the data you have in a table or in a query would be better off in an Excel spreadsheet where you could use all of Excel's number crunching capabilities. Or you may want to create a form letter in Microsoft Word and mail it to a bunch of your clients. The names and addresses are in Access and you need to know how to get them into your Word documents.

Important Message Regarding Importing and Exporting

Importing and exporting data to and from Access is going to be easiest when you are using other Microsoft products. This is not a commercial for Microsoft, just a fact. They have produced a very well-integrated set of applications in the Microsoft Office Professional suite. So your imports and exports will be more successful and less time-consuming when accomplished using the Office software components: Word, Excel, Access, and PowerPoint.

Copy Cat, or Cut-Up?

You can copy or cut data from Access and paste it into other applications such as Microsoft Excel and Microsoft Word. To copy or cut data from Access, open the database object (most likely a table or query) that holds the information. Select the data that you want to copy or cut.

You can select a record by clicking on the record selector or select an entire field column by clicking the **Field Selector**. If you want to select the entire table, click **Select All** in the upper-left corner (there is an easier way to place an entire table or query into Excel, so hold that thought).

Cut or Copy? Cutting data from a table or query removes it and places it on the Windows clipboard. Copying the data makes a duplicate of the information and places it on the clipboard.

Once you've selected the data, you probably want to go ahead and paste it into the other application; so you need to start that application if you don't already have it running. You can start an application via the **Start** button on the Taskbar. Once the application is running, choose the spreadsheet (in the case of Excel) or document into which you want to paste the information.

In Excel or Word you can click **Paste** on the toolbar or click the **Edit** menu and then click **Paste** to place the Access data into a spreadsheet or a document. When you paste the data into Excel spreadsheets you will find that the text formatting that you assigned to the information in Access is carried over into Excel. Access information pasted into Word will appear in a table format.

Paste or Paste Special?

You can paste Access data into Word so that it does not create a new table; click the **Edit** menu, then click **Paste Special**. Choose **Unformatted Text** in the **Paste** dialog box and then click **OK**. The text will be placed in your Word document as regular text.

Drag and Drop Can Be a Real Delight

For those of you who are really adept with your mouse you can also drag and drop Access tables and queries into Microsoft Word and Excel. To place an Access table in Word, open both the applications (Word and Access) so that they are side-by-side on the Windows desktop (click the **Restore** button on each of the application windows and then you can drag each window to a new location using their respective title bar).

For instance, let's say you want to place the Customers table that you have in Access into a document in Word. No problem. Open the appropriate Database window (Fromage Boutique), and then drag the table icon into the appropriate place in the Word document.

You can drag an Access table and drop it right into a Word document.

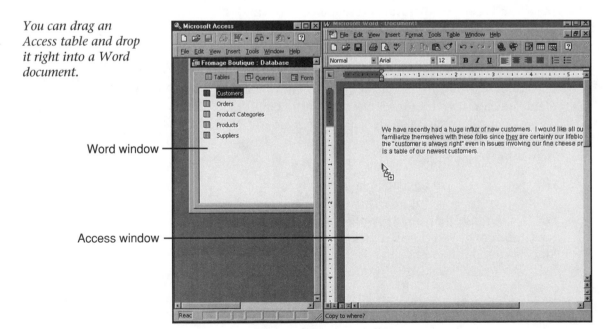

OfficeLinks Is Not Corporate Golf

While copying and pasting can take care of some of your data transfer needs, you are more than likely going to want to involve Access data in some fairly big data export deals such as data analysis in Excel or a mail merge in Word. Yeah, I know, learning one piece of software is hard enough, now you're expected to be familiar with a couple of others. Such is life in our technological age, and before you run outside and shake your fist at the sky, screaming for a return to a simpler time when there was no personal computer, let me tell that moving major chunks of Access data into Excel or Word is very easy.

The Access toolbar provides a drop-down button that can whisk your data into Excel or Word—the OfficeLinks button. Click its drop-down button and you are given three choices: Merge It (with Word), Publish It with Microsoft Word, or Analyze It with Microsoft Excel.

Merge It

When you select **Merge It** from the OfficeLinks drop-down list, the currently selected table or query in the Database Explorer will be used to supply the data for a Microsoft mail merge. The Microsoft Mail Merge Wizard appears and allows you to link the selected data (in a table or query) to a currently existing form letter or other Word document. You can also choose to create a document from scratch.

You can use the Microsoft Word Mail Merge Wizard to get your table or query data in shape to use in a form letter or other duplicate document that you created in Word.

Merging Data with Word

A mail merge is the merging of the information in your database records, such as names and addresses, with a form letter or an envelope. A letter or envelope is produced for each of the records in the database table or query. The actual creation of the letter or the envelope is done in Microsoft Word.

If you choose to use an existing Word document, a dialog box opens that allows you to select the specific document. Select the document and then click **OK**. Word will open and a link allowing data exchange between the Access table and the Word document will be created. Field codes to be placed in the Word document will be based on the field names in the Access table or query.

If you decide to create a Word document form scratch, a new document is opened in Word and the same data exchange link is made to the table or query. Both avenues provide you with a quick way to take Access data and place it in a form letter, or envelopes, or even mailing labels with a minimum of hassle.

Publish It with Microsoft Word

This OfficeLinks choice takes the data in the currently selected database object and places it in a new Word document as a text file. This is a great way to take report information and place it in Word. Having the data in Word in a text format gives you greater flexibility in presenting information from Access in a written report or other summary document.

Analyze It with Microsoft Excel

When you click **Analyze it with MS Excel**, Excel is opened and the currently selected table or query is placed into a spreadsheet. The spreadsheet that is created by this method will have the same name as the table or query in your Access database.

Excel offers an incredible array of mathematical functions and charting possibilities. So it's definitely a good idea to use the Analyze It feature when you have a query or table where you will need to do a lot of mathematical massaging to get the answers that you need. Once you have your table or query in Excel in a spreadsheet format, you can even use Excel's powerful Pivot Table feature, which supplies you with a way to view data from different perspectives and then chart it.

A pivot table in Excel looks very much like a cross-tab report in Access. It allows you to group the data in rows and columns and then pivot on certain categories of information. For instance, a pivot table detailing monthly sales by regional sales office, could pivot so that the data is shown by individual salesperson or by regional office, or even by time— by month. So in essence, the purpose of an Excel pivot table is to give you different views of the same spreadsheet data.

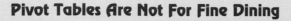

Pivot Tables Are Not For Fine Dining

Pivot table views are not unlike some of the groupings that you create when you work with Access reports. You can view data as a summary of certain information or you can break it down to be more specific. This is the special talent of the pivot table—views of the same data in a cross-tab format that ranges from the very general to the specific. There is a Pivot Table Wizard available in Access that allows you to create pivot tables; however, because of Excel's greater number crunching abilities and charting capabilities, it may make more sense to export the information to Excel and work with it there.

This Data Door Swings Both Ways

As you can see, Access is quite flexible when it comes to importing and exporting data. And as you become more familiar with the capabilities of Access and the other software packages that you use on a regular basis, you may find that you haven't always placed information in the right place. These easy-to-use importing and exporting features allow you to get that data in the right format, whether it is an Access table, an Excel spreadsheet, or a Word document. The whole point of putting information where it is best suited will save you time as you work with it and give you that extra hour at lunch that you need for shopping or hitting a bucket of balls at the golf range.

The Least You Need to Know

➤ You can easily import a spreadsheet into a new Access table using the Get External Data command.

➤ Once you have the spreadsheet in Access, you can use the Table Analyzer to normalize the new table. You can also use the Table Analyzer to check tables that you originally built in Access or another database and have found that they contain data duplication in certain fields.

➤ The normalization process breaks the original table into smaller related tables, which is exactly what you want in Access. Then you can use the tables and their relationships to build queries, forms, and reports.

➤ You can copy or cut data from Access and place it in nearly any other Windows 95 application. The data can be pasted as formatted or unformatted text.

➤ The OfficeLinks button on the database toolbar is your ticket to easy exports to Microsoft Word and Excel. You can set up a mail merge with Word using Access data, place Access objects in Word as text files, or place a table or query in Excel as a spreadsheet.

265

Chapter 19

Keeping Your Database Running Smoothly

In This Chapter

➤ Use the Performance Analyzer to fine tune your databases

➤ Document your database objects

➤ Compress a database

➤ Repair an ailing database

Society is obsessed with the notion of excellence; no matter what your vocation, you're urged to strive to be the best, to be part of a winning team. And every trade has tools to assist practitioners in their search for excellence. Astronomers have incredible tools, such as the Hubble Space Telescope, to help them in their search for new galaxies. Bodybuilders use scientifically formulated diets and engineer-designed equipment to stay pumped up. And database gurus, well, they use a bunch of great tools that Access offers for keeping their database objects in tiptop shape.

An Award Winning Performance

One way to keep your databases running well is to use the Database Performance Analyzer; this Access tool can be used to optimize the performance of any of the database objects in a particular database. You will find that if you've been careful setting up your database tables, they probably will not need to be analyzed for performance (you can always use the Table Analyzer on them).

It is the other objects that you create, based on those tables—such as forms, queries, and reports—that will benefit the most from the optimization process provided by the Performance Analyzer. The main benefit of the Analyzer is increased speed. You optimize a query, report, or macro, and they do their jobs faster. To use the Performance Analyzer, open the database that you plan to optimize. Then click the **Tools** menu, point to **Analyze**, and then click **Performance**.

And the Object Is...

See Them All You can view all of the objects in the database at once by selecting the **All** tab in the **Performance Analyzer**.

It may take a moment for the Analyzer to set things up. The first dialog box that appears, and the first choice that you must make, deals with the object that you wish to analyze. A tab for each object type enables you to view the objects that you have created in each category (table, form, report, macro, and so on). Once you've decided on what type of object you want to optimize, click the object's check box in the **Object Name** box. For instance, let's say you want to optimize a report that you built. Select the **Report Tab** and then click the report in the **Object Name** box.

The first step with the Performance Analyzer is to choose the objects you want to optimize.

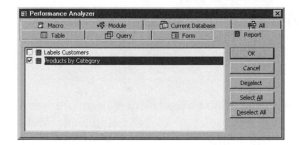

You can also select all the objects in a particular category in the **Object Name** box by clicking on the **Select All** button. Once you've chosen which objects you wish to optimize, click the **OK** button to continue.

Diagnosis and Treatment—Optimizing an Object

The Analyzer scrutinizes the selected object, and if you watch the screen closely, you can see that it also looks at all the objects associated with the one that you are currently analyzing. For example, when you analyze a report, the Analyzer takes a look at where the data for the report came from (the tables or queries).

Once the analysis is complete, you are presented with the Analyzer's recommendations for optimization. A dialog box appears and gives you a list of possible fixes that will improve the performance of the database object.

Absolutely Perfect

If your database object was well constructed (because you followed all the tips in this book), the Office Assistant will tell you that the Analyzer had no tips to offer you. Congratulations!

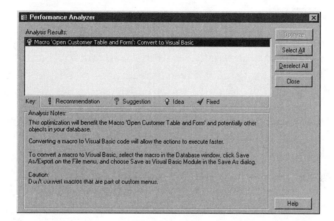

The Analyzer offering advice on a macro.

When the Analyzer's Optimization box appears, the optimization tips come in three flavors: Recommendations, Suggestions, and Ideas. To view the details on a particular optimization, click it, and the information will be displayed in the Analysis Notes box of the Performance Analyzer dialog box. It wouldn't hurt to mention the fourth icon that appears in the Optimizer key, Fixed, which is represented by a check mark. We will discuss the Fixed icon and how to make it appear in the Optimizer window a little later in the chapter.

Suggestive Icons

Each of the different optimization tips is represented by an icon: Recommendations by an exclamation point, Suggestions by a question mark, and Ideas by a light bulb.

Analyzing the Analyzer

The Performance Analyzer doesn't supply you with information on how to optimize Access itself or the computer system that you are running it on. Increasing a computer's memory always increases software performance, but there are also other things that you can do to keep your software and hardware working in harmony. For example, use the Windows 95 and Windows NT system tools, such as the Disk Defragmenter and Scan Disk, to keep your hard drive operating optimally.

Give It to Me Straight

Each of the optimization tip types have their own idiosyncrasies. Recommendations are the most straight forward and will usually result in a performance gain if you implement them on the object. Suggestions usually have some kind of potential trade off associated with them, and you should look closely at the Analysis Notes before implementing them.

Let's say that you were trying to optimize a particular report. A typical Recommendation or Suggestion provided by the Analyzer would probably suggest changing the way that the data was compiled for the report. Usually you would require the report to pull data from several related tables. A possible Recommendation or Suggestion to optimize the report would be to construct a query that pulls the data together in one place. Then when you build the report from the query the report runs optimally.

Any Ideas

The third type of optimization tip is the idea. Ideas provide you with more general information (unlike the Recommendation or Suggestion). For instance, the analysis of a macro or a module may result in an optimization Idea regarding the inclusion of a certain type of code statement at the beginning or end of the macro or module. However, anytime that you work with macros and modules, compiling issues arise, so Ideas don't give you the whole story and require a little more research and thought before you can carry them out.

Make It So

Once you've viewed the details of each of the optimization possibilities, you will want to use some and reject others. Recommendations and Suggestions can be performed by the Performance Analyzer. Select the Recommendation or Suggestion, then click the **Optimize** button in the Performance Analyzer dialog box.

The Analyzer will create the recommended or suggested object, or carry out any other steps that were detailed in the Recommendation or Suggestion. Once a Recommendation or Suggestion has been carried out by the Analyzer, it will display the Fixed icon, a check mark, next to the tip, letting you know that the optimization has been carried out.

Only the Lonely

You must perform Ideas by yourself (I guess you could have a couple of friends gather around your computer for moral support). Click **Idea** and view the suggestions that it gives you in the Analysis Notes box. Once you have a handle on what you need to do, you can close the Analyzer dialog box via the **Close** button and begin the optimization on the particular object.

Optimizations performed by the Analyzer (and by you if you implement an Analyzer Idea) may not obviously appear to increase the performance of your database. However, they do speed up the inner workings of the various database interactions and provide a more stable database for your use.

Other Performance Enhancers

There are other ways to optimize your database objects rather than relying exclusively on the Performance Analyzer. You are already familiar with the Table Analyzer (it was used to help normalize your database table back in Chapter 18), which is an excellent way to improve the overall database management capabilities of a database. Tables are the building blocks for all your other database objects, and so should be constructed carefully. The other database objects can also be tweaked to improve performance as follows:

➤ To optimize queries, use the Group By command on as few fields as possible.

➤ If you create a Crosstab query, use fixed column headings.

➤ To optimize a form, avoid overlapping the controls it contains.

➤ Use bitmaps and other graphics sparingly in your database forms.

➤ In reports, avoid sorting and grouping data on expressions you create via the Expression Builder.

➤ Base subreports on a query rather than several tables and limit the subreport to those fields that are absolutely necessary to impart the information.

Documenting a Database Object

Once you have honed your objects with the Performance Analyzer and your own database construction savvy, you can use the Object Documentor to print out a detailed report on a particular object. The report provides a great deal of information regarding the object: the date it was created, the date it was last modified, details on its makeup (the fields in the table, the controls in a form, or the actions in a macro), and even who has permission to delete, read, or change the object.

Object Documentor, Read All About It The reports that the Object Documentor provides tell you everything that you need to know about a particular database object.

To start the Object Documentor, click the **Tools** menu, point to **Analyze**, and then click **Documentor**. The Documentor is very much like the Performance Analyzer; it provides you with an opening dialog box that allows you to specify the object type and the particular object that you want to document. Click the appropriate tab to select the object category. Then click the check box for the specific object that you want to document.

The Object Documentor provides you with a detailed report on the attributes of a particular database object.

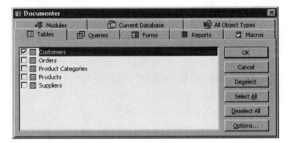

Once you've made your selections, click the **OK** button. The Documentor will look at the object and build a report detailing its attributes.

Getting the Complete Scoop on Your Tables

The anatomy of a table documentation report would include the date of creation; the date of last modification; and information on each field including field type, size, and whether or not the field has a Display Control (if so, the documentation would supply information on the Source Field and the Source Table).

And the Answer Is...

The documentation report will appear in the Print Preview Window. This gives you a chance to take a look at it and decide if you want to print it. After you've given it the once-over, click the **Print** button to send the report to the printer.

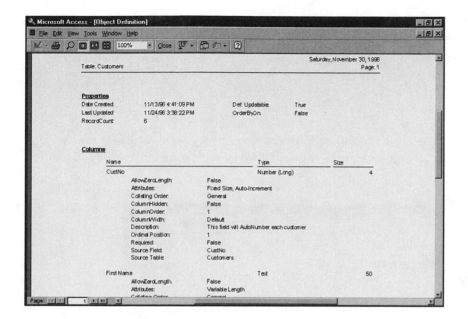

A Documentation Report for a table gives you information ranging from the attributes of each field in the table to the relationships that the table has with other tables in the database.

Object documentation reports can provide you with detailed information on how to improve a particular object, or how to build a new object based on the attributes of the one you've documented. You can even impress your friends and colleagues (maybe even your boss) by providing them with the documentation reports of some of your better built objects; let them learn more about Access by seeing a real genius at work.

A Quick Weight Loss Plan for Your Database

Even though you've optimized your database objects, your database can still get flabby over time. If you delete tables from your database, the file becomes fragmented and uses the space on your hard drive inefficiently. This can cause your database to run more slowly. Access, of course, provides a diet plan for the overweight and sluggish database. You can compact the database, which defragments the file and frees up disk space. It will also, yes, you guessed it, improve the performance of the database.

Ready with the Mouse, Take a Deep Breath, and Compact

To compact a database, close the current Database Explorer Window. Your menu selections will dwindle to File, Tools, and Help.

Caution: Database in Use

If you work in a multi-user environment (a network where a number of people can use the database file) make sure that no one is currently using the database you want to compact.

Click the **Tools** menu, point to **Database Utilities**, then click **Compact Database**. A dialog box—Database to Compact From—opens allowing you to specify the database file that you want to compact.

Select the database that you want to compact.

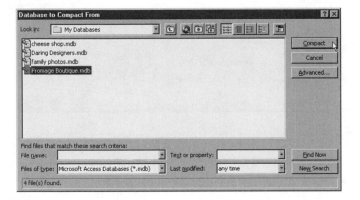

Click the database that you wish to compact (this may require you to switch to a different directory or drive), then click the **Compact** button. Access will open a new dialog box, Database to Compact To, and ask you to specify a database name to save the compacted database under. Since you are compacting the database to save disk space it makes sense to allow the compacted file to overwrite the fragmented, flabby file. So click the same database name that you selected in the Database to Compact From dialog box.

Once you've selected the appropriate database name, click the **Save** button in the Database to Compact To dialog box. If you use the same database file name, you will be asked if you wish to replace the original file; sure, you don't want that old couch potato lying around, click **Yes**.

Access will compact the database and save it under the current name. Now your database will run better, take up less disk space, and look good in a bathing suit (both male and female databases go to the beach; so don't try to catch me on that gender insensitive stuff).

My Database Has Fallen and Can't Get Up

No matter what kind of shape you keep your databases in, they can become damaged. For instance, if you're working on a particular database and one of your coworkers just happens to kick your computer's electrical plug out of the socket, the database could sustain damage. Unfortunately, this damage is not always obvious.

In most cases, Access can detect whether a database is damaged when you try to open it or try to compact it. And at that time it will prompt you as to whether or not you wish to try to repair the problem. It would make sense to fix the database immediately, because the problem will only get worse. You may, however, run across a situation where you are using a database that is acting totally wacky, but Access doesn't detect the fact that the file is damaged. No problem, you can still try to repair the database.

Let's Backup a Bit

Before you try to repair a database, you may want to make a backup copy of it. The repair process can be risky business and sometimes your database just doesn't pull through. So it makes sense to have another copy that you can use to try to save some of the data if the repairs don't work out.

You can use the Windows Explorer to copy the database file. All you have to do is close the database file and then start the Windows Explorer. Select the database file in the Windows Explorer Window, then click **Edit**, and then click **Copy**. To stick a copy of the file into the current directory click **Paste**, and the file will be named *copy of (your filename)*.

Database Doctor

Now you can scrub up and get ready to operate. Remember that this process is designed to repair a database file that has become corrupt due to hardware considerations such as a faulty drive or the loss of power while you were working on the database. Do not use this feature on a database that is functioning normally. To begin the repair process, make sure the database is closed. Again your menu choices become limited, as they did when you compacted the database.

All Users Shut Down, Please

Make sure that no one in a multi-user environment is currently working on the damaged database. It has to be closed by all the users who work with the file if you want to repair it.

Click the **Tools** menu, point to **Database Utilities**, then click **Repair Database**. The Repair Database dialog box will open. Select the database that you wish to repair and then click the **Repair** button. Access will churn up your hard drive a little bit and then report on the status of the repair. In most cases you will be told that the repair was successful. Congratulations! (If things don't work out, you always have the backup.)

The Care and Feeding of a Database File

Obviously there is more to database management than the creation and manipulation of your database objects. You should take the time to optimize the performance of your objects, and occasionally compact the database file. You should also put together a backup schedule for your database using some kind of backup utility. Keep in mind that *without data, there ain't no database*. Maintain and protect your files and your database and your business will prosper.

The Least You Need to Know

➤ You can enhance the performance of your entire database, particularly queries, reports, macros, and modules, using the Performance Analyzer. It will provide you with optimization tips that will help you improve the design of your objects.

➤ Analyzer Recommendations and Suggestions can be carried out automatically to improve the object's performance. Ideas require you to become involved hands-on in the object optimization process.

➤ The Object Documentor provides you with a detailed report on the design parameters of a specific database object. The report can be printed and tells you everything from date of creation to specifics about each component (such as a field or action) that makes up the object.

➤ Over time, your database file can become fragmented. Use the Database Utilities and compact the database file to free up disk space.

➤ There is always a slight chance that a database file can become damaged. The Repair command can be used to fix the problem. Before attempting to repair a database file, however, make sure that you have made a backup copy of the database.

Chapter 20

The Little Engines that Can—Making Macros

In This Chapter

➤ Design simple macros

➤ Create macro actions

➤ Use macros to take the drudgery out of some repetitive Access tasks

➤ Chat for hours about all the great stuff macros can do

In my youth, I was always amazed at the incredible products that you could find in a box of *Cracker Jacks*. There were noise makers, yo-yos (okay, really small yo-yos), and secret decoder rings. With the ring you (and any of the millions of kids around the country that had the ring) could write and decode secret messages just like spies in the movies.

Macros Revealed

Access has its own secret code that can greatly enhance your ability to manipulate data in your databases—macros. Macros exist as lines of code that can be used to complete specific database tasks for you. Macros are the easiest way to automate some of those things that you seem to be doing over and over. A macro is basically just a string of actions that are fired off in sequence when you run it. This lends itself to a lot of possibilities.

Access makes it easy for you create macros and actually provides a lot of help. To create a new macro make sure you have the Database window open for the database that you want to use. Click the **Macro** tab to select it.

Now comes the moment you've been waiting for. Put away that *Cracker Jack* toy and click the **New** button to begin your exploration of macros.

Designing a Macro

When you click the **New** button, the Macro window appears. This window is a little different than the design windows that you used for some of your other objects like forms and reports. The top half of the Macro window consists of two columns: the Action column and a Comment column. The Action column will hold the actual commands that make up the macro. The Comment column allows you to make optional notes related to each of the actions that you place in the macro. The lower half of the Macro window displays the arguments that are contained for each action. For instance, an action that opens a certain form will display the form's name in the Action Arguments Form Name box. Obviously, other information concerning the action will also appear in the Arguments box and these are best seen by constructing an example macro.

Let's say that you have a database that has a customers table and a customers form. You use the form primarily as a way to enter data easily into the table. A simple macro can be constructed that will open the customers table, then open the customers form, and then tile the two database objects on the screen. This may sound difficult, but the simple action macro is really quite easy to create.

Getting In on the Action

To add an action to a macro you click in the first row of the **Action** column. A drop-down arrow will appear in the box. When you click the arrow a list of built in macro actions is displayed. Now think this macro through. You want a macro that will tile two windows on the desktop—a table window and a form window. There's just one small problem here. You've probably noticed that when you open a database object, such as a table, form, or query, the Database window also stays open on the desktop. The first action in this macro, then, should be a command that minimizes the Database window. That way, when the table and form are opened by the macro, the desktop will be empty (except for the minimized Database window, which will no longer be an issue). So to place this action in the macro, you would click the drop-down arrow, scroll through the actions list and select **Minimize**.

Placing an action in the Macro Action column.

Be Responsible For Your Actionsem

The actions that you place in a macro can be previously created macros rather than actions from the drop-down list. This allows you to link a large number of actions together in one macro; each action consists of a macro that can consist of a number of actions. Since each of the previously created macros have probably been tested by you, this method allows you to quickly build a powerful macro from known actions.

Once you select the action, a description of it appears on the right of the Actions Argument box. This particular action (Minimize) will minimize the currently opened window when the macro is started. Since you will start our macro from the Database window, it will minimize the Database window (which is good because that's what you want it do).

Once you place an action in the Action column you can click in its **Comment** box to add information regarding the particular action. For instance, you may want to enter a comment for the Minimize action so that you remember it will minimize the Database window when you activate the macro.

Macros Can Be a Drag

Actually, in the case of macros, being a drag is a good thing. You can set up actions that open specific database objects by dragging the object's icon from the Database window into the Macro Actions column. Sounds pretty incredible, doesn't it? Certainly makes the example that you are working on simple. You want to add an action to the macro that opens a customers table, so all you have to do is drag the right icon into the Macro Design window.

To see the objects in the Database window and the Action column in the Macro window at the same time, you will have to tile the two windows. Click the **Window** menu, then click **Tile Vertically**. This arranges the windows side-by-side, making it easy for you to drag the object icons to the appropriate place.

279

To create an action that opens a particular database object select the appropriate object tab in the Database window. In our example you would click the **Table** tab. Now all you have to do is drag the icon for the particular table (Customers) to the Action column (that's right just drop the Table icon under the Minimize action).

Once you release the mouse, a new action will appear in the Action column. This action will open the object that you dragged into the Macro window. In this case you dragged in a table icon so the Action will read *OpenTable*. In the Action Arguments box the Table Name will appear as well as the view for the table and the data mode, which in this case is edit.

The new action and its associated arguments.

New action —

Action Arguments —

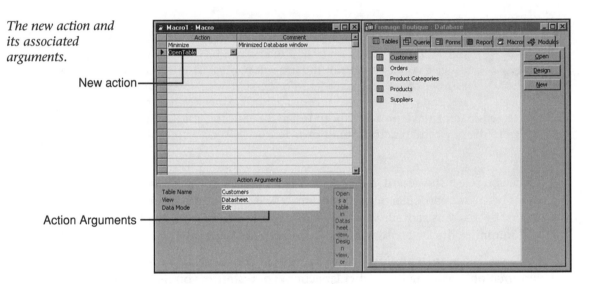

You can place as many *open object* actions into the macro as you need. In our example, you also wanted to open the Customers form, so you would drag the icon for this object into the Actions column below the previously placed action.

Creating Macro Actions for Menu Commands

So far, you've seen how to create an action that minimizes a window and an action that opens a particular database object, but this macro thing won't get you very far if you can't add actions that fire off different menu commands. Access has you covered. To add a menu command to the Action column, click the drop-down arrow in the **Action** box. Scroll down through the list of actions to **RunCommand** and select it.

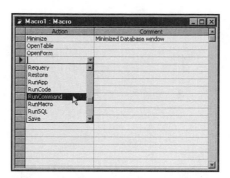

Placing the RunCommand action in the Macro Action column.

Once you have the RunCommand action selected you have to set the Action Arguments so the right command is fired off by this part of the macro.

Setting Action Arguments

The Action Arguments give a particular action its specificity. For the RunCommand action you have to tell Access where to find the particular command that you are talking about. This information consists of the Menu bar where the command resides and the specific command itself.

Click in the **Command** box in the **Action Arguments** box (it's in the lower half of the Macro Design window). A drop-down arrow appears that will give you a list of all the Access menu commands. You want the command **Tile Horizontally** (normally found on the Window menu), so scroll down through the command list until you find it. Once you find it, click it.

That's all there is to it. You specify the command (Tile Horizontally) and then you're ready to roll.

Now that you have a macro that will actually do something, it's important to save it. Click **Save** on the Macro toolbar. Type an appropriate name in the Save As dialog box and then click **OK**. After you save the macro, you can close the Macro Design window.

A new macro with a lot of action; make sure you save it!

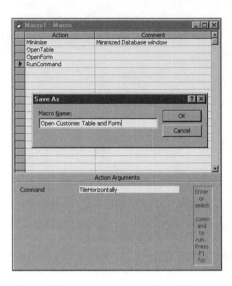

Playing a Macro

Your newly created macro will appear on the Macros tab of the Database Explorer. To play a macro, you select the macro in the Database window, and then click **Run** or double-click the macro name. In the case of your sample macro you will end up with the Customers table and the Customers form tiled horizontally on the desktop.

The result of the Customers Macro.

The Customers form ———

The Customers table ———

Minimized Database window ———

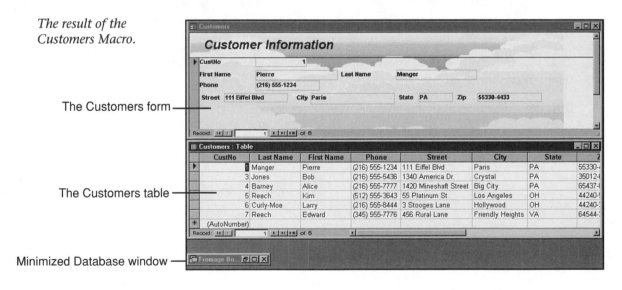

You can obviously design macros that are much more sophisticated than the example that you've been reading about. Whether you build simple or complex macros, it sometimes helps to scribble your ideas down on a piece of paper so that you can start to assemble the chain of events that you want to take place when the macro is played.

Modules Can Be Scary

Access offers another programming object for the advanced user—modules. While macros may seem quite straightforward to even the casual user of Access, modules are another story entirely. Creating modules is the pinnacle of database geekdom and requires a strong knowledge of the Microsoft Visual Basic programming language.

Modules are groupings of Visual Basic code that allow you to rewrite the way an application looks and is used. For instance, modules could be employed as the building blocks for a point of sale system that uses the power of Access to create invoices and manage inventory. The actual users of this system would be using a custom interface (menus, dialog boxes, and so on) and may not even be aware of the fact that they are using Access to get the job done.

The Least You Need to Know

Macros allow you to streamline and enhance your database management chores. Before embarking on an intense journey of discovery with macros, it will be well worth your while to make sure that you fully understand the ins and outs of the more common Access objects, such as tables, forms, queries, and reports. Working with software should never be considered drudgery, so always consider the possibilities of these "little engines that can" as you design and redesign your databases.

➤ Macros provide a way to automate repetitive tasks that you perform during database management.

➤ Macros consist of sets of actions that you define in the Macro Design window. These actions can be used to fire off a string of commands when you invoke the macro, or the actions ca be designed to only invoke a command when a certain condition is met, such as the completion of a form or report.

➤ The building of efficient and useful macros requires a good understanding of the other database objects and many Access commands and features (but don't be intimidated either—half the fun of working with software is discovery).

THE WORD IS "WALRUS"...

Chapter 21

What's the Password?

In This Chapter

➤ Assign a password to your database

➤ Deal with the various user-levels you can assign to a database

➤ Assign users to security groups

➤ Use the Security Wizard to set this stuff up

You've seen that Access provides numerous tools for building, managing, and fine-tuning your databases. Because of the valuable data residing in your databases, you may also want to take steps to secure them. This is especially true if you are an aficionado of tabloid news and daytime television talk shows. You are, no doubt, convinced that your coworkers are either aliens from another planet, or extremely dangerous maniacs, and you are obsessed with protecting your databases from them.

Choosing a Database Security Blanket

Access actually provides you with a couple of methods for securing your database files. You can add a password to any of your databases; then when you open the database you are prompted for the password—a simple and straightforward method of protection.

It's kind of like sticking one of those club things on the steering wheel of your car. Just don't lose the key (or the password).

If the simple password approach doesn't work for you, you can beef up security to a higher level of paranoia by defining user-levels. User-level security works by placing users into different groups, each of which have different levels of access to the objects in the database. User-level security is not unlike the methods that are used to grant permissions on a computer network.

Adding a Database Password

To add a password to your database, make sure the database is closed (if you are on a network all other users must close the database as well). Now this may seem a little odd since you just closed the database, but the first step in adding the password to the database is opening the database. Click the **File** menu, then click **Open**. When the Open dialog box appears, select the database file you want to add the password to.

Open From the Toolbar You can also use the Open Database button on the toolbar to open the database file and gain access to the Open dialog box.

Now comes the tricky part. In the Open dialog box click the **Exclusive** check box to select it. This means that you want exclusive rights to the database file.

Click the **Open** button box. Access will open the database file.

Once you select the database that you want to password protect, make sure you click the Exclusive check box.

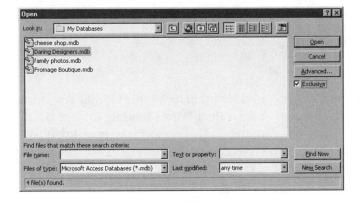

Call Security

Now that you've opened the database using the exclusive rights parameter, you can set up the password for the file. Click the **Tools** menu, point at **Security**, then click **Set Database Password**. The Set Database Password dialog box appears.

286

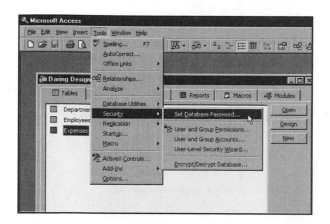

Once you have the database open, use the Tools menu to find the Set Database Password command.

The purpose of the Set Database Password dialog box is to allow you to type in a password and then verify it by typing it in a second time. In the **Password** box type your password. The password will appear as a series of asterisks (it's suppose to be a secret, remember?).

Case-Sensitive Passwords

Passwords are case-sensitive, so you may want to limit the characters in the password to lowercase. That way, you don't have to remember what was uppercase and what was lowercase (it's hard enough just remembering the password).

Now you need to verify the password. Press the **Tab** key to move the insertion point to the Verify box. Retype your password.

Wrong Password?

If you make a typo while verifying your password, Access will alert you to the fact when you click **OK** in the Set Database Password dialog box. Just click **OK** to close the typo alert box and type your password into the Verify box.

Once you've verified your password, click **OK**. Now the database is password protected; when you or any other user attempt to open the database a dialog box will appear demanding the password. One thing that you should keep in mind is that if you forget the password for the database, you are basically doomed. You won't be able to open it.

But, hey, you're memory is probably like a steel trap (a non-rusty steel trap), so there is no chance that you would forget the password. Even if you do, I know that you're smart enough to write the password down and keep it in a safe place. Let's take a look at what happens when you try to open a password-protected database file.

Opening a Password-Protected Database

When you open a password-protected database, the Password Required dialog box appears. Type in your password and then click **OK** to open the database file.

Access needs your password to open the protected database.

If you type an incorrect password, or if someone tries to get into the database without knowing the correct password, Access states the obvious—*Not a valid password.*

Access won't open the database until you type in the correct password.

You're only recourse is to click **OK** and try the password again. If you type it in correctly (it's case-sensitive, remember), you open the database.

Guess the Secret Word, and Win $200

If the above title conjures up an image of Groucho Marx and a duck, you certainly weren't born yesterday, and so you should know that this database password stuff isn't going to work if you don't keep your password a secret. There is also the additional burden of being the keeper of the database. Once you password it, you own it. You have exclusive rights to the file.

Check This Out...

Junking the Password

You can *unset,* or remove, a password for a database file. First, you must open the database and select the **Exclusive** check box in the Open dialog box. Then click the **Tools** menu, point to **Security**, then click **Unset Database Password**. Enter the correct password in the dialog box that appears and then click **OK**. The database will no longer require a password when you open it.

If this idea of exclusivity scares you, there are other ways to protect and limit access to a particular database file. You can set different levels of security for each user of the database. Of course, please understand that setting user-levels is only necessary if you are sharing a database with others on a network. If you are running a database on a stand-alone PC you really don't need to worry about security (if you do worry about security on a standalone PC, even a password isn't going to protect your files once you've opened them).

Another thing to remember is that if you work in a multiuser environment—a network—you will probably have a network administrator that will grant you your network security rights as well as your database rights. However, even if you are not in charge of the databases and their security, it doesn't hurt to know how the various levels of security are assigned.

Assigning User-Levels to a Database

The process for setting up user-levels is fairly straightforward. Someone has to be in charge, and an administrator account will have to be created. The administrator will be the person who assigns the levels of access to all the other users. It's starting to sound like some futuristic police state in a sci-fi movie, where big brother is watching—isn't it?

Join a Group

Security levels for your database will be defined by groups; each group can have a different level of access to the objects in the database. The default groups already defined in Access are User and Admins. So to begin the securing of a database the users have to be assigned to a group. The Admins group will have complete access to the database. The User group will have limited access to the database.

For instance, you may only assign yourself and one other person to the Admins group, which will have full access to the database and its objects—an administrator's level of use. People assigned to the User group will have limited access to the database and its objects. The whole matter is really as simple as that.

Techno Talk
blah blah
blah bla
bl

Create Your Own Groups

If you don't want to use the default user groups that Access provides you—User and Admins—you can create new groups. Click the **Tools** menu, point to **Security**, then click **User and Group Accounts**. The dialog box that opens allows you to create and delete users and groups.

Open the database that you want to work on. To assign yourself and other users to a group, click the **Tools** menu, point to **Security**, then click **User and Group Accounts**. The User and Group Accounts dialog box provides you with all the tools to assign individuals to the various groups.

Group Therapy for Users

The User and Group accounts dialog box has three tabs: User, Groups, and Change Logon Password. The User tab is where you assign new Users to the groups. For instance, let's say you want to include yourself in the Admins group. In the User tab of the User and Group Accounts dialog box type your name in the Name box, then click **New**.

The New User/Group box opens with your name in it. All you have to do is press the **Tab** key and then give yourself a Personal ID in the Personal ID box. Your Personal ID or PID is used to identify you in the user list. The PID must be at least four characters (a maximum of 20) and it is going to be case sensitive when used. So, as you did with database passwords, pick something you can remember and keep it in lowercase. Once you've established the PID for you are other users, then you can assign the use to any of the groups that appear in the User tab.

Creating New Groups

The Groups tab is where you create new groups. For instance let's say you want to create a group that will access to almost all the objects in the database (such as a Human Resources department) but you will still not assign them all the rights that the Admins group has. Just click the **New** button and then assign the group a name and a PID as you did for a new user. When you return to the User tab the new group will appear in the Available groups box.

The User and Group Accounts dialog box allows you to create new groups and assign users to the various groups.

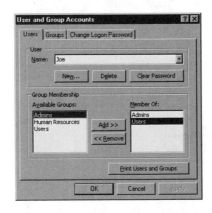

I haven't really mentioned the Change Logon Password tab. It is used to create a new password or change an old password for a particular user. When new users are initially assigned to the various groups, the Logon Password will be blank, so a proper password will have to be set up.

Once you've established the user and group accounts for the database, you are ready to move to the next step in the process—assigning the various levels of security for the database objects. Access makes this stage of the game easy on you, it's just a matter of invoking the Security Wizard and letting it take care of the details.

Learning to Share

This whole database security thing is only necessary if you are going to share the database with other users. Users who can access a database over a network are assigned to a workgroup. The workgroup parameters are held in the Access 95 Registry in Windows. Sounds confusing doesn't it? You should probably do a little in-depth research in the Access 97 Help system before pursuing multiuser security-levels.

Using the Security Wizard

To start the Security Wizard, click the **Tools** menu, point to **Security**, then click **User-Level Security Wizard**. The first dialog box in the Security Wizard lists the different object types found in a typical database (tables, queries, forms, and so on). Each object type has a check box that is currently selected. To preclude certain object types from the security set up, deselect the check box with a click.

The User-Level Security Wizard let's you select which objects in the database you would like to secure.

It's a Clone!

The Security Wizard creates a secured clone from your original database, which is not modified. So if this security thing doesn't work out, you always have the original file to fall back on.

Once you've determined which objects should be secured, click **OK**. The Security Wizard will create a secure duplicate of your original database file and allow you to save it under a new name. When you open the new database you will be asked to logon using your user name.

The first time the newly cloned, secure database is opened, only the users in the Admins group will be able to access the protected objects in the database. This does not pose a problem, however, because the administrator can then grant the necessary permissions to the user group using the User and Group Accounts feature.

A Cautionary Remark

When you assign user-levels to a database, the file is encrypted. This means that you will have a heck of a time getting to your data, if something goes wrong or if the security-levels are not assigned properly. This is why the Security Wizard duplicates the original file.

Protecting Your Secret Codes

One good reason for assigning user-levels to databases is to protect the macros and modules that have been built for the database. As you know, modules and macros can be used to dramatically change the interface and capabilities of a database. By protecting modules and macros using user-levels, the chance of someone inadvertently changing the code and therefore ruining the module or macro is reduced to nil.

The need for passwords and user-levels really should be dictated by the value of the data in your database. If you are working with extremely sensitive, highly proprietary data, it may make sense to use a database password, or assign user-levels in a multiuser environment.

However, if you are working with a database that holds data that someone could find in the public phone book, don't bother worrying about security. You really have to decide for yourself, how important your data is. And whatever you do decide, don't let it keep you up at night.

The Least You Need to Know

➤ You can make a database your own by assigning a password to it. When you open the database file, you will be prompted for the password.

➤ You assign a database a set of user-levels, which give the various users different levels of access to the database objects.

➤ User-levels are established by groups. Each group has a different level of access to the database.

➤ The administrator (an account that is created for a database) has the ability to assign the various levels of security to the groups.

➤ Don't get involved in database security unless you have to. You really have to decide if your data is important enough to warrant dealing with user-levels and passwords.

Have It Your Way— Customizing Access

Hold the pickles, hold the lettuce, special orders don't... Wait just a minute here; why is it that whenever you think of customizing something, fast food jingles pop into your head (our popular culture has certainly gone to the dogs, or is that burgers)? Well, we're going to skip the drive-thru this time and take a look at how you can customize certain aspects of the Access application window. You've learned all sorts of ways to optimize the objects that you create in Access; so why not set up the user interface (the toolbars and some of the other defaults) so that you can work quickly and efficiently.

Adding a Button to a Toolbar

As you already know, the toolbars provide you with quick access to many of the commands that you use when working with your database objects. Each database object has

Check This Out...

Customize Any Toolbar The steps outlined here for adding a button to the Table toolbar will work for any of your toolbars.

its own toolbar. You may have found that as you work with each specialized toolbar there are commands not available that you would like to be able to get at.

Piece of cake! You can easily add buttons to any of the Access toolbars. You can even create buttons that run macros that you have designed. Let's take a look at how to customize a typical toolbar—the Table toolbar.

I'm Missing a Button

When you open a table, the Table toolbar will appear. It contains a set of buttons that are designed to help you with the maintenance of your tables; there are Sort buttons, Filter buttons, a bunch of buttons. But what if you want to use a particular command and there's no button for it? You can always fall back on the menu system to fire off your command, but it would, of course, be easier if you could just click the toolbar.

The Secret Order of the Right Click

Access makes it quite easy for you to add a command button to a toolbar. Place the mouse pointer on any toolbar; that's right—any toolbar. Now you get to perform a mouse manipulation that many desire but few have mastered; click the right mouse button (pretty easy, huh).

Right click a toolbar to access the Toolbar menu.

To add buttons to a toolbar currently showing in the application window, click **Customize**. The Customize Toolbars dialog box appears. The Customize Toolbars dialog box has three tabs: Toolbars, Commands, and Options. The Toolbars tab allows you to select the toolbars that you want to show in the Access workspace. The Commands tab is where, you add buttons that represent the various Access commands to a specific toolbar. The Options tab controls the size of the buttons on the toolbars, whether ToolTips show and whether or not you want the menus to do special things when you open them (Menu animations). Since you want to add a button to a toolbar, click the **Commands** tab. Now you can concentrate on the buttons.

The Commands tab offers you buttons for just about every command you could imagine.

Life Isn't Always a Drag

Adding a button is as simple as a quick drag of the mouse. But first, let's take a look at what the Commands tab is all about. The Commands tab is made up of two areas: A Categories box that lists the different categories of Access commands, and there's a Buttons box that displays a group of buttons that relate back to the currently selected category in the Categories list.

For instance, the first category in the Categories list is File. The buttons that are displayed in the Buttons box are for commands that relate to files. There's a new Database button, an Open database button—both commands that are used to deal with files.

Buttons for Every Occasion

Each of the categories in the Categories list relates to a particular database function. For instance, the Toolbox category includes all the buttons that normally would be found on the Toolbox. The object categories such as All Tables, All Queries, and All Forms, allow you to make buttons for specific objects in your database.

While the name of each button is present in the command list, you may want more information on a specific button and its associated command. No problem, just click the button and then click the **Description** button in the **Commands** tab. You get a great thumbnail sketch of what the particular button will do.

Sewing on the Button

The process of getting the right button and the correct command on a toolbar is very straightforward. Select the category of commands that you want to use in the Categories list. A list of buttons will appear in the Buttons box. Decide which button you want to add to the toolbar and drag it onto the toolbar, preferably placing it in an open space. For instance, if you are building your tables, you might want to stick the Relationships button on the Table toolbar so you have quick Access to the Relationships window.

Click **File** in the Category box. Then scroll down through the Command list until you see the Relationships button. Drag the **Relationships** button onto the toolbar and that command will be available whenever you need it. That's all there is to it. The button, and the command associated with it, will be available on the toolbar. You can add as many buttons to a toolbar as you like; however, if you add too many to the toolbar, not all the buttons will be visible at the same time in the application window. You will have to scroll the toolbar to the right or the left to access all the buttons.

Deleting Buttons

To delete a button from a toolbar open the **Customize Toolbars** dialog box via the shortcut Toolbar menu. Click and drag any toolbar that you want to delete from the toolbar. The button will disappear. When you completed your deletions, click the **Close** button to close the Customize Toolbars dialog box.

Adding a Macro to a Toolbar

You can also add buttons to your toolbars that open or run objects you have created. You can create a button for a table, query, form, and even a report. However, you may find that macros are the best choice as far as buttons for objects go; one click and a macro button and all the actions in the macro are fired off.

To add a macro, or other object to a toolbar, click the object category in the **Categories** list—in this case **All Macros**. A list of the macros that you have created for the currently opened database will appear. Simply drag the macro onto the toolbar. The ToolTip for the new button (which looks like a scroll) will read *Run macro* followed by the name of the macro.

An Icon for Every Object

Each of the database objects has a particular button icon associated with it. Tables use the datasheet icon; queries use the double datasheet icon; forms use the form icon; reports use the notebook icon; and macros use the scroll icon.

Once you have finished adding buttons to a toolbar, click the **Close** button in the Customize Toolbars dialog box. The buttons that you add to a toolbar are saved with the toolbar and will be available whenever that particular toolbar appears in the application window.

Tying It On with the Toolbars

An alternative to adding buttons to your toolbars is to display more than one toolbar at a time. Each of the toolbars is specific to a task, such as creating and maintaining tables, or designing and running macros. So it may be easier for you to just give yourself access to more than one set of commands (via multiple toolbars), rather than trying to create the ideal toolbar by dragging a lot of unrelated commands onto it.

Surf the Web with Style

One of the coolest new toolbars available with Access 97 is the Web toolbar. It gives you quick access to the Command buttons and features found in Microsoft Internet Explorer. Jump to Web pages, even search the WWW with a click of the mouse from inside of Microsoft Access.

You already know that to get a list of available toolbars you must right-click any currently visible toolbar, click **Customize**, and then make sure the **Toolbars tab** is selected on the Customize Toolbars dialog box. A list of all the toolbars available in Access appears in the Toolbars tab of the dialog box. To place any of the toolbars in the application window, click the toolbar's check box.

Blank Utility Toolbars Await Your Commands

You will find that two Utility toolbars are listed with the other Access toolbars. The Utility toolbars are empty toolbars that you can modify for a particular purpose.

The Toolbars dialog box gives you access to all the available toolbars and various toolbar-related commands.

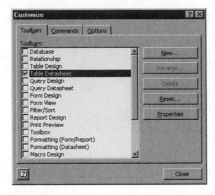

Check Your Buttons

Command buttons are also available in the dialog box. The Close button closes the box. The New button allows you to create a new toolbar. The Reset button returns the selected built-in toolbar to its original state (it gets rid of all the extra buttons you've stuck on it). The Rename button allows you to change the name of a toolbar that you created. The Properties button gives you access to the Properties dialog box, which allows you to tie a particular toolbar to a particular database object. For instance, you can have a special toolbar appear when you open a particular form or table.

Creating a New Toolbar

So you've tried everything. You added buttons to an existing toolbar, you stuck more than one toolbar in the application window, but it just didn't work for you. Well, when all else fails, you can create your own personal toolbars. Click the **New** button in the **Toolbars** tab. You are asked to name your new toolbar.

Access asks you to name your new toolbar.

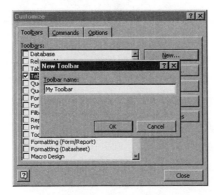

Type in a descriptive name for the toolbar, and then click **OK**. The new toolbar will appear in the application window. It won't look like much. To flesh it out, you will have to add buttons to it. You can assign your new toolbar commands that give it a very specific, use or you can make it a more general, jack-of-all-trades type toolbar.

Deleting Custom Toolbars

You can also delete custom toolbars that you no longer need. Click the toolbar you want to get rid of in the **Toolbars** tab. The **Delete** button will become active. Click the button to delete the table. And don't worry, Access will not allow you to delete any of the default toolbars. When you select them in the Toolbar dialog box, the Delete button does not become active.

Positioning the Toolbars

You can drag any of the toolbars to new positions in the Access window. Click the handle portion of the toolbar (it's on the far-left and is designated by two parallel lines) and then drag the toolbar to where you want it. For instance, you can take one of the horizontally displayed toolbars and place it vertically along the left or right side of the application window.

Custom-made toolbar

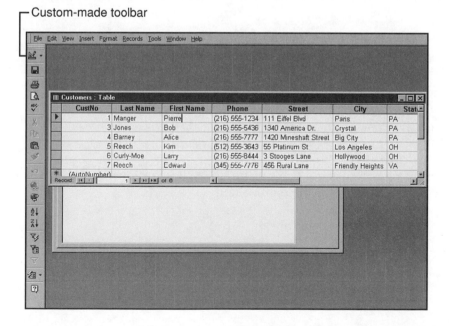

You can place your toolbars anywhere in the application window.

The toolbars are very flexible as you build and maintain your database. Having the commands that you use most often one click away can make the entire database process a lot easier to deal with.

Create Custom Menus

Custom menus can also be created in Access via the Commands tab of the Customize Toolbar dialog box. You can drag a new menu to the Menu bar and then add various commands to it. The Access help system will provide you with additional information on creating and editing custom menus.

Setting Options In Access

Customizing your toolbars is one step to having it your way. Another group of Access parameters that you can customize to your own liking is Options. These Options range from what items are displayed in the application window such as the status bar and the toolbars, to what happens in a table when you hit the Enter key.

The Options dialog box breaks down these customizable items into ten categories: General, View, Datasheet, Edit/Find, Tables/Queries, Forms/Reports, Keyboard, Module, Hyperlinks/HTML, and Advanced. Each of the categories has its own tab on the dialog box.

Cancel Bad Choices

If you set options that you don't like, just click the **Cancel** button in the **Options** dialog box and this will return you to the application window with no harm done.

To open the options dialog box click the **Tools** menu, then click **Options**. To access a particular category of options, click the appropriate tab.

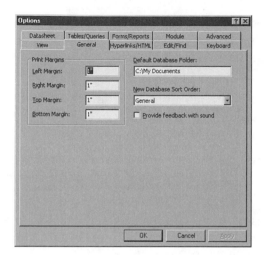

The Options dialog box gives you control over a number of Access settings.

It's All Up to You

Most of the options that you set in the options categories are either by check boxes that you select, drop-down boxes where you select from a list, or text boxes where you type in the needed parameter. Taking the time to sort through the various options can help you set Access to run the way you prefer.

View   This tab allows you to select whether to show the status bar and other application window items, such as hidden objects. It also controls how the Macro Design window is displayed and certain attributes of the toolbars such as the color and size of the buttons.

General   This tab lets you set the print margins for your objects—left, right, top, and bottom. You can also choose the default database directory in the tab.

Hyperlinks/HTML   This tab is where you set parameters that are related to your Web-ready database objects. There is an area to designate the HTML template you want to use for the creation of your HTML objects and there is also a box where you designate the path to your directory on an Internet server.

Edit/Find   This is where you set the default behavior of the Access Find/Replace feature. You select the type of search (fast search or general search) and also what types of actions require confirmation from you during a Find or Replace operation such as changes in records or deletions.

Keyboard   This tab handles the effect of certain keyboard actions. You can decide if the mouse pointer should advance to the next Field after pressing Enter, or what happens in a table when you press the arrow keys.

Datasheet Setting the color and look of your datasheets is the purpose of this Options tab. It gives you control over the font, the color of the background, and the style of the gridlines. You can also choose different cell effects such as Flat, Raised, and Sunken.

Tables/Queries This tab gives you control over the default field size and the default field type in your tables. You can also set query parameters such as Show Table Names and Output All Fields.

Forms/Reports Set the default form and report templates using this tab. Selection behavior for selecting controls (how much of the control you have to touch to select it) is also set here.

Module This tab deals with the look of the Module dialog box. Attributes such as text color, font, and font size can be set. Certain coding options are also controlled here such as Compile on Demand.

Advanced This tab lets you set parameters involved with object linking and embedding. You can also decide how Access should open databases: in either an exclusive or shared capacity.

A Little Help from My Friend

When you are working with the tabs of the Options dialog box you can get limited help on the options available to you. Click the **Dialog Help** button, (it looks like a question mark) at the top of the dialog box, and then click the mouse pointer on any area of the dialog box. For instance, let's say that you are in the Hyperlinks/HTML tab and aren't quite sure what a Server URL is. Click the dialog box **Help** button and then click the **Server URL** box.

Use the dialog box Help button to get help on specific items in a dialog box tab.

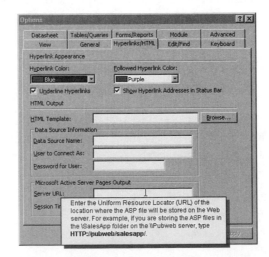

Access gives you a brief description of the area that you clicked. Being able to get immediate help on a specific option will really make it easier for you to choose your settings.

Make Access Work for You

It makes good sense to take the time to set up Access so you are comfortable with its look and feel. Database management is going to consume a lot of hours, so being at ease with the interface will make the trials and tribulations that you are going to face a little more palatable. Believe it or not, working with software packages can be fun. Go now, you Access guru, and prosper!

The Least You Need to Know

➤ You can customize any of the Access toolbars. You can add buttons and delete button—right click any of the toolbar to access the Toolbar menu, then click **Customize**.

➤ You can create toolbar buttons for any of the macros that you design. This gives you quick access to their actions.

➤ You can create your own toolbar from scratch, if you like, and populate them with a customized set of command buttons.

➤ You can place additional toolbars in the application window via the Toolbars dialog box. Once you have your toolbars in the application window, you can drag them to pretty much any place you like.

➤ The Options dialog box is your one-stop shopping for the control of the Access window's look and feel. Click the particular tab where you want to change the settings and have it your way!

Chapter 23

Surf's Up Dude—Access on the Internet

In This Chapter

➤ Save your Access objects as HTML to get them out there on the Web

➤ View Web-ready objects

➤ Decide whether your objects should be saved as static or dynamic HTML

➤ Place hyperlinks in tables that take you directly to a Web page

As far as small talk goes, the Internet is red hot. You can't get into an elevator or stand in the checkout line at the grocery store without overhearing conversations about how cool it is to cruise the Net and surf the Web. And while the Internet and probably its most used component, the World Wide Web (WWW), are categorized in the mental junk food category along with television, they are actually powerful and useful avenues for the movement of information.

This book has stressed time and time again that good database management is all about taking care of information (data). So, it's only natural that Access databases would give you the option of taking advantage of the biggest information reservoir in our planet's history–the Internet.

If you think back, you've already dabbled with the Net a little back in Chapter 3. Microsoft supplies you with Help menu choices that directly connect you to software support and information sites on the World Wide Web. And if you remember the mechanics of connecting to the Web, Access pulled in Microsoft Internet Explorer to give us a hand dealing with the actual Web pages. Now, as you embark on a survey of other ways to use the Net and the Web with Access, you will find that Internet Explorer will continue to play a part in the process.

Weaving a Database for the Web

Access 97 takes full advantage of the net. You will find that you can easily make your databases Web-ready, or save database files over the Internet using File Transfer Protocol (FTP). All these incredible net-related features can be used from right inside Access. And yes, there's more. You can actually place a special field, or hyperlink, in your tables that will whisk you (or another user of your database) right to a particular site on the World Wide Web. Let's take a close look at how Access makes it easy for you to swim, and not sink (maybe even surf), on the Internet and the WWW.

Access 97 is Net-Ready

All this great Web and Internet stuff is built right into Access 97. You will find that the other members of the Microsoft Office family such as Word and Excel also have these incredible Internet-related capabilities.

Going Hyper with HTML

WWW Pages consist of text, graphics, and other items that have been tagged with the Hypertext Markup Language (HTML). The purpose of HTML tags are to format the information for viewing with a Web browser (such as Internet Explorer). Using HTML to design a Web page is really no different than using a word processing package, such as Microsoft Word to design a flyer or brochure. Items in a brochure, for instance, are tagged to be bold, a certain font size, or a certain color. And a brochure may also include linked graphics that are tagged to show their directory location on your computer.

Access Cracks the HTML Code

Basically, HTML tags for the Web operate in the same general way as the word processing tags for a print document. The problem with Web documents, however, has been that you had to learn HTML to set them up; you had to know what the codes did. It was programming.

The great thing about Access is that it HTML codes your database objects when you save them as Web-ready items; you don't have to do the tags yourself. You get HTML formatted database objects with just a few clicks of the mouse!

HTML is Easy with Microsoft Office 97

All the components of Microsoft Office 97 offer you this quick HTML conversion for Web documents. Microsoft has also developed a Web design tool called Microsoft FrontPage. It is not a component of Microsoft Office, but is considered to be a part of the Office family of products. FrontPage helps you design your own Web pages with little (or almost no) understanding of HTML. Wizards and templates are used to build very sophisticated home pages and Web sites for business or home use.

Exporting an Access Report to HTML

Okay, let's give this HTML thing a try and see what happens. Let's say that you're building a Web site for your business. Your business just happens to be a cheese shop (this cheese shop analogy is really getting ripe). Now, you want to create an HTML object that will tell your customers (when they're browsing your Web page) who they should contact if they have questions about one of your product lines (the lines being: cheese, meats, implements, and gourmet crackers).

Your employee information and your product category information would reside in tables in your database. So, the best way to get the information together that you need for your Web site would be to generate a report from the tables. Reports also look nicer, so when you convert it to HTML, it will end up looking better than a table or query would.

A report generated to show employees and the product lines they manage.

Product Line Contacts			
Product Line	Cheese		
	First Name	Last Name	Email
	Marvin	Curdle	mcurdel@cheese.com
Product Line	Gourmet Crackers		
	First Name	Last Name	Email
	Walter	Rits	crackerboy@cheese.com
Product Line	Implements		
	First Name	Last Name	Email
	James	Cutlery	cutlery@cheese.com
Product Line	Meats		
	First Name	Last Name	Email
	Bobbi	Bison	bbison@cheese.com

Doing the Save As Thing

Once you have created a report or other object , it is fairly easy to convert it to HTML. Make sure that you have the Database window open and that you have the correct object tab selected, in this case Report. Then all you have to do is make sure that you select the report that you want to save as HTML.

The rest of the job is pretty much mouse work. Click the **File** menu, then click **Save As/ Export**. You are then faced with the choice of either saving the report to an external file or database, or saving the report in the current database using a different name. We want to save this puppy as an external file (HTML, remember?), so click **To an External File or Database** and then click **OK**.

Saving the Report from Itself

The Save As dialog box will appear and this is where you will save the report or other database object in an HTML format. There are several steps in the process, but they are pretty straightforward, so don't despair along the way.

Save In box

The Save As dialog box is your avenue to Access HTML Objects for your Web pages.

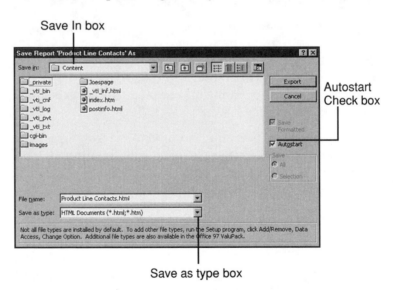

Autostart
Check box

Save as type box

In the Save In box, you designate where you want to place the file, meaning where you want this new file to end up. Once you designate the exported file's resting place, then you need to make sure that the file is saved in HTML format. This is done in the Save As Type box. Click the drop-down arrow for this box, and then select **HTML Documents (*.html;*.htm)**.

AutoStart Your HTML Engines

Once you designated the type of file you want the export to give you (HTML in this case), you are almost ready to click **Export**. However, Access offers you a nice perk in the Save As dialog box. Since you are going to save this report in HTML, Access figures you might want to take a look at it as it would appear on the Web. Access is probably right. Clicking in the **AutoStart** check box will automatically open the new HTML object in Internet Explorer once the Export process is completed. Notice also that the Save Formatted check box is automatically selected when you choose HTML as the file format. This makes sense since you will want this new file to be in the HTML format and therefore Web-ready.

Internet Explorer, Ready and Willing Web Browser

Internet Explorer is an integral part of Microsoft Office 97. Make sure that you install Explorer from your Office 97 CD-ROM or disks. You need it to take advantage of the powerful Web capabilities of Access and the other Office components.

Dressing Up Your HTML Objects with Templates

Now you can take this export business to the next step. Click **Export**. The HTML Output Options dialog box will appear. This dialog box allows you to specify whether or not you would like to use a *HTML Template* to enhance the look of your object.

These templates can provide you with navigation buttons to move through a multi-page report, or they can make sure that special graphics, such as a company logo, end up in the header section of the report. Access offers you a number of ready-made HTML templates to take advantage of. Once you've selected a template (or decided not to use one) click **OK**.

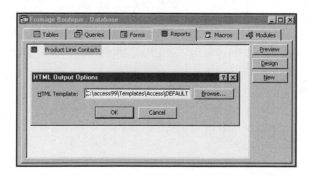

The HTML Output Options dialog box lets you choose a template to dress up your new Web-ready object.

Check This Out...

Where Are My HTML Templates? Your HTML templates will be in the Access directory that resides in your main template directory for Microsoft Office. Use the browse feature in the HTML Output Options dialog box to find and select your templates.

Explorer Takes Center Stage

Once you've ended the Export process, your computer will probably take a couple of seconds to process your new HTML file. Then, amazingly, Internet Explorer will open up and show you the fruits of your labor (this is because of Autostart, remember?). The great thing about this whole HTML export thing is that the new objects that you create can be incorporated into existing Web sites, providing easy-to-update information for the people who use your home page on the Web.

Your new HTML object will appear in the Internet Explorer Window.

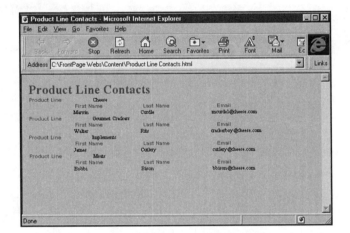

Your Web Page at a Standstill–Static HTML

Exporting Access Objects as HTML is a great way to get information on your Web site. However, you probably noticed that saving a table as HTML via the Save As command only creates a fixed view of the object (such as a table). It's kind of like a photo of the information and the new HTML object cannot be updated. In fact, if you wanted to show new data in your HTML table, you would have to edit the table in Access and then use Save As again to show the updated information on your Web page.

This type of HTML is called *Static*. It is the easiest way to make an Access object Web ready. A table in Static HTML is not unlike a picture of your college roommate taken twenty years ago; you have to take a new photo to update his image to his new look (because he's probably put on 20 pounds and lost most of his hair).

The Exciting Potential of Dynamic HTML

Although it demands a much greater understanding of Web publishing, (when compared to saving Access objects as static HTML files), Access does provide you with a way to set up Access objects so that you can place them on the Web and update them easily. For instance, you may have a Web page where you provide an Access form that allows customers to type their name and address so you can send them your latest catalog. This information would obviously have to end up in an Access table. The file format used to create Access objects that can be updated on the fly via the Web is called *Dynamic HTML*. Dynamic HTML comes in two file flavors HTX and ASP.

HTX (HTML extension file) is a type of file that contains all the Web formatting information that a HTML does, but it does not contain the static data found in the HTML file. Rather, the HTX file works with a Internet Database Connector file (idc) that gets the information entered into the Web form to the appropriate Access database table. Access can also save your database objects as *ASP* (ActiveX Server Page) files. This file format takes advantage of *ActiveX Controls*, which are very much like OLE objects in that they can be used to receive information from another application outside of Access (check out Chapter 17 for a discussion of OLE). ActiveX controls were primarily created to enhance the connectivity of applications such as Access with the World Wide Web. This means that an ActiveX object, such as a table or form, in a Web page can collect data via the Web and then deposit it in the appropriate Access file.

Not For Absolute Beginners

To build Dynamic HTML links to your databases using HTX and ASP files you must have access to an Internet server that is using Microsoft Internet Information Server software. Microsoft Office 97 comes with a wizard, the Web Publishing Wizard, which allows you to easily create a new Web page that will incorporate the HTX and ASP objects that you build in Access and make them work with Microsoft Internet Information Server. Obviously, using the Web as a data source also requires that you have a basic understanding of how a Web page works, and then some expertise with the HTML language.

Taking It Home with a Home Page

Hopefully, you now have a feel for the fact that HTX and ASP files are basically two different routes to pretty much the same result—active HTML objects. The whole point of these types of files is to help you build a truly interactive home page that links Web

313

input (data coming from the WWW) to the objects in your Access databases. Again, as I said during our discussion on macros, you need a very good understanding of Access and its various objects before you tackle active HTML objects. Acquiring information from the Web dictates that the HTML objects be well designed, and that certain security issues (such as user access) be well understood before attempting to build a home page that interfaces with Access.

Going Hyper with Hyperlinks

Wouldn't it be great if you could set up a field that would whisk you to a site on the WWW? Well you can; you set up your field as a *hyperlink*. Hyperlinks chain or connect two items together, such as documents. For instance, when you click the Hyperlink you are taken to the next document, picture, or other item. You might have a field in a database table that lists important documents related to your business. Clicking on the hyperlink field will take you to the actual document, which could reside in Microsoft Word.

Hyperlinks versus OLE

Hyperlinks and OLE objects have certain aspects in common. They can both be used to get to information that resides outside of your current database table or form. Hyperlinks, however, do not truly link or embed themselves to your database fields as OLE objects do. Hyperlinks are just a quick path to another place or item.

Hyperlinks to the Web

Using Hyperlinks in your database tables that reference sites on the WWW is a great way to tie your Access databases into the information superhighway. Let's say that you work at a computer consulting firm and that one of your jobs is to keep track of the software that the company purchases. No problem—you can set up an Access database that tracks all the purchases. The tables in the database would probably include a table for the software vendors and maybe a table for the actual software packages you purchase.

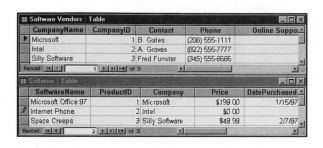

Some of the tables that you might want to have in your Software database.

Wouldn't it be great if you could set up the Software Vendors table so that there would be a field that when clicked on would take you to the particular software company's home page? Well, sure it would and this is a great way to explore how Access uses hyperlinks to connect to the WWW.

Creating the Hyperlink Field

Creating the link is actually very easy. All you have to do is open your table in the Table Design view. Create a new field for your hyperlink and then make sure that you set the field type as (yes, you guessed it) Hyperlink.

So, getting back to our example again, you have a table for your software vendors. Once you are in the **Edit view**, create a new field. Let's say you call it Online Support. You would type this into the Field Name box. Then you press **Enter** and that takes you to the Data Type box. Click the drop-down arrow that appears in the **Data Type** box and select **Hyperlink**.

Setting the field type as Hyperlink.

Setting up the data type (Hyperlink) is actually the easy part of the process. Once you return to the Datasheet view of the table you are going to have to specify the actual document or place (such as a Web site) that you want the hyperlink to take you to.

Specifying the Web Address in the Hyperlink Field

URL Back Story You will find that URLs that end in *.com* are sites related to companies. Sites that are related to an educational institution will have an URL that end in *.edu*. Government site URLs end in *.gov*.

The information that you place in the Hyperlink field in the table specifies the document, spreadsheet, graphic, or Web page, that you would like the field to take you to when you click it. Hyperlinked items can reside on your local drive, network, or on the WWW. In our example we want the field to take us to the Web support site of a software company listed in our vendors table.

Web sites on the WWW are located by their URLs. *URL* stands for Uniform Resource Locator and URLs serve as the addresses for all the sites residing on the Web.

For instance Microsoft's Web site has a URL of **http://www.microsoft.com/**.

So, let's say that you want one of the fields in our table to connect us to Microsoft's home page. All you have to do is type **http://www.microsoft.com/** in the field.

The Hyperlink field contains the Web site address.

CompanyName	CompanyID	Contact	Phone	Online Support
Microsoft	1	B. Gates	(206) 555-1111	http://www.microsoft.com/
Intel	2	A. Groves	(822) 555-7777	http:///www.intel.com/
Silly Software	3	Fred Funster	(345) 555-6666	
*	(AutoNumber)			

Copy URLs From Internet Explorer

If you hate typing long URLs into your hyperlink fields, you can use Internet Explorer to give your fingers a rest. Open a particular Web site using the Web toolbar in Microsoft Access. You can pull the site right from your favorites list. This will open Internet Explorer and display the Web page. Select the URL that appears in the Explorer's Address box. Then press the Control key and the letter C simultaneously (Ctrl + C). This will copy the address to the Windows clipboard. Then all you have to do is return to the hyperlink field in your database table and paste the URL into the field using the Edit/Paste commands.

Notice that the when you place the mouse pointer on the field, a small hand appears. This means that the hyperlink is ready to go.

Surfing via Your Hyperlink

Once you have the hyperlink addresses entered into the table, all you have to do is click a particular field (the one with the Hyperlink in it) and it will open Internet Explorer and take you to the correct Web site. This provides you with a database table that is connected to a wealth of information concerning a particular product, a company, or some other piece of knowledge that you like to be able to get to quickly.

Access and the Global Network

Hopefully you now have a feel for the incredible possibilities that Access offers you through its connectivity with the Internet and the World Wide Web. These features, such as HTML and Hyperlinks, tie you into an incredible global network that is just swimming in information.

Not only does Access tie you into this huge information loop, but it also gives you the tools to publish your own information in a Web ready format. Move over Buck Rogers because Access is going help blast us right into the twenty-first century—the Information Age and beyond!

The Least You Need to Know

➤ Saving your database objects in HTML format allows you to quickly create Web-ready objects for a home page.

➤ HTML files can come in two flavors: Static and Dynamic. Static HTML is very much like a photo of the object, it cannot be updated. Dynamic HTML provides you with an object that can be updated with data that is input into a form or table that is part of a Web page on the WWW.

➤ Hyperlink fields can be used to quickly jump to a document, spreadsheet, or site on the World Wide Web.

➤ The Hyperlink field type is created in the Design view of your table.

➤ You enter the location or Web address of the Hyperlink destination in the Datasheet view of a table.

➤ Access offers you an excellent connection to the WWW and all its incredible informational resources.

Installing Access 97

A Very Easy Installation

Installing Microsoft Access 97 and the other components of Microsoft Office 97 really couldn't be any easier. As a matter of fact, the first time you insert the CD-ROM, it automatically starts itself.

Install
Microsoft
Office

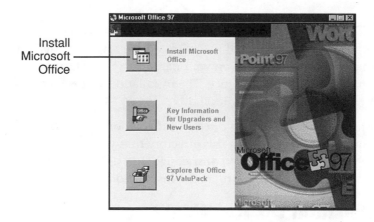

The opening screen that the Microsoft Office 97 CD-ROM provides is all you need to get started.

To install the software, all you have to do is click **Install Microsoft Office**.

If you purchased Access as a standalone product, or if you are doing the software installation from disks, the procedure for installation may differ slightly. Take a look at the Getting Started booklet that is in the box with your software for help.

Welcome to the Installation

Microsoft welcomes you to the installation, so all you have to do is click on **OK**. Then you are asked to furnish your name and the name of your organization. You can provide just your name or just the organization name. What you type into this particular box isn't all that important; it is really up to you and will not influence the rest of the installation. Once you provide the information, click **OK** to continue.

You Need a Key

The next step in the installation process will ask you for the CD-ROM key. You can usually find it on a sticker somewhere on the jewel case that the CD-ROM came in. Type in the number and then click **OK**.

Directory, Please

At this point, you are asked where you would like to install the software. Meaning what directory do you want to put all this stuff in on your hard drive? The default drive for the installation is C:\Program Files\Microsoft Office. The installation will even create this directory if it doesn't currently exist on your local drive.

You don't have to install the software in this directory, if you don't want to. For instance you may have a previous version of Office in this directory that you would like to keep (I'm not sure why you would, but that's okay). Just designate a different directory, if that's your choice, and then click **OK** to continue the installation.

What Kind of Installation Do You Want?

Now you are faced with three choices involving the type of installation that you want. You can choose **Typical**, which will install the most used components of the software. This is the easiest way to get the software onto your computer.

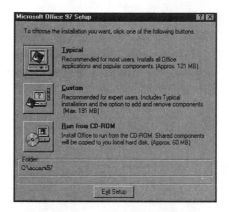

Three different ways to install the software are available.

The *Custom* installation allows you to select all the software components that will be installed. This can be useful if you want to preclude certain software items from the installation. However, the custom installation does require that you know what all these different software things do. For example, if you don't know the difference between a graphics import filter and a cigarette filter (a very non-PC reference) you better stick with the Typical installation.

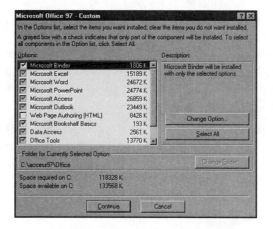

A custom installation requires a good understanding of the various Office software components.

The third choice, *Run from CD-ROM* will install a bare minimum of files on your local drive (files used to launch the various applications on the CD) and will then run the Office software directly from the CD. This can work out fine, if you are hard up for disk space; however, you must have the CD in your CD-ROM drive whenever you want to use the software.

Finishing the Installation

Once you make your choice of Typical, Custom, or Run from CD-ROM, the Office installation will check your local drive for previous versions of Microsoft Office. The Upgrade Wizard will offer to remove old Office components. If you say **Yes**, all the old stuff will be cleaned out of the various directories this stuff gets installed into. If you say **No**, previous Office components will remain intact. If you are installing Office 97 and want a fresh start, meaning you want all the old Office stuff to go away, say **Yes**.

It's All Over but the Applause

Once you've made all your choices, the Office installation process will copy all the files from the CD-ROM to the directory you designated on your local drive. Once the installation is complete, Office will let you know. All you have to do is click **OK**, and you're ready to start doing some serious computing.

Final Notes on Software Installation

Once you start using your software, you may find that you would like to add components that were not installed during your initial run-through with the software. This doesn't pose a problem. Just insert the CD-ROM back into the CD-ROM drive. A window will automatically open showing you the files and folders on the CD-ROM. Click the **Setup** icon. You will be walked through the steps that allow you to add components to your previous installation or remove items that you don't feel you need. Again, this requires a good understanding of what all these software components are, but if you feel confident about what you're doing, proceed.

Once you get the software installed, I think you will agree that Office 97 and it's components (you know, like Access, the subject of this great book) are incredible productivity tools that are easy and fun to use. Good luck with all your computing!

The Workstation Primer: Windows 95 and Windows NT

While you're probably raring to tackle Access and learn all about databases, you may be new to the Windows environment, or are upgrading from Windows 3.1. It probably wouldn't hurt to take a few moments to get familiar with the environment that Microsoft Access runs in—Windows.

The "new" Windows currently comes in two flavors. Windows 95 and Windows NT Workstation 4.0. Both of these operating systems are built to run the new 32-bit application packages such as Microsoft Access 97. This means that the operating system takes full advantage of your computer hardware—the memory, processor, and so on— as you work.

The differences between Windows 95 and Windows NT Workstation are not readily apparent to the end user—people like you and me who just want to run our application packages and get our job done. In fact the only real difference that you may encounter is the way you log into your computer if you are on a network. Windows NT requires that you press the **Control**, **Alt**, and **Delete** keys simultaneously to access the user login box (the place where you type your user name and password). Windows 95 does not.

Windows 95 versus Windows NT

There are other differences between Windows 95 and Windows NT that may influence which of these operating systems you choose to use. Windows 95 offers backward compatibility with most DOS software packages (yeah , that old stuff you have—probably games). Windows 95 also embraces plug-and-play hardware configurations, meaning it is much easier to add a new sound card or a modem to a computer running Windows 95. Windows 95 is considered the best bet for the home user and Windows NT workstation is slanted more toward the corporate end user who is connected to a Windows NT network server. Both operating systems have their pluses; you can't really tell them apart by the interface, however.

What Does NT Stand for?

NT stands for New Technology. It was one of the first 32-bit graphical user interfaces and actually existed in earlier versions before the advent of Windows 95.

To make this primer more useful and less confusing we will ignore the fact that there are two 32-bit Windows operating systems that look very much alike, but do have some major internal (and hidden) differences. Let's just call these guys Windows and get down to business.

The Interface

Microsoft Windows is a perfect example of a *GUI* (its not as sticky as it sounds)—a Graphical User Interface—which embraces the mouse as the chief mode of navigating in and around your software packages. The great thing about Windows is that all the applications that run in the environment share a common "look and feel," which makes it easy for you to learn and use new software packages.

Access 97 is no exception to this rule. It fully embraces the Windows interface and takes full advantage of all the computer processing stuff that goes on behind the scenes in this powerful, yet user-friendly operating system (meaning Windows 95 and Windows NT are both easy to deal with).

The Windows Desktop

As you gaze out over the Windows Desktop (that's what the screen is called now—it takes up most of the real desktop anyway) it seems like a placid, glassy lake. Little does the unsuspecting computer novice know that just below the surface there's a software tsunami waiting to arise.

You have probably noticed that all the program groups that you used to see on your Windows 3.1 (and Windows for Workgroups 3.11) desktop are gone. They have been replaced by a Start button that supplies you with a pop-up hierarchy of your software packages. Your old program groups can be found by clicking on **Start** and then clicking on **Programs**.

What Is this Stuff?

Even though the Windows desktop seems pretty spartan compared to its predecessors (Windows 3.1 and Windows for Workgroups 3.11) there are some landmarks. I'm betting that there are at least a couple of icons floating on that sea of tranquillity.

Desktop Folder

My Computer icon

Software icon

Recycle Bin

Internet icon

Start button

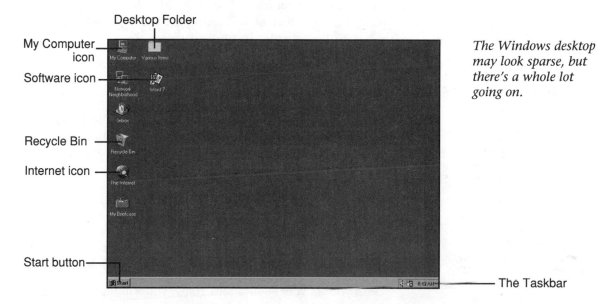

The Windows desktop may look sparse, but there's a whole lot going on.

The Taskbar

Going from the top of the desktop to the bottom (starting on the left) one of the first icons you will run into is a small computer labeled as *My Computer*. When you double-click the My Computer icon you can see all the folders and files on your computer's hard drive. You can use My Computer to copy and delete files; you can also use it to start applications.

Techno Talk

To start an application using My Computer locate the executable file for the software (it usually has the file extension ".exe") and double-click this file. You can also drag this executable file out onto the desktop and a Short-cut icon will be created for the application.

Would Someone Please Take Out the Trash?

Another icon that you'll find on your desktop is the *Recycle Bin*. In days past, we would have called this the Trash Can. However, in this era of Reduce, Reuse, and Recycle, we call the place that our deleted files are sent to, the Recycle Bin. The neat thing about this is that when you delete a file—such as a no longer needed database file—it is automatically sent to the recycle bin. This gives you the chance of undeleting the file if you've made a mistake. Otherwise you can empty the Recycle Bin, and this will clear space on your hard drive for other files.

All Task Masters Belly Up to the Taskbar

Check This Out...

Open Applications on the Taskbar Another cool thing about the Taskbar is that since it shows you all the applications you currently have open (and is always visible on the desktop), you can use it to switch quickly between the software packages. Just click your choice and it switches you there.

Another very important area of the desktop is the *Taskbar*, and the most important part of the Taskbar is the Start button. The Start button gives you access to all your program groups and program icons. So you use the Start button to launch your applications.

For instance, you may want to start Access, the subject of this clever and informative book. No problem; you just click the **Start** button and then click the **Access** icon (zero to 100 mph in two seconds with two clicks of the mouse!).

Once you get your applications going, you will find that there are many strange and wonderful Windows accoutrements: boxes that you use to save files, menus that pull down and fire off commands, and toolbar buttons that launch complex features with one click. Sound amazing? It is.

Windows Geography 101

For those of you that were dragged kicking and screaming from DOS into the Windows environment, I've got news for you the cursor is no longer with us. But its memory lives on in the next generation...

The Insertion Point

In Windows the cursor has been reborn as the *insertion point*. The insertion point is a vertical blinking bar as opposed to the old horizontal cursor. The insertion point is where you insert your new text, pictures, or other neat stuff. As you type, the text chases the insertion point across the page. (Run, Point, Run.) You will be seeing a lot of the insertion point in Access when you do data entry.

Multi-tabbed Dialog Boxes

One of the many differences between Windows 3.1 and the new 32-bit Windows operating systems is the way you supply your various applications with information. Although dialog boxes were a part of the Windows 3.1 interface, you will find that they have a decidedly different look now because they have tabs.

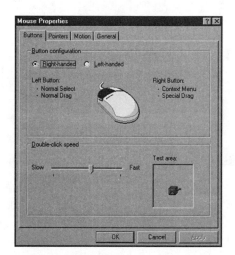

Tabbed dialog boxes allow you to make your choices regarding various software and hardware features.

The tabs on the dialog boxes allow you to access a subset of the features or commands controlled by the particular dialog box. This makes it easier for you to set the various Windows parameters that control your hardware and software.

Hardware and Software Settings

Getting to the place where you can determine various hardware and software settings and how they relate to the Windows interface has never been easier. Click the **Start button**, then point the mouse at **Settings**. Now all you have to do is click **Control Panel**.

The Control Panel is where you can change the settings related to items like your mouse or modem. You can use the Control Panel to add and remove software components of Windows. This is also the place where you add the software drivers for that new modem or sound card that you bought and have recently installed.

The Windows Control Panel lets you set various hardware and software settings.

Display Properties

The way you configure the Windows interface (colors, screen saver, wallpaper) is different now too—you won't find a main group icon on the desktop that lets you get to your desktop settings the way you could in Windows 3.1. To choose your desktop settings, move your mouse to an empty place on the desktop and then click the right mouse button. A Shortcut menu will appear and all you have to do is select **Properties**. The Display Properties dialog box will appear.

The Display Properties dialog box contains different tabs that allow you to control the background, colors, and screen saver that you see as you use Windows. Once you select the parameters you want, just click **OK** (if you want the new parameters to go into effect before you close the dialog box, click **Apply**).

The Display Properties dialog box allows you to control the background color, your screen saver and other parameters related to how Windows looks on your screen.

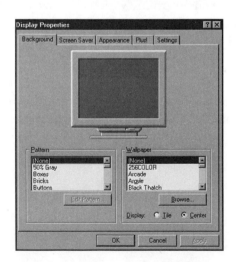

File Management

You will be surprised to find that the Windows 3.1 File Manager is no more. These latest and greatest versions of Windows (95 and NT 4.0) offer the Windows Explorer as the chief file management tool.

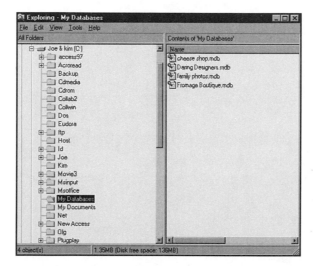

The Windows Explorer will help you manage your files.

The Explorer window is divided into two panes. The box on the left (All Folders) shows all the drives and directories that you have access to. When you double-click a particular directory, its contents are displayed in the right box (Contents of).

A menu system provides you with the means to move, copy, and delete files. You can also easily create new directories, or change the names of current directories and files. Under the Tools menu is an excellent Find feature that really makes it easy to find a file or groups of files on your local drives or network. You will find that once you get used to it the Explorer is a much more versatile tool than the Windows 3.1 File Manager.

Building on the Basics

Now that you've had an introduction to the Windows interface, you're ready to start grappling with the concepts and commands associated with database management. Flip to the beginning of Chapter 1 and start your Access 97 journey in earnest.

Speak Like a Geek: The Complete Archive

Action Arguments　They give a macro action its specificity. For example, for a particular command such as the DoMenuitem you need to set an action argument that tells the macro which menu item to do or select.

Actions　These are specific commands or other macros that you place in the Macro Design box. When you run a macro all the actions in the macro are fired off in their appropriate sequence.

Administrator　The owner of a database that has been assigned user-level security. The administrator assigns the rights and maintains the various groups associated with the database.

Alphanumeric characters　The letters of the alphabet and other non-numeric symbols.

AutoForm　A form that uses all the fields in the table as it displays the data one record at a time. Click the New Object button on the toolbar to create an AutoForm.

Best Fit　Double-clicking on a column divider in a datasheet widens the column to the left of the mouse pointer to accommodate the longest entry that has been entered in it.

Bitmap Image　A particular file format for graphics. It is the standard format for the Windows environment.

Bound control　A control in a form or report tied to a particular field in the associated table or query. The opposite of the Bound control is the Unbound control.

Chart　A graphical representation of numerical data in a table, query, form, or report. Charts for Access objects can be created using the Graph 5.0 program that ships with Access 97 and the other members of Microsoft Office software package.

Combo box   A box that provides a drop-down list of choices in a table form, or report, and also gives you the option of typing in an entry not found on the list.

Command button   A button that can be placed on a form to invoke certain commands such as printing. Command buttons can also be tied to macros.

Compact   The act of defragmenting a database file to increase its performance. Compacting a database file also frees up disk space on your hard drive.

Control   A dynamic box in a form or report that calls data from a specific field in a table or uses a formula designed in the Expression Builder to calculate an answer.

Control Format   You can format controls so that they display their contents with a certain number of decimal places or as currency. Control formats are set in the control's Properties box.

Criteria   Conditional statements that you devise for queries.

Crosstab Query   This query displays its results in a spreadsheet-like format presenting the data in rows and columns. This type of query works well when you want to follow a certain field such as name across the crosstab to view items associated with a particular person or thing.

Database Documentor   An Access 97 feature that can provide a detailed report on any of your database objects. The report includes date of creation and specifics on such things as the fields in a table, or the actions in a macro.

Database object   This refers to the different items that can be part of a database. Objects can consist of data manipulation and viewing containers such as tables, forms, and reports, or objects can be mini-software programs that you create using macros and the Visual Basic application language that comes with Microsoft Access 97.

Detail area   The main area of the design window for forms and reports. The Detail area is where the controls representing fields or calculations are placed when a form or report is being designed.

Dialog Box   Software packages use these boxes to gather information from the user.

Drag and Drop   The easiest way to move a selection a short distance. Select an item and then drag it to the new location.

Dynamic HTML   Access objects (tables and forms) exported as .htx or .asp files can be used to receive new data via the Web. Data input received through these objects updates the associated table in your Access database. (*See* HTML)

Export   The act of moving data out of Access and into other applications. You can cut and paste information from Access directly into other applications. You can also export Access tables into Excel where they are treated as spreadsheets.

332

Expression Builder   A tool for building mathematical formulas and other expressions that can be placed in controls on forms and reports.

External Data   Information that resides outside Access in another format. Access is capable of importing external data that is stored in Excel and Lotus spreadsheets.

Field   This is a particular piece of information, such as a name or address, found in the data record.

Field Properties   Control parameters that dictate how information in a field will be stored, handled, or displayed.

Filtering Records   A method of viewing certain records in a datasheet. You can filter by selection where you select an example of a field parameter you want to view by, or you can filter by form, where you type in a filter parameter into a specific field.

Folders   These things used to be called directories and will contain your data and software files.

Footer   The area at the bottom of a printed page. It is also the bottom area in the form and Report Design views. Items placed in the page footer area will repeat on every page of the form or report.

Form   This object supplies a record-by-record view of your database records. Forms are excellent for data input and editing.

Freezing Fields   This allows you to freeze a particular column in a datasheet so that it remains in view when you scroll to the extreme edges of the data area.

Glossary term   In the Help system, click these highlighted terms and a definition of the word or topic appears in a Glossary box.

Groups   Areas of a report where certain information is grouped together, such as a subtotal for a set of selected fields. A group can also refer to users that have been placed in the same security-level for a database.

Header   The area at the top of a printed page. In the Form and Report Design views, the header area is at the top of the design area. Items placed in the page header area will repeat on every page of the form or report. You can also have section headers and group headers in reports that are used to place information at the top of a summary group or report section.

Home Page   The main page that is displayed when you connect to a Web site.

HTML   HyperText Markup Language is the set of tagging codes that is used to publish material electronically for the World Wide Web. HTML basically tells a Web Browser like Internet Explorer how to display the text and graphics that are contained in the Web document or home page.

Hyperlink   In Access a field type that allows you to jump to another document or item. Placing a URL in a Hyperlink field allows you to connect to Web sites on the WWW by clicking on the field.

Import   The act of taking data that resides outside Access and placing it in a new or existing Access table.

Input Mask   A defined pattern for all the data that is entered in a particular field. Input masks are assigned to fields during table design.

Insertion Point   This blinking, vertical line points to where you are in a text box, field, or other text area. In former days this thing was called the cursor.

Internet   A global system of linked computers—basically this mega-network began as an experimental project that allowed universities and military computers to maintain contact during times of National emergencies. The Internet is now a resource for people like you and me and allows the exchange of email, the transfer of files, and the browsing of Web sites.

Internet Explorer   This is Microsoft's Web browser. It is also an integral part of the software tools found in Microsoft Office 97.

Label   The tag for a control in a form or a report. The label will usually contain the name of the field that the control is associated with.

Landscape   The page is oriented with the width greater than the length. This would be 11" by 8.5" for a typical piece of paper.

List box   A box that provides a drop-down list of choices in a table, form, or report.

Local Drive   Windows 95 way of referring to the hard drive on your computer. You can have more than one local drive; it depends on how many fixed disks have been physically installed on your computer.

Macro   A set of actions that you put together to automate repetitive tasks. Macros can be built that open specific tables or forms; or open a form, wait for data entry, and then print the form.

Mail Merge   This involves creating a word processing document such as a form letter and exporting data from Access to provide the address information for the letters. Mail merges can be used to create letters, mailing labels, and envelopes as well as other document types. A mail merge, which is handled by the Mail Merge Wizard, does require that you have Microsoft Word installed on your computer.

Mailing Labels   A special kind of database report that creates mailing labels for you. A specific Wizard exists for the creation of mailing labels.

Many-to-Many relationship   A relationship between tables where each record in the first table has many possible matches in the second table, and the records in the second table have many potential matches in the first table.

Menu Bar   This pull-down system gives you access to your software commands and features.

Module   A mini-program built with Visual Basic code. Modules require programming; they can be used to automate tasks and radically alter the user interface for a particular database.

Normalization   The act of taking a table that has fields in which data is repeated and breaking it into smaller related tables. Access has automated the normalization process via the Table Analyzer.

Object Linking and Embedding (OLE)   The process of placing information in an application that has originated in another application. Linking ties outside information to an object such as a table, but the linked file resides outside the database table. Embedded information, such as a graph or a graphic, becomes part of the database file that it is placed in increasing its size.

Objects   Items that originate in source or server applications and are linked or embedded into a destination application. Objects can consist of a spreadsheet, graph, or graphic image, just about anything that can be created in an application. Object can also refer to database items such as tables, forms, and reports.

OfficeLinks   A set of commands that make it easy for you to export data from Access to other Microsoft products. You can use OfficeLinks to export tables to Excel or create a mail merge using Access data in a Microsoft Word form letter.

OLE field   A special field that is placed in an Access table that uses linked or embedded objects as its source. For instance an OLE field in a table could hold embedded photos.

One-to-Many relationship   A relationship between tables where a record in the first table can be matched to more than one record in the second table.

One-to-One relationship   A relationship between tables where each record in the first table can be matched to only one record in the second table.

Optimization   The Performance Analyzer can be used to optimize any of your database objects; it provides tips and strategies for increasing object performance—recommendations, suggestions, and ideas.

Options   A number of parameters associated with the Access application window. Options can dictate a wide array of things ranging from whether or not the status bar is shown to the default size of fields in datasheets or forms.

Page Setup   This menu command gives you the capability to determine the orientation (portrait or landscape) and the margins of the pages you want to print.

Password   A security device that makes you the owner of a particular database. You must type your password every time you open a database. It is a security device for your database files.

335

Pivot table   A flexible crosstab formatted spreadsheet in Excel that allows you to drag the columns and rows to new locations, pivoting the data. This allows you to group and summarize the data in the spreadsheet in different ways. You can export an Access database into Excel and then create a pivot table or you can create a pivot table in Access.

Portrait   The page is oriented with the length greater than the width. This would be 8.5" by 11" for a typical piece of paper.

Primary key   A field that uniquely identifies each of the records in a table. The table will be indexed automatically by the primary key field.

Print Properties   Global settings that affect all your print jobs. The Print Property dialog box has three tabs: Paper, Graphics, and Device options. Remember that when you set the print properties you are affecting all the print jobs from all your software packages.

Properties   This is usually associated with controls in forms and reports. The properties of a control would dictate the source of the control such as a particular field. An input mask would also be the property of a control in a form.

Query   A way to ask a table or tables certain questions. A select query lists the records that satisfy a certain question or parameter. An action query actually does something to a table such as deleting records that satisfy a certain request. Queries can also be used to return totals or the answers to other of mathematical expressions.

Record   A collection of data pertaining to a particular person, place, or thing. It appears as a row in a datasheet.

Relational database   A database that groups information in discreet tables. Relationships will exist between the tables in this type of database. An example would be a small business database where the customer information, product information, supplier information, and employee information all reside in different tables, but can be tied together by queries, forms, and reports.

Repair   Database files can be corrupt or damaged. Use the Repair command to try and fix any damage that a file may have suffered. Since this process does entail some risk to your data make sure to create a copy or backup the database file before beginning the process.

Report   This object pulls together data from a table or a number of tables and presents the information in a readable, well-designed format.

Sections   Additional areas that you can add to a report. For instance you can add a group section that provides a subtotal for certain information or provides some other type of summary information.

Sorting   This is the capability to reorder table records numerically or alphanumerically in either ascending or descending order.

Start button   Used to start your applications; it gives you access to all your program groups and application icons.

Status Bar   This area of the application window gives you specific information about what's going on with the software.

Static HTML   Database objects saved as .html files provide you with an object that can be viewed on the World Wide Web. However, the object is really nothing more than a photo of the current Access object. Static HTML objects cannot be updated directly only viewed.

Subform   A form that you can place in a control on an already existing form. This allows you to see data from two different tables as you work with the form.

Subreport   A previously created report that can be placed in a control on a second report. Subreports are excellent vehicles for placing a short summary report on a longer more detailed main report.

Table   An object consisting of information in rows and columns and is used for data input and editing in your database.

Taskbar   The Taskbar, which resides at the bottom of the Windows desktop, shows you which applications you currently have open; click an application to restore it to the desktop.

Template   A blueprint or foundation for a database that can include ready-made tables, forms, reports and other database components.

Title Bar   It tells you the name of your application and can be used to move the software window on the desktop.

Toolbar   A quick access mechanism that provides a one-click method of invoking a variety of the software's features and commands.

Toolbox   A group of design tools used to create forms and reports in their respective design views.

URL   Short for Uniform Resource Locator, the URL provides the address that you use to locate a particular Web site on the World Wide Web.

User-levels   Different degrees of access to a database's objects. User-levels are assigned to user groups. The group that you belong to will dictate your level of access to the objects.

Visual Basic   A Windows programming language. Visual Basic for Applications is a common language used by several Microsoft programs such as Access and Excel.

Wizard   An interactive feature that walks you through the steps involved in a particular process such as creating a form. Wizards use a series of dialog boxes to get answers to specific questions and then create a particular object or complete a particular task based on those answers.

The World Wide Web (WWW) An electronic patchwork of interconnected HTML documents on computers all over the world. The Web is navigated via a Web Browser, which allows you to view the various pages present.

Zoom The capability to increase or decrease the degree of detail that you can see on an object that is displayed in the Print Preview window. You can zoom out to see the design of the entire page, or zoom in to view specific data.

Index

X-Y-Z

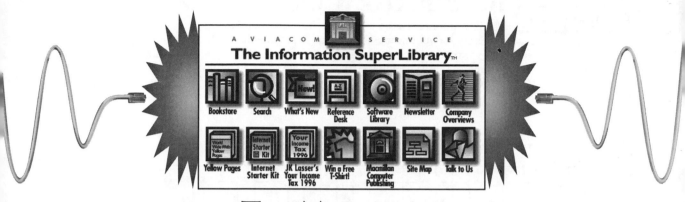

Complete and Return this Card
for a *FREE* Computer Book Catalog

Thank you for purchasing this book! You have purchased a superior computer book written expressly for your needs. To continue to provide the kind of up-to-date, pertinent coverage you've come to expect from us, we need to hear from you. Please take a minute to complete and return this self-addressed, postage-paid form. In return, we'll send you a free catalog of all our computer books on topics ranging from word processing to programming and the Internet.

Mr. ☐   Mrs. ☐   Ms. ☐   Dr. ☐

Name (first) ☐☐☐☐☐☐☐☐☐☐☐☐☐ (M.I.) ☐ (last) ☐☐☐☐☐☐☐☐☐☐☐☐☐☐☐☐

Address ☐☐☐☐☐☐☐☐☐☐☐☐☐☐☐☐☐☐☐☐☐☐☐☐☐☐☐☐☐☐☐☐☐

☐☐☐☐☐☐☐☐☐☐☐☐☐☐☐☐☐☐☐☐☐☐☐☐☐☐☐☐☐☐☐☐☐

City ☐☐☐☐☐☐☐☐☐☐☐☐☐☐☐☐☐ State ☐☐ Zip ☐☐☐☐☐ ☐☐☐☐

Phone ☐☐☐ ☐☐☐ ☐☐☐☐ Fax ☐☐☐ ☐☐☐ ☐☐☐☐

Company Name ☐☐☐☐☐☐☐☐☐☐☐☐☐☐☐☐☐☐☐☐☐☐☐☐☐☐☐☐☐☐☐

E-mail address ☐☐☐☐☐☐☐☐☐☐☐☐☐☐☐☐☐☐☐☐☐☐☐☐☐☐☐☐☐☐☐

1. Please check at least (3) influencing factors for purchasing this book.

Front or back cover information on book .... ☐
Special approach to the content .... ☐
Completeness of content .... ☐
Author's reputation .... ☐
Publisher's reputation .... ☐
Book cover design or layout .... ☐
Index or table of contents of book .... ☐
Price of book .... ☐
Special effects, graphics, illustrations .... ☐
Other (Please specify): _____ ☐

2. How did you first learn about this book?

Saw in Macmillan Computer Publishing catalog .... ☐
Recommended by store personnel .... ☐
Saw the book on bookshelf at store .... ☐
Recommended by a friend .... ☐
Received advertisement in the mail .... ☐
Saw an advertisement in: _____ ☐
Read book review in: _____ ☐
Other (Please specify): _____ ☐

3. How many computer books have you purchased in the last six months?

This book only .... ☐   3 to 5 books .... ☐
2 books .... ☐   More than 5 .... ☐

4. Where did you purchase this book?

Bookstore .... ☐
Computer Store .... ☐
Consumer Electronics Store .... ☐
Department Store .... ☐
Office Club .... ☐
Warehouse Club .... ☐
Mail Order .... ☐
Direct from Publisher .... ☐
Internet site .... ☐
Other (Please specify): _____ ☐

5. How long have you been using a computer?

☐ Less than 6 months   ☐ 6 months to a year
☐ 1 to 3 years   ☐ More than 3 years

6. What is your level of experience with personal computers and with the subject of this book?

	With PCs	With subject of book
New	☐	☐
Casual	☐	☐
Accomplished	☐	☐
Expert	☐	☐

Source Code ISBN: 0-7897-1051-X

7. Which of the following best describes your job title?

Administrative Assistant .... ☐
Coordinator .... ☐
Manager/Supervisor .... ☐
Director .... ☐
Vice President .... ☐
President/CEO/COO .... ☐
Lawyer/Doctor/Medical Professional .... ☐
Teacher/Educator/Trainer .... ☐
Engineer/Technician .... ☐
Consultant .... ☐
Not employed/Student/Retired .... ☐
Other (Please specify): _____ ☐

8. Which of the following best describes the area of the company your job title falls under?

Accounting .... ☐
Engineering .... ☐
Manufacturing .... ☐
Operations .... ☐
Marketing .... ☐
Sales .... ☐
Other (Please specify): _____ ☐

9. What is your age?

Under 20 .... ☐
21-29 .... ☐
30-39 .... ☐
40-49 .... ☐
50-59 .... ☐
60-over .... ☐

10. Are you:

Male .... ☐
Female .... ☐

11. Which computer publications do you read regularly? (Please list)

_____
_____
_____
_____
_____
_____
_____
_____
_____
_____

Comments: _____
_____
_____

Fold here and scotch-tape to mail.

Check out Que® Books on the World Wide Web
http://www.mcp.com/que

As the biggest software release in computer history, Windows 95 continues to redefine the computer industry. Click here for the latest info on our Windows 95 books

Make computing quick and easy with these products designed exclusively for new and casual users

Examine the latest releases in word processing, spreadsheets, operating systems, and suites

The Internet, The World Wide Web, CompuServe®, America Online®, Prodigy® —it's a world of ever-changing information. Don't get left behind!

Find out about new additions to our site, new bestsellers and hot topics

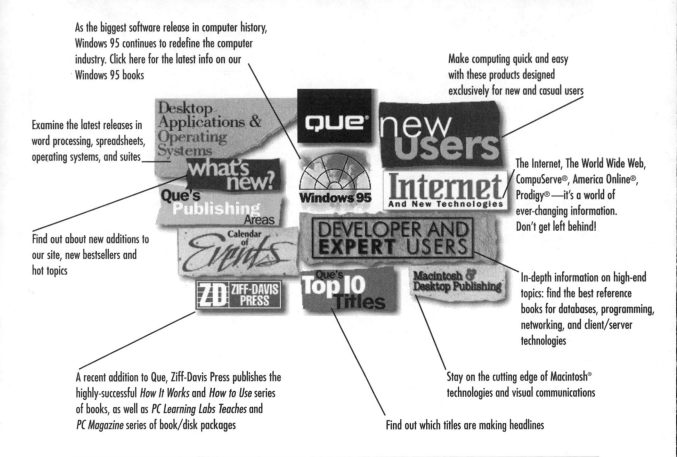

In-depth information on high-end topics: find the best reference books for databases, programming, networking, and client/server technologies

A recent addition to Que, Ziff-Davis Press publishes the highly-successful *How It Works* and *How to Use* series of books, as well as *PC Learning Labs Teaches* and *PC Magazine* series of book/disk packages

Stay on the cutting edge of Macintosh® technologies and visual communications

Find out which titles are making headlines

With six separate publishing groups, Que develops products for many specific market segments and areas of computer technology. Explore our Web site and you'll find information on best-selling titles, newly published titles, upcoming products, authors, and much more.

- Stay informed on the latest industry trends and products available
- Visit our online bookstore for the latest information and editions
- Download software from Que's library of the best shareware and freeware